The
50

30

The 50

Football's Most Influential Players

JON DRISCOLL

First published by Pitch Publishing, 2020

Pitch Publishing
9 Donnington Park,
85 Birdham Road,
Chichester, West Sussex,
PO20 7AJ
www.pitchpublishing.co.uk
info@pitchpublishing.co.uk

© 2020, Jon Driscoll

Every effort has been made to trace the copyright.
Any oversight will be rectified in future editions at the
earliest opportunity by the publisher.

All rights reserved. No part of this book may be reproduced,
sold or utilised in any form or transmitted in any form or by
any means, electronic or mechanical, including photocopying,
recording or by any information storage and retrieval system,
without prior permission in writing from the publisher.

A CIP catalogue record is available for this book
from the British Library.

ISBN 978 1 83680 012 5

Printed and bound in the UK on FSC® certified paper in line
with our continuing commitment to ethical business practices,
sustainability and the environment.

Typesetting and origination by Pitch Publishing
Printed and bound by CPI Anthony Rowe, UK

Contents

Acknowledgements 10
Preface 11

1. Charles Alcock 13
2. Nicholas 'Jack' Ross 19
3. Jorge Brown 26
4. Billy Meredith 31
5. Vivian Woodward 36
6. Walter Tull 43
7. Lily Parr 48
8. Dixie Dean 53
9. José Andrade 58
10. Stanley Matthews 63
11. Giuseppe Meazza 69
12. Tom Finney 74
13. Obdulio Varela 80
14. Alfredo Di Stéfano 86
15. Ferenc Puskás 91
16. Pelé 98
17. Lev Yashin 106
18. Jimmy Hill 110
19. Garrincha 116
20. Bobby Charlton 121
21. Eusébio 129
22. Billy McNeill 134

23. George Best 140
24. Johan Cruyff. 145
25. Franz Beckenbauer 151
26. Viv Anderson 156
27. Kenny Dalglish. 162
28. Mario Kempes 169
29. Justin Fashanu 175
30. Paolo Rossi 180
31. Michel Platini 185
32. Diego Maradona 191
33. Hope Powell 199
34. Marco van Basten 205
35. Paul Gascoigne 211
36. Brandi Chastain 219
37. Eric Cantona. 224
38. Jean-Marc Bosman 231
39. George Weah 236
40. Cafu 241
41. Zinedine Zidane 247
42. Ronaldo 256
43. David Beckham 262
44. Cristiano Ronaldo 271
45. Xavi Hernández 278
46. Lionel Messi 284
47. Mesut Özil 289
48. N'Golo Kanté 295
49. Megan Rapinoe 302
50. Raheem Sterling 307

Bibliography 314

Dedication:
To the Driscolls

'The history of football is made of players, not managers. Real Madrid had Di Stéfano and Puskás, so they won. Milan had Van Basten and Gullit, so they won. I don't think it was the managers who made them win. It was the players.'

Arséne Wenger, *The Italian Job* (Gianluca Vialli & Gabriele Marcotti)

Acknowledgements

WRITING THIS book has been an absolute pleasure; thank you for reading it. There were lot of books for me to read and videos to watch but they were all about football so it's not exactly hard work.

Thanks to everyone at Pitch Publishing for the opportunity and for your support and guidance: Jane Camillin, Alex Daley, Andrea Dunn, Michelle Grainger, Graham Hales and Duncan Olner.

My wife, Alison, cast her expert historian's eye over the first draft, which was invaluable. Thanks also to Graham Hunter and Jacqui Oatley for their expert opinion and to Guillem Balague, Philip Barker, Rob Carter, Dave Farrar, Terry Gibson, Mark Hirst, Gareth Jones, Sid Lowe and Rich Rowling for either asking or answering questions. And thanks to anyone who joined in the twitter polls and questions @driscollfc.

Preface

I MUST begin by thanking Neil MacGregor of the British Museum for his inspirational *A History of the World in 100 Objects*. It is a monumental work, but he makes one schoolboy error. Obviously, the best object invented by humans is the football, at least since the 'Olduvai stone chopping tool' allowed us to crack open bones and suck out the protein-rich marrow, but somehow it doesn't make it into MacGregor's 658-page masterpiece. The nearest thing is the 'ceremonial ballgame belt' – believed to be from Mexico, from between AD 100 and 500. The one in the British Museum was probably used for the pre-match build-up – like the tracksuits players wear for the Champions League music. Later pictures show the players wearing something similar to reinforced pink Y-fronts, as they try to land a rubber ball in their opponents' court, using only their buttocks, forearms and hips. Occasionally, the losers would be killed. Today, we have social media.

Despite his mistake, MacGregor does understand the importance of sport to humans: 'One of the striking characteristics of organised games throughout history is their capacity to transcend cultural differences, social divisions and even political unrest. Straddling the boundary between the sacred and the profane, they can be great social unifiers and dividers. There are few other things we care about so much in our society today.' So why did he prefer the Statue of Ramesses II to Dixie Dean's leather-panelled casey?

The history of football has been told through results, events, coaches and tactics, but it is a game made by players, and I wanted the players to tell the story. Some of *The Fifty* changed the world: without Charles Alcock football would be a different game, and Jean-Marc Bosman should be toasted by every super-rich modern star. Some left a stamp greater than their contribution on the pitch: Johan Cruyff was the first name on my team sheet. The three times European Player of the Year became a great coach and advocate for a style of football that dominates the top level of the sport still, after his death. I almost made the mistake of regarding Pelé as simply a great footballer until I re-read his autobiography and realised the importance of a black man being the greatest game's greatest star before Nelson Mandela was sent to prison or Martin Luther King made his 'I Have a Dream Speech'.

Lily Parr was only one of Dick, Kerr's Ladies, who filled football grounds until the women's game was deliberately crushed by the FA, but I chose her not only because she was paid in Woodbine cigarettes but because she was an openly gay footballer decades before any male player dared to come out. Walter Tull was a war hero who was racially abused by football fans; over a century later, Raheem Sterling is fighting the same fight.

Some of the players were so good they wrote their own page in history: Matthews, Maradona and Messi set new standards. You will have to read Jimmy Hill's chapter to decide whether I put him in just for laughs.

The list isn't perfect; it was like completing a moving puzzle. The Brits dominate early on, before I spread my gaze wider. It was painful to leave out some of the best-ever footballers, and I'm sorry if I missed your favourite player.

1

Charles Alcock

HUMANS HAVE kicked balls at or through targets for thousands of years, but it took the enthusiasm of the Victorian Brits for rules-based sport to turn football into a game ready to conquer the world. As America and Australia demonstrate, it was by no means inevitable that the beautiful round-ball game known now as football (or soccer, if you prefer) would come to bestride the globe. That is where Charles Alcock comes in.

There is a reference to a game in which participants invade their opponents' territory with a ball, played in Derby in AD 217. It was locals versus occupying Romans, although we don't know the score, or the rules. We do know that versions of football survived, always under threat of being banned by disgruntled authority.

The trouble was that it was a deadly business. Henry de Ellington was perhaps the first documented football fatality in 1280. This is what we know: 'Henry, son of William de Ellington, while playing at ball at Ulkham on Trinity Sunday with David le Keu and many others, ran against David and received an accident wound from David's knife of which he died on the following Friday. They were both running to the ball, and ran against each other, and the knife hanging from

David's belt stuck out so that the point sheath struck in Henry's belly, and the handle against David's belly. Henry was wounded right through the sheaf and died by misadventure.'

In 1321 William de Spalding successfully persuaded the Pope to give him indemnity for killing his friend, also called William, in a football match. There were frequent attempts to ban the games, especially during times of war. In 1531 Henry VIII, no less, got in on the act:

'Foot balle is nothing but beastly fury and extreme violence whereof proceedth hurte and consequently rancour and malice do remayne with thym that be wounded, wherefore it is to be put to perpetual silence.'

Despite such threats, folk football outlived the Tudors, and in 1660 Francis Willughby chronicled it in his *Book of Games*: 'They blow a strong bladder and tie the neck of it as fast as they can, and then put it into the skin of a buls cod and sow it fast in. They play in a long street, or a close that has a gate at either end. The gates are called gaols. The ball is thrown up in the middle between the gaols, the players being equally divided according to their strength and nimbleness.

'Plaiers must kick the ball towards the gaols, and they that can strike the ball thorough their enemies gaol first win. They usually leave some of their best plaiers to gard the gaol while the rest follow the ball. They often breake one another's shins when two meete and strike both together against the ball, and therefore there is a law that they must not strike higher than the ball.'

Shrove Tuesday, an apprentices' holiday, became a traditional football day, but the drowning of a player in the River Derwent in 1796 highlighted a problem: it was too dangerous. As the industrial revolution gathered pace and people started to work in factories, their bosses objected to broken bones, and as glass became affordable, householders objected to broken windows. The new middle classes drove football to the margins of society.

CHARLES ALCOCK

One surviving hotbed was the English public school system. 'Flannelled fools at the wicket and muddied oafs at the goal,' was how the great poet and novelist Rudyard Kipling described his sporting contemporaries. Did the common folk have the public schools to thank for codifying and civilising the game? In his excellent history of the formation of British football, *Beastly Fury*, Richard Sanders rejects that: 'Public schools were a prison from which football would have to escape before it could be reborn.'

The educational institutions of the British Empire were strange places, and Sanders argues the stubborn adherence to each school's unique version of the game, coupled with toxic snobbery, hampered the coordination and consolidation of rules. For football to have a future in Victorian Britain and beyond, it needed laws that encouraged players who *did* mind if they broke a bone.

At Cambridge University in 1848, old boys of various public schools tried to write a compromise rulebook. Dedicated football clubs were springing up around the country, most notably Sheffield FC, which also produced a set of rules in 1858. It was a painful process and would ultimately lead to a split: one code became modern football; the other remained a more violent game, in which the ball could be carried, and attackers caught in front of it would be offside. Rugby school became the rallying point for this code.

The argument was unresolved when the Football Association was formed in 1863, in a series of meetings at the Freemasons Tavern in London. Francis Campbell of Blackheath said if they banned the practice of hacking an opponent's legs, he would be 'bound to bring over a lot of Frenchmen who would beat you with a week's practice'.

At first the FA struggled to assert itself on the country's football clubs and schools. Its rules were an unloved hybrid that resembled modern rugby as much as football. Then, thankfully, Charles Alcock enters the story.

THE FIFTY

Charles and his brother John were born in Sunderland but brought up in Chingford, Essex, and went to Harrow School, where they were keen footballers. They set up Forest FC, which later became the famous Wanderers FC. John was the administrator – he was at the founding meetings of the FA in 1863 – and Charles the acclaimed player. Charles's friend W.G. Grace, the best cricketer and most famous sportsman of the day, wrote, 'The way Alcock used to knock over a fellow when he was trying to pass him I shall never forget. Alcock made Catherine-wheels of those fellows.' Alcock was around 6ft tall and a burly 13 and a half stone, large for his day but dwarfed by Grace.

Charles brought his playing reputation and diplomatic skills to the thorny issue of blending existing laws from the FA, Sheffield FC and the public schools to create a version of the game that could thrive. The rugby men split and loyalty to the Football Association is why the game was also referred to as 'soccer'; the word is not the Americanism often assumed.

Alcock's influence didn't end there. He became FA Secretary while still Wanderers' star player and he was a prolific journalist with his *Football Annual*, *Football* and *Cricket* publications. It was at a meeting in his office at the *Sportsman* that he persuaded the FA to hold a challenge cup competition, for which all clubs in the country would be invited to compete. As an ex-Harrow man, he had been inspired by his school's Cock House competition, although some speculation suggests his friend Grace might have shared some part in the germination of the idea.

The first games kicked off in November 1871 and Jarvis Kenrick of Clapham Rovers scored the first goal against Upton Park FC. Barnes beat a Civil Service team that had only eight players. Wanderers didn't enter until the second round, when they beat Clapham 1-0. Their next two games finished 0-0 and they progressed each time because of the other club's withdrawal.

So Alcock led out Wanderers in the first FA Cup Final at The Oval, home of Surrey County Cricket Club, of which he was secretary from that year until 1907. Their opponents were Chatham-based military side Royal Engineers, who had the considerable advantage of regular training sessions, and were prepared to offer positions to servicemen based on their sporting ability – essentially, the first semi-professional club!

The wholly amateur Wanderers won, helped by a broken collarbone suffered by Royal Engineers' Edmund Creswell, who stayed on the pitch but contributed little. Morton Betts scored after 15 minutes and, despite Wanderers having eight forwards and the engineers seven, that was the only goal.

Wanderers won five of the first seven FA Cup finals, although Alcock only played in the first. In 1873 they were joined by Arthur Kinnaird, who won three cup finals with Wanderers and two with Old Etonians. Kinnaird was a founding director of Barclays Bank and FA president for 33 years. In Wanderers' 1877 victory over Oxford University, Kinnaird was the goalkeeper and carried the ball over the line for Oxford's goal. He later persuaded his fellow FA committee men to scrub it from the records, and it stayed that way for over a century.

Alcock, meanwhile, invented international football, of a sort. He set up five fixtures between England and Scotland and advertised for players in the *Glasgow Herald*. The Scotland team that took the pitch was controversial because it contained many London-based players such as Kinnaird, with others reluctant to travel south, possibly because of the different laws. Alcock persisted and Queen's Park – Glasgow's premier club – took up his challenge to play by Association rules. The match was played in Partick, Glasgow, in November 1872 and is now recognised by FIFA as the first international.

Alcock was injured but he picked the team. The English were bigger and stronger but the club-mates who made up the Scotland side were better coordinated and passed more effectively. The match finished goalless, but it was rapturously received by spectators and press alike. The teams met again at The Oval the following March. Queen's Park brought only seven players and recruited London-based Scots, including Kinnaird. England won 4-2. Alcock was injured again and was listed as one of the two umpires. He missed out again as Scotland won in Glasgow in 1874 but finally won his only official cap at The Oval in 1875 and scored in a 2-2 draw, at the age of 32.

This giant of Victorian sport was more than just a footballer. His energy and diplomacy were vital in arranging cricket's first Test match to be staged in England. It was played at The Oval and his friend Grace dominated with a century, as England beat Australia. We will hear more from Alcock, the administrator, shortly but it is worth one more note – he also captained the France cricket team against Germany in Hamburg.

2

Nicholas 'Jack' Ross

THE EARLY days of organised football were dominated by the amateur clubs of London. That was fine for gentlemen like Charles Alcock, who came from a wealthy shipping family, had an income from journalism and a £250-a-year job as secretary of Surrey. Arthur Kinnaird was richer still, coming from landed gentry before turning to banking. Contrast that with our next player, who was born into a large, working-class Edinburgh family. He was regarded as the best defender around, but is so far from famous that even his name is disputed.

Nicholas John Ross was born in 1862. A majority of sources refer to him as Nick and he signed a letter with his full name, but most contemporary football reports refer to him as Jack. His mother was a shop worker and his father was a stonemason, who died while Jack was an adolescent. He and his brother Jimmy were part of a wave of talented Scots who helped transform football from the pastime of public school old boys to a professional sport followed by millions.

As organised football grew in the industrial towns of northern England, clubs realised people would pay to watch. The details of when, where and to whom the first payments were made are unclear because clubs could be thrown out of the cup, and possibly the FA itself, if they were caught. Payments could be made for expenses and for 'broken time' if a player missed work for a match, which created a grey area. In the more established sport of cricket, W.G. Grace, supposedly a great amateur, was raking in a fortune (including the extraordinary sum of £9,703 for a testimonial in 1896). Military side Royal Engineers won the FA Cup with players who trained together on work time, while senior figures in the club admitted the corps deliberately recruited good sportsmen.

Preston North End's Major Billy Sudell took it to new levels. He had persuaded the club to switch from rugby to football in 1880, but they struggled against the established Lancashire teams, suffering a 16-0 defeat to Blackburn Rovers. Sudell's solution was to turn unashamedly to professionalism. Northern clubs already openly advertised for players in the *Glasgow Herald*, so Sudell went to Edinburgh and signed up Hearts' belligerent skipper Jack Ross. The leading football writer Jimmy Catton described Ross as the greatest full-back, but added, less flatteringly, 'Ross's teeth were discoloured, almost green at the gums, and he hissed through them as he played.'

Players were given jobs: Ross was, in theory, a slater, but it never got in the way of his real work of leading Preston's beautifully balanced machine. He played 'scientific' football; or in modern parlance – he read the game.

The teams from the North and Midlands, with barely concealed professionals, soon became too strong for the southern amateurs. Old Etonians' victory over Blackburn Rovers in the 1882 FA Cup Final was the last hurrah of the old guard. The following season Blackburn Olympic beat Old Etonians, whose skipper Kinnaird was remarkably sporting, agreeing to unscheduled extra time despite having an injured player. Not all amateurs took their demise as gracefully.

After Preston played the London amateurs Upton Park, a complaint was made to the FA that the Lancastrians were professionals and should be expelled. Sudell was summoned to the FA in London and admitted everything. His argument was essentially, 'So what, everyone's doing it.'

Preston were thrown out of that season's cup but not expelled from the FA. The battle was at last in the open, with amateur and professional hardliners standing firm and Alcock leading the compromisers. Preston, Burnley and Great Lever withdrew from the FA Cup the following season. The advocates for professionalism threatened to form the breakaway British Football Association, and the amateurs gave ground.

At first they tried to cling to the class distinctions seen in cricket where 'Gentlemen' and 'Players' used different changing rooms, entered the pitch through different gates, and the professionals referred to their social superiors as Mister. The first professional to play football for England, James Forrest of Blackburn Rovers, wore a blue shirt, while his amateur teammates were in white.

The FA briefly imposed a residency requirement, preventing clubs signing players and putting them straight into cup games. Preston were again expelled from the 1885/86 competition, along with Bolton Wanderers, as each complained about the other breaching the regulations. With Preston out of the way, Blackburn Rovers won the FA Cup in 1884, 1885 and 1886.

Violence was commonplace. At least twice Preston won games, only to be attacked by mobs of opposition fans. Jack's younger brother Jimmy joined him at Preston and sparked a riot when they went back across the border to play Queen's Park in Glasgow. It was the last match the great amateur side played in the English FA Cup, but they would win the Scottish Cup twice more. Preston were surprisingly beaten by West Bromwich Albion in the semi-final and Aston Villa lifted the trophy.

Preston tried again and on 15 October 1887 they played Hyde in the first round. Sudell was irritated that the Cheshire side refused to reschedule the match and put out his full-strength team. Jimmy Ross hit seven and Jack one in a 26-0 victory that remains an English record.

That match highlighted a problem. Preston had wanted it rescheduled because of fixture congestion. The professional clubs needed regular income, so played in local cups and arranged friendlies whenever and wherever they could get a paying crowd. The FA Cup was undoubtedly the top prize, but not knowing how many games a club would play was disruptive.

On their way to the 1888 final, Preston scored 49 and conceded only three. They were unbeaten in 43 matches when they faced West Brom again, this time at The Oval. Sudell made a monumental mess of the preparations. The players went to watch the Oxford–Cambridge Boat Race on the Thames that morning and were cold and hungry by the time they kicked off. He also had them photographed with the trophy before kick-off while their shirts were still clean.

Apparently that irritated the referee, FA president Major Francis Marindin, who wished the West Brom players well in their dressing room – after checking they were all English. Cambridge University captain Tinsley Lindley said to Ross after the game, 'Well Jack, you cannot expect to win when playing against 11 men and the devil.'

Jack was as tense as Sudell was complacent, according to Albion's Billy Bassett: 'Jack Ross lost his cool that day. That was the key. I managed to keep my cool and the cooler I kept, the rasher Ross got.' In the build-up to Jem Bayliss's winning goal, Ross charged at Bassett and reportedly somersaulted clean over him. Bassett admitted the best team lost. 'I have never seen a side that compared to that Preston North End team at their best. I do not pretend for a moment that we deserved to beat them.'

The night before the match, Aston Villa's William McGregor held an historic meeting with representatives of 11 other clubs from the North and Midlands. The rail network was now good, workers had won the right to Saturday afternoons off and the government was providing education to create a literate populace. Conditions were right for football to follow US baseball and English cricket and form a professional league. Before even agreeing on the number of points for winning and drawing, Accrington, Aston Villa, Blackburn Rovers, Bolton Wanderers, Burnley, Derby County, Everton, Notts County, Preston North End, Stoke, West Bromwich Albion and Wolverhampton Wanderers arranged home and away fixtures for the 1888/89 season.

By the time the Football League kicked off on 8 September 1888, Jack was an Everton player. He had been approached by a committee member after the FA Cup semi-final and offered £10 to join the Merseyside club. He moved in the summer and became the highest-paid footballer. It was bad timing. He made his debut in a 2-1 win over Accrington in front of 12,000 fans at Everton's Anfield Road stadium, the biggest crowd of the day. They won their first two games, but so did Preston and West Brom.

Fears that Preston were past their best were soon dispelled. They didn't drop a point until Accrington held on for a 0-0 in the seventh round of matches. By the time they beat Jack's Everton team 3-0 in December, they were runaway leaders. They beat Everton again in January, and went unbeaten in all 22 league games, clinching the title with three games to spare. No other team went through an English top-flight season unbeaten until Arsenal in 2003/04. Jimmy also scored as Preston finally won the FA Cup, beating Wolves 3-0 in the final. The teams from the new league were dominant; Chatham, the last southern amateur side involved, lost 10-1 to West Brom in the quarter-final.

An incident at Everton's game with West Brom set Jack against his new club. The visiting skipper complained the ball wasn't properly round, and when Jack asked for a replacement he was told by a club official to 'mind your own business and go to your place'. Luckily, Sudell didn't hold grudges if there was a chance to strengthen his team. Jack returned and Preston kicked off the league's second season with a 10-0 win over Stoke. They weren't invincible this time, but held off Everton, and Jack got his Football League winner's medal.

Preston became victims of their own success. Clubs from big towns and cities had the support and therefore the financial muscle to recruit their own stars. Everton signed more Scots and beat them to the title the following season. Sunderland were the next champions: their 'Team of All the Talents' also had a distinctly Scottish influence. They and Aston Villa were the dominant forces until the turn of the century. No doubt the Preston players' hard-drinking also played its part.

Sudell's determination not to go without a fight ended in disgrace. In 1895 he was arrested for embezzlement and falsification of accounts. He had redirected £5,326 from the Goodair Mills factory, where he was the account manager, into the football club. He was sentenced to three years in prison.

Jack caught the flu and, during an 18-0 win over Reading in the FA Cup in January 1894, he was persuaded to shelter in the dressing room until a downpour had passed. In February the *Lancashire Evening Post* reported, 'After last Saturday's match with Darwen, even the most ardent admirers of Jack Ross were forced to admit that he was not in fit condition to play football at present. Accordingly, on Monday he decided to stand down again for a while, and to put himself under hydropathic treatment at the best establishment at Matlock … everyone wishes him a complete and speedy recovery.'

He bought a cottage by the sea and the club sent him on a cruise to the Canary Islands to help his recovery, but he had pneumonia and collapsed and died at home that August, aged 31. Thousands lined the streets as his horse-drawn hearse passed by on its way to Preston Cemetery, where his teammates carried his coffin to its final resting place.

Jimmy moved to Liverpool in 1894 and was relegated and subsequently promoted again. He did exactly the same in three years at Burnley, before helping Manchester City win promotion to the First Division. City was Jimmy's last club; like his older brother he fell ill whilst still playing top-level football and died in 1901, aged 36.

The Ross brothers' early deaths were tragic, but not particularly unusual for working-class men of the day. They had served their purpose, helping turn football into a massively popular sport ripe for exploitation, and then they were gone and almost forgotten.

3

Jorge Brown

WE LIKE our history neatly packaged, hence the notion that Britain invented football and generously offered it to the world. It goes like this: Charles Alcock and his public school chums codified the game, before Jack Ross and a myriad of Scots professionalised it ready for export. The truth is messier. The Chinese kicked balls around; the people of North America played a form of the game before Christopher Columbus arrived, and 16th-century *calcio fiorentino* might have derived from the Roman game harpastum. It is hard to say.

We do know for sure that Brits liked to travel long before they could take footballs with them. In 1825, for example, 220 Scots sailed from Leith and Greenock to Buenos Aires to set up an experimental agricultural colony. The colony failed but many of the Scots thrived, including James Brown, whose grandchildren would dominate the early days of the Argentina national football team.

There is no record of rules-based football in Argentina until 1867, when Yorkshireman Thomas Hogg, known in Argentina as Tomás, set up Buenos Aires FC and arranged the first match in the country to be played, roughly, under the latest FA rules. It was eight-a-side with 15 of the 16 players from the British and Irish community. Hogg might have been my choice of pioneer footballer, but he seems to have preferred rugby.

Looking back it can seem inevitable that football would become the world's game. It is beautifully easy to play but impossible to master. You can have a few players or dozens. You only need one piece of equipment – and it is tremendous fun. Yet even in Brazil in the 18th century, British sailors were regarded with curiosity when they kicked a ball around the docks. 'In Bom Retiro, a group of Englishmen, a bunch of maniacs as they all are, get together, from time to time, to kick around something that looks like a bull's bladder. It gives them great satisfaction or fills them with sorrow when this kind of yellowish bladder enters a rectangle formed by wooden posts.' That is a Brazilian scoffing at other people taking football too seriously; bear that in mind when we get to the 1950 World Cup.

Football failed to become the leading sport in most of the English-speaking world. America and Australia had their own codes, which became associated with national pride; Melbourne Rules were written in 1859 and Australian Rules in 1863, before the Football Association's. The American variation was first played in 1869 and soccer, as it was known, later had competition from another easy-to-play game for the masses – basketball, which was first played in 1891. In Canada the weather suited ice hockey. In Ireland there was a concerted political push to drive out English games, so hurling and Gaelic football thrived. Elsewhere in the Empire, ex-pat Brits were happy to have football codes that were less appealing to their local populations than the round-ball version that was beginning to sweep the old country.

It was a different story where English wasn't the first language. In southern Spain, Captain W.F. Adams recorded in 1874 that he and his men had 'marched out from Huelva on Wednesday. Played foot-ball with some railmen at about an hour out. The only diversion we truly had.' Spain's first football club, Recreativo Huelva, was set up by Scots Alex McKay (or MacKay) and Robert Russell Ross, who had been attracted to Spain by the nearby copper mines.

In Italy, clubs such as Milan Foot-Ball and Cricket Club, and Genoa Cricket and Football Club were formed by English ex-pats. Torino Football and Cricket Club was set up by Turin native Edoardo Bosio, who had worked in England and caught the football bug. The complex reasons for football's successes and failures are examined in forensic detail in David Goldblatt's extraordinary book *The Ball is Round*.

The pivotal figure in Argentina is another Scotsman, Alexander Watson Hutton, who arrived in Buenos Aires nearly 50 years after James Brown, and died there, aged 82, having earned the sobriquet 'The Father of Argentine Football'. He had lost both parents and two brothers to tuberculosis and was looking for a place to escape to when he was hired as a teacher by St Andrew's Scots School. He soon fell out with the austere governors about sport and corporal punishment and set up the English High School. His willingness to engage with the local middle classes saw him prosper.

It was another Scottish teacher, Alec Lamont, who established the first Argentinean football league in 1891, but it folded a year later and the intervention of Watson Hutton was again required. This time the league was around to stay. Immigrants living around the dock areas set up the likes of River Plate in 1901 and Boca Juniors in 1905, and the game spread beyond Buenos Aires.

The dominant club in those early days was Watson Hutton's own: Alumni, which was made up largely of EHS pupils and old boys. Handily for the success of both the school and the club, old James Brown's youngest son – also James – had nine sons of his own. They enrolled at EHS and Watson Hutton taught them to play football. Jorge was the leader but seven of Mr Brown's boys played for Alumni, as did their cousin Juan

Domingo Brown. Five of the Browns played for the newly formed Argentina national team: Jorge, Ernesto, Eliseo, Alfredo and Carlos Carr.

Jorge was there throughout the club's ten title wins between 1900 and 1911. As well as his great ability, his leadership was crucial, according to his team-mate Carlos Lett: 'The secret of Alumni's success was the friendship and comradeship existing among the players rather than their skills with the ball. In football, a drop of "bad blood" between two team-mates would also extend to the rest of the team, and, fortunately, this never happened, largely due to the Brown brothers' temperament, particularly Jorge's.'

Argentine football was well below the standard of English teams such as Southampton, who toured in 1904, and Nottingham Forest, who came a year later. But Alumni – now with Watson Hutton's son Arnold in the forward line – struck a first blow for the nation in 1906, beating a South African touring side that largely consisted of British ex-pats. It would be convenient to claim that Argentine football had arrived, but when Everton and Tottenham later toured they were too strong, upsetting the locals with their physical approach.

In 1910 Jorge captained Argentina to victory over Uruguay and Chile in the Copa Centenario Revolucion de Mayo, a tournament recognised as the forerunner to the Copa America – 20 years before the World Cup began and 50 years before the first European Nations' Cup Final. Ernesto and Juan Domingo were the other Browns. Arnold scored in the final and Harry Hayes, a son of English immigrants, was top scorer. Arturo Jacobs, Haroldo Grant and Carlos Wilson show the British influence was still present, but the other names were Spanish.

Alumni didn't play in the 1912 season and Watson Hutton Senior dissolved the club. As amateurs, they were racking up debts and struggling to compete as others professionalised. Jorge Brown moved to Quilmes where he won his final championship medal.

THE FIFTY

That's why I chose Jorge for *The Fifty* over Alexander Watson Hutton, el Padre de la Futbolera. Football thrived in Argentina because the local population took control. In parts of the world where the Brits ruled, the elite stuck to their rugby and cricket. Where they traded without conquering, the masses took to football, as they had in England. Jorge Brown represents that transition between the Brits and locals. Without him, his brothers and people like them, we might never have heard of Alfredo Di Stéfano, Diego Maradona and Lionel Messi.

4

Billy Meredith

WHEN JACK Ross was lured from Preston to Everton to become football's best-paid player on £10 a week, Billy Meredith was working down a North Wales coal mine. He spent eight years in the pit during a time of industrial strife that saw miners forced to take a 25 per cent pay cut. Then he became the most famous footballer of his age.

Meredith played for his home-town club Chirk and, to make ends meet during a miners' strike, also played occasionally for Northwich Victoria, in the new English Second Division. Northwich withdrew from the league after the 1893/94 season, in which they won only three matches. They did better when Meredith played, which was noticed by another Second Division club, the newly restructured and renamed Manchester City.

City's representatives were not welcomed when they went to Chirk to find Meredith and had to buy beer to placate angry miners. Billy's mother wasn't impressed by his proposed new career and advised him to stay at the mine. He did for a year, also playing for City part time. For the avoidance of doubt, no current Manchester City player doubles up as a coal miner.

Meredith scored on his City debut, and got two in his second match, against Newton Heath in the Football League's first

Manchester derby. He was top scorer in his first season with his new club and was captain by the age of 21. City were promoted in 1899 after making a late-season signing, Meredith's football hero Jimmy Ross. They played two seasons together in the First Division. Jimmy died before City were relegated in 1902. The club and Meredith bounced back up and went on to win the FA Cup in 1904 and have a serious tilt at the Football League title in 1905. An elegant goalscoring outside-forward, he was renowned for his skill and speed, and for his quirk of chewing a toothpick as he played. With football's popularity growing, Meredith became as famous as the music hall stars of the Edwardian era – but he was more than just a terrific footballer.

To explore Meredith's role in the history of football, we need to rewind to Jack Ross's move to Everton. Ross's £10-a-week deal was probably twice that of any other player in the game. Major Sudell didn't like it, and, although he later made peace with the player, he went to war with the system, which he believed was biased in favour of clubs from cities and big towns.

The result was the outrageous 'retain-and-transfer' system introduced in 1893/94, meaning that once a player had registered with a club he couldn't sign for a rival without his original 'owner's' permission, even after his contract expired. Sudell didn't benefit because he went to prison in April 1895, but restrictions on footballers' basic liberties persisted in England, and consequently elsewhere, until Jean-Marc Bosman changed everything in 1995. The first attempt to organise the players collectively against the clubs, the Association Footballers' Union, ended in rapid and abject failure.

Clubs still weren't satisfied and they successfully lobbied for a maximum wage. A limit of £4 a week was set in 1901. This was a serious restriction on the top stars, falling well below the figures the Rosses had commanded and Meredith's near £7 a week – at least that was the official line.

The ex-miner would be at the forefront of football's next industrial dispute – but not until he had been at the centre of a major scandal. City were chasing Newcastle for the 1905 title and faced FA Cup winners Aston Villa in their last league fixture. What started with mud-slinging – literally – descended into a brawl and soon to the break-up of Manchester City's first great team. It wasn't Meredith's style to be at the forefront of the fisticuffs, but he was later accused of offering Villa captain Alec Leake £10 to throw the game. Leake confirmed a conversation had happened but said he took it as a joke. Meredith was suspended for a year without pay. At first he came out fighting.

'Such an allegation as that of bribery is preposterous. I could never risk my reputation and future by such an action.' He blamed anti-Manchester City bias among football's top brass and added, 'Had I been anyone but a Welshman I would have been better dealt with.'

It is worth treating fervent denials with scepticism because Meredith was guilty. When he felt the financial squeeze and City's directors, who were being watched by a hawk-like FA auditor, left him to suffer, he blew the whole racket and gave the details of how City had cheated their way around the maximum wage.

'From 1902 I had been paid £6 a week and [George] Livingstone had been paid ten shillings more than that in wages,' he wrote. 'The season we won the cup I also received £53 in bonuses for games won and drawn. The team delivered the goods, the club paid for the goods delivered and both sides were satisfied.'

Meredith's testimony was devastating for Manchester City. The club's board and secretary were suspended, along with 17 players, who were also fined. City held an auction to sell players, but in May 1906 they agreed Meredith could leave for nothing because they couldn't deliver a benefit match he had been promised. He didn't go far. Meredith, Herbert Burgess, Sandy Turnbull and Jimmy Bannister all signed for newly promoted Manchester United, the club formed from Newton

Heath. The new players were suspended for half of that season, but in 1907/08 United ran away with the title, finishing nine points clear. They won the FA Cup in 1909, moved to a new stadium at Old Trafford in 1910 and won the league again in 1910/11.

But in the turbulent career of Billy Meredith, simply being the best forward of his generation wasn't enough. He became involved in attempts to reform the players' union. In their first title-winning season, United's game with Newcastle attracted 50,000 fans and yet the players were still receiving a maximum wage of £4 – plus whatever their clubs dared to sneak them in extras. The 'retain-and-transfer' system also created a market which in 1905 saw Middlesbrough pay Sunderland £1,000 for striker Alf Common in a desperate attempt to stave off relegation (though, ironically, relegation was scrapped that season when the divisions were reorganised). Players' rewards were scant by comparison.

Unfortunately for the union men, the FA and club owners outmanoeuvred them and a threatened strike was called off. Players were threatened with suspension for union membership and, although most caved in, Meredith and his Manchester United team-mates stood strong, for a while. They dubbed themselves 'Outcasts FC' and won some concessions from the authorities and were allowed to play again. The union survived but was ineffective for years. Key restrictions stayed in place: players couldn't move without permission from their club, and wages were kept low even though attendances were high.

Meredith wrote of his fellow professionals, 'The unfortunate thing is that so many players refuse to take things seriously but are content to live a kind of schoolboy life and to do just what they are told ... instead of thinking and acting for himself and his class.'

He also took aim at the FA toffs: 'They have always treated the player as though he were a mere boy or a sensible machine.

When they were displeased they just cracked the whip or gave him a slap.'

The class warrior remained a class footballer. In an age and environment where heavy drinking was rife, he was a teetotaller. He offered his dedication, rather than the notion of God-given talent, as the reason he should be paid more than his team-mates. His professionalism gave him remarkable longevity. He was too old to fight in World War One but kept playing football and was still going when the Football League restarted. He fell out with United over money and in 1921 moved back to City. He finally finished playing for City in 1924, having made his debut for Chirk in 1892. Between United and City, he played 720 games and won a then-record 48 caps for Wales, retiring after helping his nation win the British Home Championships in 1920, aged 45.

Meredith found personal success and adulation but failed to change football in the way he wanted. The game's ruling class knew when to give ground and when to strike back. Football's finances didn't change fundamentally until Jimmy Hill turned his strangely brilliant brain to the matter decades later. Footballers were ripped off for generations, although you might look at Premier League wages and give thanks that Meredith and co didn't get what they wanted. Going to football matches in Britain remained affordable and spectator numbers swelled. Would England's unique four-division professional structure have developed if big clubs had been able to monopolise the best players as they do now? The maximum wage also prolonged the existence of the great amateur footballers, such as Vivian Woodward.

5

Vivian Woodward

WHILE BILLY Meredith tortured defenders and administrators in equal measure, there was another great player of the pre-1914 era who was cut from very different cloth. Vivian Woodward was five years younger and, although his career was much shorter than Meredith's, he had time to score 29 goals in 23 official England internationals – a national record until the 1950s. While the Welshman was confronting, cajoling and double-crossing the game's powerbrokers, Woodward was invited to join the board at both Tottenham and Chelsea. The difference was that he was a gentleman, son of an architect and Freeman of the City of London, one of a dying breed: the great amateur footballer.

The nearest southern equivalent to the pioneering clubs of the North and Midlands was Royal Arsenal, which turned professional in 1891 and changed its prefix to Woolwich. Consequently, the club was expelled from the London FA, which was dominated by rabid anti-professionals like Nicholas 'Pa' Jackson. Jackson was the leader of Corinthian FC, a celebrated touring club for amateur gentlemen intent on spreading the gospel of 'sportsmanship, fair play and a love of the game'.

I suspect Meredith would add 'rampant class snobbery' to that list. The extraordinary C.B. Fry was the most celebrated Corinthian: an England international at football and cricket, long jump world-record co-holder and acquaintance of Adolf Hitler. Fry put it this way: 'Football in the Midlands and the North was played by wage earners, whereas in the South most of the strong clubs were composed of relatively leisured men.'

Corinthians would never take a penalty kick nor defend their goal if they conceded one. Their nobility, or otherwise, should be considered in the light of their view that the law reflected the rise of the working class, or, as Fry put it, 'It is a standing insult to sportsmen to have to play under a rule which assumes that players intend to trip, hack and push their opponents and to behave like cads of the most unscrupulous kidney.'

The opponents of professionalism got a good press, mainly because they owned and wrote it; both Jackson and Fry were influential sports journalists. Not everyone in southern England was so opposed. Woolwich Arsenal, unable to play in London FA events, tried to drum up interest in a professional league in the South. They failed and were on the brink of folding until they were rescued by the Football League in 1893. Perhaps they regretted not waiting because, while they struggled with long journeys and small crowds, the Southern League was founded with professionals and amateurs competing together.

Millwall Athletic were the first champions in 1894/95. They turned down an offer from the Football League and successfully defended their title. Southampton St Mary's usurped Millwall's Southern League dominance, winning six titles between 1897 and 1904 and twice losing the FA Cup Final with a mixed team of professionals and amateurs. In 1902 Fry was in the Saints XI, beaten in a replay by Sheffield United.

Woodward was an excellent cricketer and one of England's finest tennis players. He played football for Clacton Town, where his father was a board member, until he outgrew the

North Essex League and signed for Tottenham in 1901. His arrival went unheralded, even by the player himself, who stated he would turn up when it was 'convenient to play'. He usually missed the start of each season because of cricket commitments and didn't like to play at Christmas.

A measure of the strength of the Southern League was that Tottenham won the FA Cup that year, also against Sheffield United, while finishing fifth. You can watch highlights of the match. William 'Fatty' Foulke, gargantuan by the standards of the day, with trousers hitched distressingly high, is easy to spot, despite wearing the same coloured jersey as his outfielders. Estimates of the size of the crowd at Crystal Palace range from 110,820 to 114,815; it was football's biggest at that point, although I'm not sure how reliable the counting process could have been. The replay was played at Bolton, and on the train back south Lord Arthur Kinnaird, now president of the FA, drank beer from the FA Cup with a Tottenham-supporting bricklayer.

Woodward started playing football more regularly; he made his England debut in 1903 and scored twice against Ireland. He netted the winner when he faced Meredith for the first time as England defeated Wales 2-1 at Fratton Park, Portsmouth – one of only six meetings between the two greats. Woodward was described as 'the human chain of lightning, the footballer with magic in his boots'. The *Sporting Chronicle* added, 'Woodward is a great initiator, the personification of unselfishness ... quick to grasp the ever-changing situation of the game.'

The elegant architect was the obvious choice to captain the Great Britain team at the 1908 London Olympics. The FA had started organising amateur internationals in 1906 and England beat France 15-0 with four from Woodward. The football competition at the 1908 games was the first with recognisably national teams. In 1900 Great Britain had been represented by London amateur club Upton Park, who won the gold medal (don't be confused by the name: it had nothing to do with West Ham United, which was formed from Thames Ironworks).

No European footballers travelled to St Louis in 1904, but in 1908 Great Britain entered a team of leading amateurs, mainly southerners, but also containing the likes of Harold Hardman, a Manchester United outside-forward and future club chairman. They were all English and were interchangeably referred to as England and Great Britain.

To modern eyes, the competition doesn't seem properly global – every team was European and the standard varied tremendously. Denmark beat France 'B' 9-0 in their first game and the supposed France 'A' team 17-1 in the semi-final. Former Tottenham manager-turned-writer John Cameron surmised that, 'The French are never likely to do much at our winter game. They were much too polite and too fond of smoking the eternal cigarette. They puffed away to the start of the match, and in the interval had another smoke, finishing up the day by repeating the practice.' Woodward scored as Great Britain won the final in front of only 8,000 fans at London's White City.

The Southern League was declining, although the Football League's maximum wage allowed southern clubs to occasionally poach players, particularly older stars keen to become managers. Tottenham's ambitions almost ended in catastrophe as they fell out with the Southern League but failed to be elected to the Football League. They were rescued when Stoke got into financial difficulty and resigned, opening up a place in the Second Division.

Woodward nearly missed Spurs' first Football League game, against Wolves in September 1908, because it was scheduled for 5pm on a Tuesday and he was committed to playing cricket. The 20,000 fans were glad he made it when he scored their historic first goal, six minutes in. He led Spurs to promotion but didn't play for the club in the First Division. He left in the summer of 1909 to concentrate on his architectural practice. He turned out for Chelmsford briefly but was soon tempted back to the big time by a new club in west London.

Chelsea had a stadium first and a team second. Gus and Joseph Mears bought Stamford Bridge Athletics Stadium with a plan to redevelop and rent it to Fulham FC. Fulham had other ideas and Gus Mears was contemplating selling it to the Great Western Railway when he was persuaded by his colleague Fred Parker to set up his own club. Chelsea FC were formed in March 1905. They first asked to join the Southern League but, after Fulham and Tottenham objected, they applied instead to the Football League. With remarkable speed, they kicked off in the Second Division that September, having recruited a team with Fatty Foulke in goal. Given the trials and tribulations of other southern clubs, it is interesting to wonder what it was about millionaire Gus Mears that persuaded the Football League to admit Chelsea so quickly. They were promoted at the second attempt but went down again in Woodward's debut season, 1909/10, after losing to Spurs on the final day.

Class divisions were stark in Edwardian football. While Meredith and his fellow professionals fought for a fair share of gate receipts, Woodward was a genuine amateur, refusing to claim match expenses, which could be higher than professionals' match fees. Match officials called him 'sir' and in a game for Spurs against Millwall the referee hadn't seen whether the ball had crossed the line from a Woodward shot, so he asked the player and took his word that it had.

Woodward's attitude was lauded as much as his skills. Sports journalist Jimmy Catton wrote, 'His game was all art and no violence.' Tall and slim, he was targeted by the hard men of the game, as another writer Arthur Haig-Brown put it, 'It is a thousand pities that his lack of weight renders him a temptation which the occasionally unscrupulous half-back finds himself unable to resist.' (See Pelé, Best, Van Basten ...)

Chelsea were promoted in 1912 before Woodward again led Britain at the Olympics, this time in Sweden. The team had two First Division players, Arthur Berry of Everton and Bradford's Harold Walden, but another two from the Isthmian League and one from Stockton in the Northern League. Walden scored eight goals as Britain retained their title with Denmark again taking silver.

The Southern League's heyday was over, and in 1920 the remaining strong teams joined the new Third Division of the Football League, leaving behind a semi-professional feeder league. Great Britain lost to Norway in the first round of the 1920 Olympics, leaving no doubt that the great amateur footballer had been consigned to history. Belgium won the gold medal when their opponents in the final, Czechoslovakia, walked off in protest at the performance of 65-year-old English referee John Lewis.

By then Woodward had stopped playing competitively after being hit in the thigh by grenade splinters in World War One. He joined the Territorial Army at the outbreak of war but still played football, as competitive matches continued until the end of the 1914/15 season, when any pretence of the fighting being over by Christmas had been dispelled. Chelsea reached the 1915 FA Cup Final against Sheffield United; Woodward was given leave from his regiment but refused to play in place of his team-mate Bob Thompson, who had featured in every round. Thompson played despite an injury and Chelsea lost 3-0.

Woodward's last competitive goal came in a league game for Chelsea against Meredith's Manchester United. Meredith was too old to be called up. Woodward didn't wait to be asked, and in 1915 he became an officer in the 17th Battalion of the Middlesex Regiment, the so-called Footballers' Regiment. One of his fellow officers, Walter Tull, had signed for Tottenham when Woodward left in the summer of 1909.

Woodward recovered enough from his injuries to play occasional games for Chelmsford and Clacton, but his top-level career was over. Amateurs faded into the periphery of the game, although Arsenal's Bernard Joy won a full England cap as late as 1936.

Having designed a stand at Antwerp Stadium, Woodward retired from his architectural practice and became a farmer and director at Chelsea. He was an air raid warden in the Second World War. He died aged 74, telling a journalist who interviewed him in his Ealing nursing home, 'No one who used to be with me in football has been to see me for two years. I wish they would.'

6

Walter Tull

NOT EVERY amateur footballer in southern England came from wealthy stock. Walter Tull's background could hardly have been more different from that of Vivian Woodward, the man he followed into Tottenham's team in their first-ever season in Football League Division One.

Tull's grandparents had been slaves in Barbados. His father Daniel travelled to England as a ship's carpenter and settled in Folkestone, where he married a young local woman called Alice Palmer. They had six children, including Walter in 1888. Alice died of cancer when Walter was seven years old and Daniel married her cousin Clara. Walter was eight when his father died of heart disease. Clara couldn't afford to look after all of the children so Walter and his brother Edward, who was also of school age, were sent to the Children's Home and Orphanage in East London. The boys lived there together until Edward went on a money-raising singing tour and was spotted by a Glaswegian dentist who adopted him.

Walter became an accomplished sportsman and trained to be a printer. He played football for Clapton and was the star of their 1909 FA Amateur Cup-winning side. He caught the eye of Spurs, who had just lost Woodward, and was invited on their tour of Argentina and Uruguay – the one where the Englishmen's physicality so upset the locals. He was offered professional terms and played in Spurs' first-ever First Division game, a 3-1 defeat against Sunderland.

He made remarkably rapid progress. His third game was against a Manchester United side, minus Billy Meredith that day. A report in the *Daily Chronicle* lauded Tottenham's new player: 'Such perfect coolness, such judicious waiting for a fraction of a second in order to get a pass in not before a defender has worked to a false position, and such accuracy of strength in passing I have not seen for a long time. Tull has been charged with being slow but there never was a footballer yet who was really great and always appeared to be in a hurry. Tull did not get the ball and rush into trouble. He let his opponents do the rushing, and defeated them by side touches and side-steps worthy of a professional boxer.'

That is strong praise for a 21-year-old a few games into his professional career, especially as he had debuted for Clapton less than a year earlier. And yet Tull only played ten league matches for Tottenham. No one said why, but it is fair to speculate as to whether it had something to do with the racism he suffered in a match at Bristol City in October that year.

The *Football Star* reported, 'A section of the crowd made a cowardly attack upon him in language lower than Billingsgate [London fish market]. Let me tell these Bristol hooligans (there were but a few of them in a crowd of nearly twenty thousand) that Tull is so clean in mind and method as to be a model for all white men who play football whether they be amateur or professional. In point of ability, if not actual achievement, Tull was the best forward on the field.'

Tull played the next two Tottenham home games against Bury and Middlesbrough, but didn't feature again for the first team for more than a year. Some writers suggest he was dropped by club directors keen to avoid the sort of scandalous scenes that happened in Bristol. Or maybe the two contemporary reporters who praised him so lavishly were both wrong and he wasn't good enough to play.

The irrationality of racism leads to contradictions in both sport, and, as we shall see, in war. Tull seems to have been the only black footballer of his day in Britain, but there had been others. The great Scottish Cup-winning Queen's Park team contained Andrew Watson, who also played for Scotland. Watson played for leading amateur clubs in London too, and might have been paid when he played for professional club Bootle. Watson, an expensively educated son of a wealthy Scottish sugar planter and a Guianese mother, is there to be seen in photos of the Queen's Park side but so little was made of his skin colour that Arthur Wharton was long referred to as the first black footballer.

Wharton was definitely a professional. He played with the Ross brothers at Preston but left before the Football League began. He did play league games for Sheffield United in 1894/95, as understudy to 'Fatty' Foulke. If Watson's story suggests a rosy picture of racial harmony in Victorian football, consider this report in the *Athletic News* about Wharton playing for Preston:

'Good judges say that if Wharton keeps goal for Preston North End in their English Cup tie the odds will be considerably lengthened against them. I am of the same opinion ... Is the darkie's pate too thick for it to dawn upon him that between the posts is no place for a skylark? By some it's called coolness – bosh!'

In 1911 Tull was sold to Northampton Town, where he thrived in the early managerial career of Herbert Chapman, a great innovator, who would later guide Huddersfield Town and Arsenal to Football League titles. There was speculation he was close to signing for Rangers, which would have allowed him to live near his brother Edward, who was practising as a dentist – but on the outbreak of World War One Tull gave up football and joined the army.

THE FIFTY

Competitive football continued after the amateur-dominated sports of cricket and rugby had stopped and players came under feverish pressure from newspapers, serving soldiers and, naturally, from famous wealthy men who were too old to fight, such as Sherlock Holmes creator Arthur Conan Doyle. There were calls for the king to withdraw his patronage from the FA because so few footballers had joined the likes of Tull and Woodward. Lord Kinnaird helped rally would-be troops at a meeting at Fulham Town Hall in December 1914 and the 17th Service (Football) Battalion of the Middlesex Regiment was founded. They were far from overrun with recruits and the season was played out. Many members of the battalion were fans keen to serve alongside stars such as Woodward.

Tull transferred to the 'Footballers' Battalion' in 1915 and was made a sergeant. They reached the front line in January 1916, where they suffered their first casualties and Woodward was wounded. In May, Tull was treated for 'acute mania', more commonly known as shell shock, and now as post-traumatic stress disorder. He was luckier than others, who were condemned as cowards, although he wasn't given long to recover and was back at the front in September, to join the Battle of the Somme. Footballers weren't protected from the horrors of war; England international Evelyn Lintott was one of 19,240 British soldiers killed on 1 July 1916, the first day of the Somme. Later that year Tull was sent back to Britain with trench fever. During his rehabilitation he was identified as a potential officer, despite explicitly racist rules designed to prevent soldiers not 'natural born or naturalised British subjects of pure European descent' – in other words, non-white – from becoming commissioned officers.

Lieutenant Tull was mentioned in dispatches for gallantry and coolness after leading a night raid over the River Piave, into enemy territory in northern Italy. A colleague suggested Tull's name was to be put forward for the Military Cross, although no proof of this has been found. Tull returned to France in March

1918 and fought at the First Battle of Bapaume in the German Army's Spring Offensive. Reports exist of exhausted soldiers struggling to move over territory that had been the scene of so much fighting already. As one survivor put it, 'what remains of my memory of this day is the constant taking up of new positions, followed by constant orders to retire, terrible blocks on the roads, inability to find anyone anywhere.'

In one of those advances, Tull was shot in the head by German machine-gun fire. His comrades, including ex-Leicester Fosse goalkeeper Tom Billingham, tried to recover his body but were forced back and he was never found.

So what was Walter Tull's legacy? British football now has lots of black and mixed-heritage stars and you don't have to have white skin to become an officer in the British Army but progress was slow and hard-fought. His story is now told to primary school children, but I had never heard of him when I was a football-mad kid. One footballer's story can be an inspiration but it can take generations to get real change, as decades of women footballers knew only too well.

7

Lily Parr

'THE GAME of football is quite unsuitable for females and it ought not to be encouraged.'

And with that, in 1921 the FA successfully drove women to the fringes of football. There was no outright ban but a restriction on clubs allowing their stadiums to be used for women's matches. Coupled with a firm message of disapproval, it stopped the growth of women's football in its tracks. And what growth there had been. On Boxing Day 1920, 53,000 fans went to Goodison Park to watch Preston-based works team Dick, Kerr's Ladies beat St Helens' Ladies 4-0. A mark of how effectively the restriction worked was that there wasn't a bigger crowd at a women's match in England until the 2012 Olympics.

Dick, Kerr's Ladies were some team. They started playing matches against their male colleagues and then branched out to become the dominant force in the short-lived heyday of the early women's game. Their star was Lily Parr, a hard-drinking, woodbine-smoking, goalscoring winger. Parr was also openly gay in the 1920s. We won't get to another gay footballer in this book until Justin Fashanu, nearly 60 years on.

Women had played football since Victorian times. In 1895 Nettie Honeyball (possibly not a real name) established the

British Women's Football Club and a crowd of 5,000 watched a North versus South match played in Bury, although interest waned until World War One.

Young men like Walter Tull and Vivian Woodward were fighting in France and Belgium and women were recruited to work in the factories, such as Dick, Kerr's, which had been converted into a munitions factory. With the restrictions on organised men's football, women's matches attracted more fans, and with large amounts of money raised for charities Prime Minister David Lloyd George gave his blessing.

Dick, Kerr's were the best but by no means the only women's team. The Bradford Women's League had two divisions and there were plenty of other works' teams, including Lyons Tea Rooms. Attendances were good and manager Alfred Frankland persuaded Preston North End to bring Deepdale out of mothballs. On Christmas Day 1917 10,000 watched the first game at the stadium since the suspension of the men's league. The reception in the male-dominated press was mixed. The *Lancashire Daily Post* reported on a Dick, Kerr's Ladies match: 'Quite a few of their shots would not have disgraced regular professionals except in direction, and even professionals have been known on occasion to be a trifle wide of the target. Their forward work indeed was often surprisingly good.'

Frankland was a ruthless recruiter of talent, happily plundering beaten opponents. Parr had grown up playing football with her brothers and caught Frankland's eye when she played for St Helens against Dick, Kerr's, even though she was only 14. He offered her a job in the factory and told her she could earn ten shillings' expenses for turning out for the works' team – effectively a semi-professional outfit. In her first season she scored 43 goals. They recruited from further afield as well, including Frenchwoman Louise Ourry and Scot Nancy Thomson (who only died in 2010).

People turned out to watch Dick, Kerr's whenever they played: 35,000 saw them at Newcastle in 1919. The players were given free rail travel and the future FIFA president Jules Rimet helped to organise England versus France games, with the bulk of the England team coming from Dick, Kerr's. The first women's international at Deepdale was watched by 25,000, and other games were played at Manchester's Hyde Road and at Stamford Bridge. In 1920 Frankland organised an England tour of France and games were played in front of 14,000 and 16,000 spectators.

When they got back to England, they started to play fundraising games on behalf of the Unemployed Servicemen's Distress Fund, but expenses paid to players were to become a source of controversy and an attack route for opponents. As well as the 53,000 inside Goodison Park for the match between Dick, Kerr's Ladies and St Helens, another 14,000 were turned away. The match raised over £3,000. Dick, Kerr's played again at Old Trafford, with 35,000 watching. They played 67 games in 1921 and turned down over 100 other offers.

It is hard to pinpoint the exact moment when the football establishment decided enough was enough. Wartime arrangements had contributed to the growth of women's football but the biggest crowds were in peacetime. It has been suggested the football establishment was fearful that men's football would decline in popularity and there was another political dimension.

When prominent women's teams began to raise money to support miners involved in a bitter industrial dispute in 1921, the FA took a dim view. Football academic Dr Ali Melling put it this way: 'Women's football was therefore perceived as revolutionary and quite dangerous. There was a political reason for shutting it down. Women's football got too big, too soon and too class-orientated. And it was too dangerous. It scared people.'

Questions were raised about how much of the money raised reached the intended charities, though little evidence of wrongdoing emerged. The FA found female doctors happy to back their case.

Dr Elizabeth Sloan Chesser said, 'There are physical reasons why the game is harmful to women. It is a rough game at any time, but it is much more harmful to women than men. They may receive injuries from which they may never recover.' Harley Street physician Dr Mary Scharlieb said, 'I consider it a most unsuitable game, too much for a woman's physical frame.'

There was some resistance and the English Ladies' Football Association was formed, but there were disagreements and splits and it folded, leaving women's football without a governing body. The early era of mass attendances was over. Parr and the Dick, Kerr's Ladies went on a tour of Canada and the USA, only for the Canadian football authorities to ban teams from playing against them. They had more joy in the US, although class prejudice played its part again. Soccer there was already seen by some as a game for middle-class girls, and college principals were reluctant to allow them to play against British factory workers. Some of their games were against men's teams and they fared well, with one newspaper describing Parr as 'the most brilliant female player in the world'.

Her team-mate Joan Whalley later wrote, 'She was the only person I knew who could deadlift the old heavy leather ball from the left wing over to me on the right and nearly knock me out with the force of the shot.' Scotland international Bobby Walker called Parr, 'The best natural timer of a football,' and there is a much-told story of an arrogant male goalkeeper who challenged her to beat him from the penalty spot. She didn't, but he was left moaning, 'She's broken my arm.'

Dick, Kerr's factory was taken over by English Electric and the new owners stopped supporting the team. Lily and others got jobs at Whittingham Hospital and Lunatic Asylum, one of the recipients of their charity in the team's pomp. The stadium ban stayed in place until 1971. As late as 1962, the FA actively intervened to stop a women's charity match from being held at a British Legion-owned ground because Wigan Rovers also played there.

THE FIFTY

There is great sadness in this story, but I am reluctant to paint Parr as a victim. She carried on playing football with Preston Ladies until 1950, she was the first person in her family to buy a house and she lived happily with her partner Mary. It was claimed she scored 986 goals, although it is impossible to verify. She wasn't a saint. She drank a lot, and smoked strong Woodbines, once demanding to be paid her expenses in cigarettes. More than once she stole the match ball and sold it. She has a statue and a place in the Football Hall of Fame.

The real victims of this story are the generations of women who didn't get to play football in front of tens of thousands of fans, who were discouraged, warned off or mocked when they tried to play the best sport of all. Women competed at the Olympics and at Wimbledon, and between 1962 and 1972 there were six female winners of the BBC Sports Personality of the Year – but in the story of football we don't get to another woman until Hope Powell who was born 61 years later; a great shame for the great game.

8

Dixie Dean

WHEN EVERTON won the 1914/15 Football League before nationwide football was suspended for the war, a new fan attended his first game at Goodison Park. William or Billy Dean had travelled over the Mersey from Birkenhead with his dad, who was a railway worker. Billy left school at 14 and began training as a fitter on the Wirral Railway working nights to allow him time to play football in the daytime. At 16, he made his debut for Tranmere in Division Three (North) and was soon attracting scouts from bigger clubs.

Twenty-seven goals in 30 games by March in the 1924/25 season was an impressive scoring rate for those days, especially at a club that had to apply for re-election to the Football League at the end of the campaign. Post-war austerity had hit football and there was tactical trouble. The offside law (in place since 1866) meant a player would be penalised unless he had three opponents, including the keeper (or ball), between himself and the goal. Most teams played with a 2-3-5 formation and defenders came to realise that one of them could sweep and the other could press high and try to catch attackers offside. Newcastle were said to be the worst, or most cunning, culprits, with Bill McCracken perfecting the art of stepping up and demanding the offside flag. Play became bunched around the halfway line and goals per game fell, soon followed by attendances.

The laws of football are made by the International Football Association Board, which even now has half its members from the British associations. A simple change to the offside law revolutionised the game. From the start of the 1925/26 season an attacker was onside if he had just two opponents goal side of him. The transformation was stunning: an extra 511 goals were scored in the First Division alone that season. Aston Villa thrashed Burnley 10-0 in August; Newcastle hammered Notts County 6-3 in September; and on New Year's Day Sheffield United beat Cardiff 11-2. Blackburn Rovers' Ted Harper got a record 43 goals in a mid-table team. Everton's new young striker, known to fans and the media as Dixie, scored 33 in his first full season in the big time. A couple of months later he was fighting for his life.

In June 1926 he took his girlfriend for a motorcycle ride in North Wales and crashed into an erratically driven oncoming car. He said that when he realised the collision was about to happen he pushed his girlfriend off the bike and she suffered only an ankle injury. He was left in a coma with a fractured skull and jaw and smashed kneecaps. Doctors said that if he survived he would never play football again. Four months later he lined up for an Everton reserve match and scored with a header.

'As a matter of fact,' he told the newspapers, 'I think the skull fracture knitted twice as hard, so they tell me, and it considerably helped with the old heading trick.'

He played a total of 36 games in league and cup that season and scored 36 goals, but down in the Second Division there was a new record-breaker. George Camsell, recently signed from non-league Durham City, banged in 59 of Middlesbrough's 122 goals as they finished top. He didn't even take any of Boro's last five penalties after missing one in February.

DIXIE DEAN

Dean scored against Sheffield Wednesday on the first day of the 1927/28 season and at least once in the next eight games, including a 4-1 defeat at Middlesbrough, for whom Camsell got them all. Dean's goal glut continued and in February a hat-trick against Liverpool at Anfield took him past Harper's top-flight record. Everton stormed to the title with an unbeaten run of eight games, in which Dean scored 17 goals including a last-day hat-trick against Arsenal, which took him to 60 league goals for the season, one more than Camsell's record. To add insult to injury for the Boro striker, who had scored 33, his side were relegated as two points separated the bottom nine teams.

Dean made a sensational start to his England career that season, scoring 12 goals in his first five games against Wales, Scotland, Belgium, Luxembourg and France. England had been 2-0 down in Luxembourg until Dean began the comeback with his first of three goals in the 18th minute.

He didn't hit the heights of 1927/28 again, although he scored consistently whenever he played, despite Everton's ups and downs. In the next two seasons he appeared in only 29 and 25 league games and scored 26 and 23 goals; Everton went down in 1930. He stayed fitter for the next two seasons and Everton surged back up in 1931, with Dean scoring 48 in all competitions. They won the Football League again in 1932, their first year back: 47 in 40 games was Dean's contribution.

He won his only FA Cup in 1933, scoring in a 3-0 win over Manchester City while literally becoming football's first number nine. The FA experimented with shirt numbers for the first time and Everton wore one to 11, while City took 12 to 22. City's number 19, Scotland international wing-half Matt Busby, was awestruck: 'When Dixie went up for the ball, he was almost unstoppable. Defenders were absolutely terrified of him.'

Another Scotland wing-half and future managerial great, Bill Shankly, signed for Preston in 1933. 'Dixie was the greatest centre-forward there ever will be,' he reflected. 'He belongs to the company of the supremely great, like Beethoven, Shakespeare and Rembrandt.'

Apparently Dean didn't like the nickname Dixie, although if his friend Shankly was using it decades later he maybe got used to it. Two explanations are offered: either a corruption of 'digsy', a dialect word for 'tag' or, more likely, it was a comment on his skin colour. He wasn't black or, that we know of, mixed heritage, but he had relatively dark skin and curly black hair. 'Dixie' probably referenced black southern American slaves. At a match against Tottenham a racist fan abused Dean, shouting, 'We'll get you, you black bastard.' A policeman stepped forward but Dean ushered him aside and punched the fan, knocking him to the ground. The policeman was apparently satisfied that honour was done: simpler times, before seagulls followed trawlers.

In all, Dean scored 349 league goals and a total of 395 for Everton in 12 full seasons before being sold to Notts County, where he struggled with injuries until World War Two. Before he left Goodison Park, he made a point of training up his successor Tommy Lawton, another great goalscorer who won the title with Everton in 1939 and scored 22 goals for England either side of the war.

Dean's career Football League scoring record was eventually overtaken by the amazingly durable Arthur Rowley, who scored 434 between 1946 and 1965. Jimmy Greaves surpassed the record for top-division goals, but no one has topped Dean's 60 Football League goals in a season. We shouldn't forget the amazing Josef Bican, a forward in Austria's *Wunderteam*, who scored 805 goals in official matches, and we will get to Pelé's 1,000 goals later. The scoring rate stayed high, barring a post-war dip, until the late 1960s when defences mastered the new offside trap and the linesman's flag became a regular blight on football again.

His only underachievement wasn't really his fault. He played only 16 times for England, victim of an erratic selection committee and the home nations' isolationist outlook. FIFA had been established by eight European associations in Paris in 1904, and after staying clear for two years the Brits joined in 1906 and were immediately allowed to take over, with Daniel Burley Woolfall becoming president until his death in 1918, after which he was succeeded by Frenchman Jules Rimet. After playing a successful part in the staging of the Olympic football tournaments, the British withdrew from FIFA in 1928 over a row about professionalism and took no part in the 1930 World Cup.

Would one of the home nations have won it? Would Dixie Dean and his English mates have had too much power and know-how for the hapless foreigners? That was certainly the view in England, where the Football League's Charles Sutcliffe branded the World Cup 'a joke' and insisted the Home Championship decided the best team in the world.

The evidence doesn't back him up. In 1929 England were beaten 4-3 by Spain at Madrid's old Estadio Metropolitano without Dean. In May 1930 they drew with Germany in Berlin and again in Vienna against the wonderful Austrians. In 1931 they lost to France, and, although Dean was back to score as England took revenge over the Spanish with a 7-1 win at Highbury, the idea that the British were unquestionably the best was nonsense. Could they have travelled to Uruguay in July 1930 and shown the world whose game football was? Maybe, with good preparation and lots of luck, but we will never know.

Dean first took that most traditional of post-football career paths, running a pub. He later worked as a porter for Littlewoods Pools, an officially sponsored gambling operation hugely popular in the days before the National Lottery and today's Wild West of gambling. His passing was sad but poetic: Everton's legendary centre-forward had a heart attack at Goodison Park while watching the 1980 Merseyside Derby, at the age of 73.

9

José Andrade

JOSÉ LEANDRO Andrade was reportedly a drummer, a violinist, a shoe-shiner, a lover of famous women and the first world-class black footballer. Unpicking truth from myth is tricky with early stars, so we don't know for certain that his father was an escaped Brazilian slave who was 98 at the time of José's birth, but that is how the story goes.

It is definitely true that a country with less than two million inhabitants produced football's first truly global champions. As the sport reached its Olympic pinnacle in the 1920s before going it alone with the first FIFA World Cup in 1930, it was tiny Uruguay that swept the board. Do cry for me, Argentina.

Andrade moved to live with an aunt in the capital Montevideo, a thriving port city, though his was no privileged upbringing. He slept on a dirt floor as a kid and later worked as a carnival musician, dancer and, apparently, a gigolo. Andrade's good looks definitely turned heads. While he and his fellow 1924 Olympians were catching the eye of European football's intelligentsia in Paris, he was also romantically linked with two of the most famously beautiful women of the age: novelist and scandalous Moulin Rouge performer Colette, and Josephine Baker, one of the first black film stars.

JOSÉ ANDRADE

The Uruguayans caught Europe unawares. Those remarkable pioneers from Victorian Britain had taken the game to South American ports, and locals had caught football fever. By the time the Olympics could claim to be a properly global football event, the South Americans had reinvented the game.

Andrade was part of a great team, captained by *El Gran Mariscal*, José Nasazzi, a marble cutter turned Grand Marshal of the Uruguay defence. Their first World Cup goal was scored by Hector Castro, who had lost a hand to an electric saw when he was a carpenter. Their leading scorer was Pedro Cea, a coolheaded former ice salesman, who hit a hat-trick in the 1930 semi-final and the equaliser in the final.

They were watched in the Olympics final by the remarkable Gabriel Hanot, a former France international who later became national team coach, set up the legendary football journal *L'Équipe* and devised both the Ballon d'Or and the European Cup.

Hanot wrote in *Miroir des Sports*, as referred to by Goldblatt in *The Ball is Round*, 'The principal quality of the victors was a marvellous virtuosity in receiving the ball, controlling it and using it. They have such a complete technique that they also have the necessary leisure to note the position of partners and team-mates. They do not stand waiting for a pass. They are on the move, away from markers to make it easy for team-mates.

'The Uruguayans are supple disciples of the spirit of fitness rather than geometry. They have pushed towards perfection the art of the feint and swerve and the dodge, but they also know how to play directly and quickly. They are not only ball jugglers. They created a beautiful football, elegant but at the same time varied, rapid, powerful, effective. Before these fine athletes, who are to the English professionals like Arab thoroughbreds next to farm horses, the Swiss were disconcerted.'

We can't know whether Hanot's view of the Uruguayan superiority to the British was justified because this was one of football's Brexit phases and neither England nor

Scotland played against La Celeste until the 1950s (when they both lost).

Andrade was a tall, fast, strong wing-half (precursor of a defensive midfielder) but what marked him out was his elegance. Literary theorist Professor Hans Ulrich Gumbrecht wrote about the aesthetics of sports, claiming Andrade was 'responsible more than anybody else in the first third of the 20th century for putting football on the map of international sports'.

But he was no straightforward hero. Argentina were piqued that their rivals from across the River Plate had gone to the 1924 Olympics and wowed the world, while they stayed home. The two rivals played regularly (36 times in the 1920s) but the post-Paris clashes were particularly feisty. An attempt to play a match in Buenos Aires had to be abandoned because of crowd violence, and when it was rearranged the local fans threw stones over and through the fences at Andrade, who picked up the stones and threw them back. As the police tried to intervene, his team-mate Hector Scarone kicked an officer and in the subsequent melee the Uruguayans left the field and the match was abandoned.

Andrade also lived a hedonistic lifestyle which came back to haunt him, possibly blind him, and ultimately kill him. There were tales of frequent absences from the team hotel and riotous drunken nights out. His club Nacional went on a tour of Europe in 1925 that was watched by more than 800,000 people, but Andrade missed half of it after being told by a doctor in Brussels he had syphilis, an infection that is usually sexually transmitted. He is said to have disappeared to Paris on hearing the news. He reappeared in Montevideo two months later. On his arrival, a reporter said he had lost weight and had 'an air of depression'. Andrade said he was feeling 'somewhat ill' and would undergo a course of treatment.

He played on having lost some of his pace but none of his skill. When Uruguay's entertainers reached the Olympic final

JOSÉ ANDRADE

in Amsterdam in 1928, more than 250,000 applied for tickets – ten times the stadium's capacity. Uruguay beat Argentina 2-1, but in the semi-final against Italy Andrade ran into a goalpost and, some said, the injury was so serious he was later blinded in one eye. Perhaps, though, his deteriorating health, and blindness, could have been caused by syphilis.

FIFA's choice of Uruguay to host the first World Cup in 1930 made sense. They were double Olympic champions and had an economy buoyant enough to pay travel expenses of visiting teams and to build a new stadium – named the Estadio Centenario in recognition of Uruguayan independence in 1830. Only 13 nations attended. Hungary, Austria, Italy, Germany and Spain had strong teams but chose not to go. England and Scotland were making a principled stand against something or other, so the European representation was from Belgium, Romania, Yugoslavia and France, who won the first fixture 4-1 against Mexico in front of just 4,444 fans.

It was very different when Uruguay got involved. A crowd of 57,735 saw Castro's goal secure a win over Peru, before they thrashed Romania 4-0 and Yugoslavia 6-1, in the semi-finals.

Andrade was still a star and was named in the 'Team of the Tournament'. He was apparently slower but played every game including the final – another fraught showdown with Argentina, whose star defender Luis Monti received death threats from fans of both sides.

Cris Freddi argues in his *Complete Book of the World Cup 2006* the feverish atmosphere demonstrated that Uruguay was the right place for the first World Cup. 'It proved the match *mattered*. Had it been held in Europe, how many spectators would have been locked out as they were here? Would they have been searched for weapons on the way in? How many European stadia needed a surrounding moat?'

Belgian referee John Langenus agreed to take the game only if FIFA promised there would be a boat in the harbour, ready to leave within an hour of the final whistle. Uruguay scored first through Dorado but Argentina were ahead by half-time; Guillermo Stabile's total of eight goals was a tournament high. But it seems that Uruguay, to use the modern parlance, wanted it more. Cea, Iriarte and Castro all scored in a 4-2 win and Jules Rimet handed his trophy not to the skipper Nasazzi but to the president of the Uruguayan federation.

It was the end for that great Uruguayan generation. There wasn't another Copa America until 1935, and many of them, including Andrade, were gone by then. There was no football at the 1932 Olympics as the World Cup assumed dominance and Uruguay didn't defend their trophy in 1934 or play in 1938. Andrade was a spectator and honoured guest in Brazil 1950, watching his nephew, Victor Rodriguez Andrade, and his teammates reclaim Uruguay's place at the top of the world game.

José played club football beyond 1930 but post-retirement he didn't find work as a coach or broadcaster, as many of his colleagues had. Who knows from this distance how much that was because of his partial blindness, illness, spiky personality, wild lifestyle or skin colour. He drank heavily, had troubled relationships and depression. In 1956 a German journalist found Andrade living in a dilapidated Montevideo basement flat, too drunk to be interviewed. He died a penniless alcoholic in an asylum, aged 56.

10

Stanley Matthews

STANLEY MATTHEWS was arguably the greatest footballer of his generation, although a detractor might say he was more Neymar than Messi: lightning fast, graceful and skilful but at his worst too peripheral in games. It is also hard to define when the Matthews era was. He helped England beat world champions Italy in 1934, which was 22 years before he became the first European Footballer of the Year. His last professional appearance was in 1965, a few days after his 50th birthday.

The maximum wage did its job. That the acclaimed Matthews played his entire professional career for Stoke City and Blackpool shows the big clubs didn't monopolise the best players. Blackpool have never finished higher than second – in the year Matthews beat Real Madrid's pioneering European Cup winners to the Ballon d'Or. Stoke have never bettered their fourth-place finishes of 1936 and 1947. A win at Sheffield United in their last match of the 1946/47 season would have secured the title, but they lost – without Matthews, who had been sold in early May after a long-running dispute with the manager became irreconcilable. He chose Blackpool because he and his wife had bought a guest house there.

Pelé described Matthews as 'the man who taught us how football should be played'. Bobby Charlton put it like this: 'In the context of great players, going back as far as I can remember, Stanley Matthews is probably the greatest of them all ... I couldn't take my eyes off him.' I could fill a chapter with similar quotes but you can look for yourself – try *Stanley Matthews, Wizard of the Dribble* on YouTube. Look beyond the baggy shorts, the thin hair and the full-backs getting squared up (every time!) and note the balance and explosive speed. Ronaldinho came to my mind.

Stanley was the son of Jack Matthews, who earned his money through the non-traditional combination of boxing and hairdressing. He taught Stanley to box, instilling a tremendous work ethic. In an era of minimal training, the great Matthews would be out practising crossing for hours. His regime was decades ahead of its time: weights to build up what we now call core strength, running for cardio fitness and a diet focussed around fruit and vegetables. As a young apprentice at Stoke he met Billy Meredith, who told him, 'Always listen to the older players' – wise words in a time when tactical work among English teams was almost non-existent.

Matthews signed for Stoke, his home-town club, and was paid £5 a week in season and £3 in the summer. An average worker could earn around £2 a week and a standard head teacher's annual salary might be £300. Footballers were well off but not rich, yet some of the biggest-ever attendances are from that time. In six consecutive matches in 1934, Stoke's crowds added up to 399,874, including Manchester City's record of 84,569. Matthews was playing when 149,547 watched Scotland beat England at Hampden Park in 1937. It wasn't a perfectly level playing field; Arsenal were dubbed 'the Bank of England Club' as they won five titles in the 1930s, but the idea that a player of such status would stay with a mid-sized club is now unthinkable.

He was close to leaving in 1938 after manager Bob McGrory quibbled over £150. Clubs were able to pay a £650 bonus to professionals for five years' service, but McGrory initially refused to hand over more than £500. Matthews and his wife were buying a semi-detached house in the village of Trent Vale and he was determined to get the full amount, so he handed in a transfer request. Local businessmen organised a crisis meeting and 3,000 people attended. Stoke paid up and their star player stayed.

Matthews's England career spanned from the period of jingoistic self-deception to the era of crushing realisation. The brutal confrontation with World Cup-winners Italy in 1934 was dubbed the Battle of Highbury. A narrow, disputed victory saw *The Times* claim, 'The verdict is that England is still supreme in a game essentially our own.'

It was a ludicrously overblown conclusion. Games against continental opponents were largely restricted to end-of-season tours, and that year England had lost to Hungary and Czechoslovakia. In 1936 they lost to Austria and Belgium. Matthews had perhaps his best game for England, scoring a hat-trick in a 5-4 win over the Czechoslovaks at White Hart Lane in 1937. There was a free-scoring tour of Scandinavia, but most matches were against the other home nations, as pig-headed isolationism kept England away from the early World Cups.

In 1938 England beat Germany 6-3 in Berlin, an occasion most remembered now for Matthews and his team-mates giving Nazi salutes beforehand. The shame for that should belong to British Ambassador Sir Nevile Henderson, who pressured the FA in his eagerness to avoid a diplomatic incident. Senior Nazis were there in force: Hess, Ribbentrop, Göring and Goebbels, but not Hitler, who had seen Germany lose before and refused to attend. Matthews did have a brief brush with the despot though. He and team-mate Bert Sproston were in a café when the Führer's motorcade flashed by. Matthews noted the effect it had on the people around them. 'I could see the Germans regarded Hitler as a God. I had not believed before that such fanaticism was possible.' Sproston told Matthews, 'I don't know much about politics but I reckon yon Hitler is an evil little twat.'

Given the miseries of World War Two, it seems trivial to grieve for lost football, but Matthews's peak years were spent as a PE instructor in the Royal Air Force. Professional football was suspended but games were played as part of the effort to maintain morale, and big crowds turned up as Matthews played for England (in unofficial internationals), the RAF and as a guest for various club teams, including Blackpool. He didn't see active service, though other footballers, such as Tom Finney and Wilf Mannion, did.

After the war, Matthews witnessed what was then the greatest tragedy in British football. The FA Cup had resumed and in March 1946 Stoke went to Bolton's Burnden Park. Estimates suggest 85,000 tried to squeeze inside. The turnstiles were closed 20 minutes before kick-off but more supporters crammed in and collapsing barriers contributed to 33 deaths and around 400 injuries. The players weren't told of the severity of the tragedy and played out a 0-0 draw. Matthews said later he was sickened that the game was played. There was an inquiry and new safety restrictions were placed on football grounds, though sadly there are more tragedies to tell of later.

Matthews's post-war form is testimony to his lifestyle and dedication. It was Blackpool's glory era, but it appeared that it would be defined by near misses, as they lost the FA Cup finals of 1948 and 1951. We modern fans don't appreciate the importance of the FA Cup in those days, but it was at least on a par with winning the league; as one Pathé newsreel claimed, 'the most coveted football trophy in the world'.

Matthews won his only major club honour in 1953, aged 38. The build-up to the FA Cup Final against Bolton focussed on whether this was finally his moment. As Blackpool's players lined up in tangerine kit, the Duke of Edinburgh told them, 'You all look like a bunch of pansies.'

They were 3-1 down with 23 minutes to go. The match was dubbed 'The Matthews Final', but it was his England teammate Stan Mortensen who scored a hat-trick to pull it back to 3-3 before a typical Matthews run and cross set up Bill Perry's winner in the 89th minute.

That match came between his two World Cup appearances. England finally came out of hiding for the 1950 tournament in Brazil. As Obdulio Varela led Uruguay to a sensational victory, England turned up poorly prepared and suffered a humiliating defeat. Matthews's international career was a stop-start affair, partly because of war and partly because of the nature of the selection committee and its competing agendas.

He was originally left out of the 1950 squad and went instead on an FA tour of Canada, only to be summoned to Brazil at the last moment. Having travelled for 28 hours, he was left out of the win over Chile and not picked for the infamous defeat against the USA, only appearing for the Spain game, another defeat that confirmed England's elimination. The England entourage left as soon as they could along with the press corps. Matthews asked to stay and learn by watching the best teams in the world but was told to leave with the rest of the party.

His longevity meant he was at Wembley in 1953 when Ferenc Puskás and the Mighty Magyars finally stamped out English football's notion of superiority. He was still going at the 1954 World Cup in Switzerland, where England fell to Uruguay in the quarter-final. When he won his final cap in 1957, he was 42 and the European Footballer of the Year.

He played on for eight more years. As a 46-year-old in 1961, he rejoined Stoke, who were in the Second Division, being watched by paltry crowds. On Matthews's return, the attendance tripled to over 35,000, breathing new life into the club, who were promoted back to the top flight. He was knighted on New Year's Day 1965. After finally calling it quits, he played in a televised farewell game: Stanley Matthews XI versus a World XI, after which he was chaired off the pitch by Puskás and the great Russian keeper Lev Yashin.

Matthews managed Port Vale for a while but his coaching career took him abroad, including a spell running an all-black team in Soweto, in apartheid South Africa. He had played in 783 club matches in peacetime and over 100 representative matches, including 54 official internationals, but when he asked for tickets to watch Stoke he was refused. In later days football clubs would become more graceful in their treatment of ex-players and Matthews's ashes are buried under the centre circle at Stoke's current stadium, which bears not his name but that of a betting company. In Milan, they renamed the San Siro after the first great superstar of Italian football.

11

Giuseppe Meazza

IN THE 1920s and 30s, the English regarded themselves as the undisputed kings of football and were determined not to prove it. Winning a match or two each season on European summer tours was enough to top up the triumphalism. But while Stanley Matthews was drawing gasps from gargantuan crowds, Giuseppe Meazza was winning the World Cup, twice.

English football was straightforward and robust, and while great individual talents were appreciated, its playing style evolved slowly. By contrast, central European football had an intellectual curiosity, underpinned by a devotion to the old Scottish passing game. The hotbed was Vienna and its famous coffee houses, from where Hugo Meisl's Austrian *Wunderteam* sprang. Strong sides developed in Czechoslovakia, Hungary and Yugoslavia. They played each other in the Central European International Cup, later known as the Dr Gero Cup. Professionalism reached the central European powerhouses in the mid-1920s and from 1927 leading clubs played in the Mitropa Cup, driven by the need for regular income.

Italian football had similar issues of 'shamateurism' as the British, but no Billy Sudell-like figure to blow the gaff. An Italian champion had been declared since 1898, but politics and factionalism were rife and held back attempts to sort out the competitive structures. Perhaps the low point was 1925 when the Northern Championship final play-offs between Bologna and Genoa were marred by accusations of cheating, which gave way to violent clashes and gunshots were fired. In 1926 professionalism was finally legalised. In 1929 the fascist authorities established Serie A as the first national league, incorporating the impoverished south into the wider football community.

Meazza, a teenage striker with Inter, was the star of Italy's new beginning. The Milan local had been a regular scorer in the short-lived Divisione Nationale, before hitting 31 goals, ten more than anyone else, in the first Serie A season. He scored at least 20 goals a season for ten years and won the title, the *scudetto*, three times. While Dixie Dean and his British contemporaries were restricted by the maximum wage to £8 a week in 1932, Meazza was a famous international star, paid £35 a week.

It is almost fruitless to contrast players from different eras, but what becomes clear when you read contemporary reports of Meredith, Matthews and Meazza is that they were ahead of their time. Short and strong, Meazza could play comfortably with both feet when that was rare and he was acrobatic enough to perform bicycle kicks. He was an early exponent of drawing keepers out of their goal in one-on-one situations.

In *Calcio*, John Foot quotes famous architect Giancarlo De Carlo on Meazza: 'He was truly creative: he never adopted typical solutions, but scored extraordinary goals. His movements were unpredictable, impossible to foresee and he played to the crowd.' Meazza was key to the success of a controversial Italian national side during the stormy 1930s on and off the pitch.

European interest in the 1930 World Cup had been half-hearted and only Yugoslavia made it beyond the group stage. Austria missed their big moment as the *Wunderteam* were developing into a formidable unit that would enjoy a 14-match unbeaten run in 1931 and 1932, inspired by goal machine Josef Bican and playmaker Matthias Sindelar, known as the Paper Man.

FIFA's decision to take the second World Cup to Italy, where Benito Mussolini and his fascists ruled through violence and oppression, was hotly contested. Maybe they were swayed by the offer to pay visiting teams' expenses and provide free train travel for visiting fans. Champions Uruguay sent the European snub back over the Atlantic. Their bitter rivals, Argentina, sent a largely amateur team, who were knocked out after a single game, but that doesn't mean there were no Argentine stars at the tournament.

The charter of 1926 that legalised professionalism for Italian clubs also banned foreigners. That put around 80 players, mainly Austrians and Hungarians, out of work. Did anyone really believe they had all moved countries to play for free?

Clubs found a way around the new restrictions by redefining the meaning of 'foreign'. Anyone born abroad but deemed to be of Italian origin was eligible for national service and if they could fight for Italy then why couldn't they play football in Italy? Soon that became play *for* Italy.

Italy had won the Bronze medal at the 1928 Olympics, losing to Uruguay in the semis. Argentina were silver medallists and their forward, Raimundo Orsi, was offered a lucrative contract and a Fiat 509 to join Juventus. Attracting players to Europe was made easier by the late adoption of professionalism in South America, and soon Orsi was far from alone.

The Italy team that faced the USA in Rome for the 1934 World Cup opener contained Orsi, his old Argentina teammate Luis Monti, and a former Brazilian international Filo, now known as Anfilogino Guarisi. There were two more ex-Argentines in the squad, but the formidable centre-half Monti was the most significant 'signing' for Italy (and for Juve, who won Serie A from 1932 to 1935). Meazza scored the seventh goal as Italy smashed the Americans, who went home after one match. They then knocked out Spain, whose keeper, the great Ricardo Zamora, took a battering in a 1-1 draw and had to miss the next day's replay in which Meazza scored the only goal.

The semi-final saw the showdown with the much-heralded Austrians, after Meisl's team had beaten France and Hungary. It was only two days after the quarter-final replay, but the Italians won with another scrambled goal. Once again losing sides were left to complain about biased refereeing, with allegations that Meazza had fouled the Austrian keeper. They faced another central European side, Czechoslovakia, in the final, coming from behind with an excellent equaliser from Orsi, before another Argentine-born player, Enrique Guaita, and Meazza combined to create the winner for Angelo Schiavo.

It was a triumph for Italy's team, for inspirational coach Vittorio Pozzo, and for Mussolini. But England's absence had left a nagging doubt about the side's true status as the best in the world. The Italian authorities were keen to face the founding fathers of the game and, against Pozzo's advice, accepted a November match at Highbury. Mussolini offered every Italian player an Alfa Romeo car if they beat the English and a bloodbath ensued. At the start of the match, Monti had his foot broken by Arsenal's Ted Drake and England took advantage, racing into a 3-0 lead. Only after the limping Monti was moved out of defence did the world champions get a grip.

England captain Eddie Hapgood had his nose broken, Ray Bowden suffered an ankle injury and Eric Brook a fractured arm, while Drake got a bad cut, apparently from a punch. Meazza scored twice in the second half, hit the bar and later said his worst regret was not being passed to when free in the box at the end of the game. England won but nothing was proved.

A very different Italy team won the 1936 Olympic tournament and only Meazza, Eraldo Monzeglio and Giovanni Ferrari were still around for the successful defence of the World

GIUSEPPE MEAZZA

Cup in Paris in 1938. The British, Argentina and Uruguay were no shows. Austria had disappeared as a country – swallowed by Hitler's Germany. The resulting merged team without Sindelar, who refused to play, was weak and divided.

In the *Complete Book of the World Cup 2006*, Cris Freddi said the 1938 Italians were a brighter and fitter team than the 1934 version. They beat Norway and France, and in the semi-final they faced Brazil. The Italians were accused of suffocating the Brazilian flair, as national football stereotypes emerged. Meazza scored the decisive penalty, while holding up his shorts after the elastic had broken. They beat Hungary 4-2 in the final, one last pre-war triumph over the central Europeans.

Unlike Matthews, Meazza enjoyed his wealth and fame to the fullest. Slowed down by injuries, he didn't play for Italy after 1939 and had brief spells at AC Milan, Juventus, Varese and Atlanta before finishing with Inter. He died in 1979 and they renamed the San Siro stadium after him in 1980.

Outside of Italy, there is no love and little respect for the Italian sides of the 1930s: the fascist salutes, the absence of major rivals from both World Cups and the questionable refereeing of 1934 are all valid reservations. There is more respect for the Austrian *Wunderteam*, for Netherlands 1974, for Brazil 82 and, as we'll see, for the Mighty Magyars. But who won the World Cup?

The more major tournaments I watch, the more the search for greater meaning seems forlorn. I enjoy the games and I see teams finding ways to win and lose, being lucky and unlucky. Sometimes great sides emerge; sometimes the winners have found a way to survive, and we reverse engineer the legend. The World Cup isn't a lottery but it is about finding a way through, about turning up – literally and figuratively. That is what Giuseppe Meazza and Italy did – twice – and they deserve respect for that.

12

Tom Finney

IN THE 1940s and 50s there was a Messi-Ronaldo style debate about who was the greatest: Stanley Matthews or Tom Finney. Blessedly, there was no social media to amplify it. The two men were dismissive of the whole polemic; happy to room together with England and quick to praise the other's brilliance. Matthews was the wizard of the dribble, but Finney was better in the air, more likely to score and excellent in all of the forward positions. Of course, there was an English insularity to the whole debate as both men, keen students of football, recognised.

Matthews later wrote of Finney, 'To dictate the pace and course of a game a player had to be blessed with awesome qualities. Those who have accomplished it on a regular basis can be counted on the fingers of one hand – Pelé, Maradona, Best, Di Stéfano and Tom Finney.'

Finney's Preston team-mate Bill Shankly had a knack for a phrase: 'Tom Finney would have been great in any team and in any age even if he'd been wearing an overcoat.' After Sheffield United's Tony Currie had wowed the crowd in a match against Liverpool, Shankly was asked whether Currie could be compared with Finney. Shankly answered, 'Aye, he compares, but Tom is nearly 60.'

Young Tom Finney must have seemed an unlikely future star. He lost his mother when he was four and suffered constant illnesses. He loved football but remained small and frail until he had an infected gland removed at the age of 14, after which he blossomed. He soon left school and became an apprentice plumber. When Preston offered him a position on the club's ground staff – essentially an apprenticeship – Tom's father Alf refused permission, insisting he finish his plumbing training. Preston wisely allowed Finney to train with them as an amateur. By the time he turned professional, competitive football had been suspended for World War Two.

Finney's early career was spent playing wartime matches. Crowds were big but, because selection depended on players' military duties, big names would often guest for other clubs. Preston reached the 1941 Wartime Cup Final against Arsenal. The first game, played in front of 65,000 at Wembley, was drawn. A mark of the times is that Arsenal and England skipper Eddie Hapgood was disconcerted by facing a left-footed right-winger. Preston won the replay in front of 45,000 at Ewood Park, Blackburn. Preston also won the Northern Championship and, in terms of silverware, Finney's career had already peaked.

His call-up papers arrived soon after his 20th birthday, and in April 1942 he joined the Royal Armoured Corps. At first he carried on playing football and, when he was selected for an FA XI, he had his first meeting with Matthews, who was playing for the RAF.

In December 1942 Finney sailed for Egypt to join the Eighth Army of the revered General Bernard Montgomery, which had recently won the Second Battle of El Alamein, the most significant Allied success of the war thus far. Finney was soon on the pitch again. Army chiefs saw football as a useful morale booster and created a team called Wanderers, made up of the best players they could find, who then toured Palestine and Syria, playing games often against Egyptian sides. It is widely reported that Finney faced future movie star Omar Sharif in one of these matches, but the Egyptian was ten years younger than the Englishman so I suspect some licence has been taken with that particular tale.

Finney felt uneasy and shared his concerns with senior officers. 'I had a terrible guilty complex about playing. It seemed grossly unfair that football was offered to those talented enough to make the team while the others were left to get on with the fighting.' He was told he was more useful as a footballer than a soldier and was sent on a tour of Jerusalem, Beirut and Tel Aviv that involved 13 matches in 23 days. He said playing on bone-dry pitches helped improve his technique.

He was posted to Foggia, Italy, as a tank driver and mechanic and sent to the front line to replace men killed the previous day. 'The most distressing part,' he recalled, 'came when you returned to base at night to discover that some of your pals had gone down that day. It was a real eye opener. The heartache of listening to grown men, hard men, sitting up in bed crying at night; the empty feeling when a death was announced.'

Lots of footballers were killed in World War Two, including Southampton's Norman Catlin, who was on HMS *Gloucester* when it went down off Crete, and Charlie Sillett, father of future players John and Peter, who was onboard a Norwegian ship that sank in 1945. Eric Stephenson of Leeds and England was killed in Burma. Rangers' Scotland international Willie Thornton survived the Battle for the Sferro Hills and was awarded the Military Medal.

Finney did three spells in Italy, visiting his fiancée Elsie and playing wartime football on brief trips home. There was more football before he was demobilised. He was woken early one day and told he was flying to Switzerland to play in an unofficial international; because Switzerland was neutral, uniforms weren't allowed and he wore civvies for the first time in three years. He also played in front of a crowd of 30,000 in Naples against an Army XI managed by Matt Busby. FA Secretary Stanley Rous said he would try to get Finney out of the army early, but it was actually his plumbing qualifications that got him demobbed, on condition that he restart work with his old company. In fact, he continued plumbing even after the return of competitive football, building up a business with his brother to supplement his restricted wages.

Finney's professional club career began when the Football League recommenced on 31 August 1946 and within weeks he sailed to Northern Ireland for his England debut and scored in a 7-2 victory. Middlesbrough's Wilf Mannion, who had fought in the Battle of Sicily, got a hat-trick.

Finney was excelling for Preston on the right wing – also Matthews's preferred position – and England's selectors struggled to deal with their two best players competing for the same spot. After much dithering, the pair finally appeared together against Portugal in Lisbon with Finney on the left and Matthews on the right. Both scored and Tommy Lawton and Stan Mortensen got four each in a 10-0 thumping. The last time the front five of Finney, Mortensen, Lawton, Mannion and Matthews played together was England's 4-0 win in Italy in Turin. On the newsreel the commentator declares, 'Our players show the world just who's who amongst footballers.'

In Finney's first 14 internationals, England won 13 and drew one, but it was a naive and woefully underprepared side that went to Brazil in 1950. The team was picked by Football League President and Grimsby fish merchant Arthur Drewry, the only selector who made the trip. He ignored Matthews for a 2-0 win over Chile, in which Mortensen and Mannion scored, but the players were fatigued from travelling and disconcerted by eating unfamiliar food.

On 29 June in Belo Horizonte, England suffered their most humiliating defeat. The USA players were semi-professionals and had lost their last seven internationals. Three of them weren't US citizens and had been only recently added to the squad, including Scotsman Ed McIlvenny who had played for Wrexham, and Joe Gaetjens. Gaetjens was a Haiti international who declared his intention to become a US citizen and was therefore picked. He scored the only goal, deflecting in Walter Bahr's shot with his head.

US full-back Harry Keough admitted, 'The ball just hits him and you can't follow it that fast and it changed direction and speed. Nobody knew where the hell the ball went until they saw it bouncing up and down in the net.' Certainly the cameraman didn't, so we will never be able to judge how lucky it was.

England manager Walter Winterbottom thought the players became desperate and tense after that, or, as Keough put it, 'they got a little mad'. They would never live down the humiliation but still had a chance to go through if they beat Spain. Matthews was brought in but a single goal by the great Basque striker Telmo Zarra won it for Spain.

Finney and Matthews were told they couldn't stay to watch the rest of the tournament, leaving Matthews to reflect: 'We stood still, our insular attitude reinforced by the notion that we invented the game.'

There were more humbling days to come. Finney was a spectator when Hungary's Mighty Magyars left England dazed and confused at Wembley in 1953, but he did play in the 7-1 defeat in Budapest before the 1954 World Cup.

England reached the quarter-finals in Switzerland where they lost to Uruguay, with keeper Gil Merrick harshly shouldering the blame. Finney played again at Sweden 1958, scoring a penalty past the USSR's Lev Yashin in a 2-2 draw but sitting out the rest of the tournament through injury. England went home after losing to the Soviets in a play-off. Finney's last international was later that year and he finished with 30 goals from 76 matches.

When Preston were relegated in 1950, Finney was approached by an agent acting on behalf of an unnamed First

Division club and offered £2,000 to put in a transfer request. He refused and led his home-town club to the Second Division championship.

He was still running his business but a lucrative offer could have changed his financial circumstances forever. On England's 1952 summer tour of Italy, Finney was approached by Prince Raimondo Lanza di Trabia, owner of Italian club Palermo and business associate of the Shah of Iran. The flamboyant prince offered a £10,000 signing-on fee, £130-a-month wages, win bonuses of up to £100, a villa on the Mediterranean, a new sports car and free travel to and from England for Finney and his family. He was tempted and approached Preston's directors, who turned down the offer of a £30,000 transfer fee.

He played on for Preston without a fuss, and in 1952/53 they finished as runners-up behind Arsenal only on goal average. The other time he came close to peacetime silverware was the 1954 FA Cup Final. A year after the Matthews final, the story was screaming to be written, if Finney could seize the day. He didn't. He spent the week beforehand answering phone calls and worrying about tickets and walked onto the Wembley pitch exhausted. He contributed little as Preston lost to West Brom. He was twice named Footballer of the Year before he retired in 1960 – a boy of 38 compared to Matthews, who still had his second spell at Stoke to come!

The main stand at Deepdale is now the Sir Tom Finney Stand, and if you look from there to your left you'll see the Bill Shankly Kop; the two of them used to stay after training, playing head tennis and talking football. Shankly became a managerial legend but Finney was content to become Mr Preston, serving as club president. He received a knighthood in 1998 and lived in Preston until the age of 91.

13
Obdulio Varela

IF YOU ever need a captain for an all-time XI, consider Obdulio Varela, the bloody-minded Uruguayan who unceremoniously lifted the 1950 World Cup in front of 200,000 stunned Brazilians. He was 32 when his big moment came: a defensive midfielder who had never played for a club outside of his home city. He wasn't silky or fast, and he didn't spearhead any great tactical innovation. What Uruguay's second World Cup-winning captain shows is that football matches are sometimes won by inspired leadership and sheer force of will.

His mother Jauna was black and a laundress. He never knew his father and by the age of eight Obdulio was selling newspapers and shining shoes to help pay the bills. He learned football on the concrete courts of Montevideo where his muscles – built up helping his mother with the laundry – came in handy. He was given the nickname *El Negro Jefe*, The Black Chief.

He made his international debut in 1939 and won the 1942 Copa America. He won the Uruguayan league six times with Peñarol, but Varela was supposed to be a footnote in the story of Brazil's glorious summer of 1950.

While England stumbled into the World Cup grumbling about foreign food, the hosts had everything perfectly planned.

OBDULIO VARELA

The 1949 Copa America winners spent a month in a training camp, as the final touches were put to the world's most magnificent stadium: the Maracaña, still the only venue to have hosted a crowd of over 200,000. Tom Finney was amazed by a boy who was begging while juggling an orange from one foot to another. 'We knew the Latin Americans were football crazy,' he wrote, 'but the anticipated frenzy was nothing compared to the reality.'

Varela was Uruguay's captain, despite making important enemies because of his involvement in a players' strike. After his second championship win he was offered a bonus of 500 pesos, twice that of everyone else at Peñarol, but he refused it unless his team-mates got the same. Uruguay had a strong leader but indifferent form. They had snubbed the two European World Cups and lost a swathe of players, initially to Italian football, and more recently to a lucrative pirate league in Colombia. They had finished sixth at the 1949 Copa America and lost 5-1 to Brazil.

A spate of withdrawals and some odd decisions by the organisers gave the 1950 World Cup a lopsided look. Scotland were offered a place for finishing second in the Home Championships but turned it down. Turkey had also been scheduled to be in Uruguay's group but pulled out. Only 13 teams were left and rather than rejig the groups, Uruguay were left in a qualifying pool with only Bolivia, who they beat 8-0. It made sense to revive the group phase, given that teams had travelled to France in 1938 for a single game – but FIFA went too far by creating a final group – whoever finished top of which would win the World Cup, with no scheduled final.

Brazil played three games in their first group: a handsome 4-0 win over Mexico followed by a nervous 2-2 draw with Switzerland in Sao Paulo. Back at the Maracaña they beat Yugoslavia 2-0 in front of an official crowd of 142,429 but it was almost certainly more. In their next two games, the white-shirted Brazilians looked like world beaters as the best Europeans were dispatched: Sweden 7-1 and Spain 6-1. English referee Arthur Ellis described Ademir's bicycle kick in the rout of Sweden as the best goal he had ever seen. By contrast, Uruguay played a brutal 2-2 draw with Spain with a late equaliser from Varela before another comeback saw them beat Sweden 3-2. They definitely had guts.

These results created the accidental World Cup Final. Brazil faced Uruguay at the Maracaña, where a draw would be enough for the hosts to lift the Jules Rimet Trophy. Unfortunately, the nation seemed to believe the job was already done. On the morning of the game, Varela walked past a newspaper stand in the team hotel and was angered by the front pages, typified by *O Mundo* which had a picture of the Brazilian team captioned, 'These are the World Champions'. He bought a copy of every paper and summoned whichever of his fellow players he could find to his bedroom. He laid the papers on the bathroom floor and told his team-mates to join him in urinating on them. I can find no mention of who cleaned up.

It wasn't just newspapers: thousands of T-shirts were in circulation proclaiming Brazil the world champions. Gold watches had been inscribed for each player: 'For the World Champions.'

The hubris was relentless. Before the game, the federal mayor of Rio, Ângelo Mendes de Moraes, with no concept of tempting fate, addressed the crowd and the Brazilian players via the PA system: 'You Brazilians whom I consider victors of this tournament. You players who in less than a few hours will be acclaimed by millions of your compatriots … You who have no equals in the terrestrial hemisphere … You who are so superior to every other competitor,' and just to rub it in, 'You whom I already salute as conquerors.' It wasn't just the locals: Jules Rimet was there to present the trophy with a speech in his pocket praising the Brazilian victory.

Meanwhile, the sense of inevitability threatened to infect the Uruguay camp. Coach Juan López told his players to play defensively, but after he left the dressing room Varela took charge, reportedly saying, 'Juan is a good man but if we do defend then we will suffer the same fate as Sweden and Spain. When you go onto the pitch, don't look at the crowd, everyone outside the pitch is made of wood.' His words were only partly effective in calming nerves, because forward Julio Pérez wet himself during the national anthems.

A 21-gun salute led to dignitaries being showered with Maracaña concrete and on the pitch Brazil's other glorious façade was not as robust as it appeared. True to López's instruction, Uruguay defended with everything they had in the first half, and someone counted that Brazil had 30 shots. The positioning of Brazil's left-back Bigode was central to the tactical post-mortems, but he was also upset by a sly punch from Varela. That apparently shook the confidence of the player, who would become increasingly exposed against Uruguay's excellent right-winger Alcides Ghiggia.

The story seemed to be on script when Brazil scored early in the second half, through Sao Paulo winger Friaça. Again Varela took charge. Amid the frenzied celebration of 200,000 or more Brazilians, he feared his team would be overrun if they let the hosts build momentum, so he pretended to complain about a missed offside and refused to kick off until a translator had been called to let him make his case to English referee George Reader. By the time the match resumed the supporters were hushed. As Ademir put it, 'They always tried to do the opposite of what we wanted and that's how they took the initiative.'

An increasingly anxious crowd began to affect the Brazilian players; Jair described it as a 'collective drop in pressure'. Varela pushed forward and, with Uruguay on the front foot, Ghiggia began to attack Bigode. One of his crosses was swept in by Juan Alberto Schiaffino for 1-1. Brazil coach Flávio Costa later blamed centre-back Juvenal for not protecting Bigode. The 79th-minute winner came from the right again, Ghiggia running clear and beating Moacyr Barbosa at his near post.

It wasn't a particularly good goal, but nor was it horrendous goalkeeping, by the standards of the day.

Rimet described a morbid silence in the Maracaña. Again, the World Cup had been won by a team that wasn't the greatest of the age. Varela embodied the notion of getting the job done; Rimet handed him the World Cup and kept his speech in his pocket. Varela took his players to the hotel bar, followed by the nightclubs of Rio. Ademir got into his car and drove around before taking a boat to an island, where he stayed for 15 days. Brazil didn't play another international until April 1952 and didn't wear white again. With no lack of melodrama, Brazilian writer Nelson Rodrigues described the defeat as 'our Hiroshima'.

Brazil's black players, Bigode, Juvenal and goalkeeper Barbosa, were the most viciously castigated. Thirteen years later, Barbosa was presented with the Maracaña goalposts and he invited friends to his house, where he burned them on a barbeque. As an old man he said, 'In Brazil the most you get for any crime is 30 years, but for 50 years I've been paying for a crime I didn't commit.'

Varela returned to the World Cup in 1954 and scored as Uruguay beat England in the quarter-final. Unfortunately, he was injured in that game and missed the semi-final against Ferenc Puskás and Hungary, Uruguay's first-ever World Cup defeat.

Even a winning World Cup captain can be restricted by the colour of his skin and the humbleness of his background. Varela got enough prize money from the 1950 World Cup to buy a 1931 Model Ford, which was stolen a week later. He was briefly player-coach at Peñarol, taking himself off having come on as a sub in his final appearance in 1955.

Despite his obvious leadership qualities, he had no glorious retirement. The discrimination was too deeply ingrained; he didn't learn to read until after he married a Hungarian woman when he was 29. No one doubted his contribution on the pitch, but there was no influential role for the dark-skinned son of a laundress. One of his team-mates was Victor Rodriguez Andrade, nephew of José, the 1930 World Cup winner. As George Reid Andrews describes in *Blackness in the White Nation*, Uruguay was far from a nation of racial harmony, no matter how well their black footballers played: 'Even for these demigods of Uruguayan football, sport was the path to fame but not fortune.'

Varela's story wasn't as sad as José Andrade's. He and his wife Catherine lived together until they both died in 1996. There is a small stadium in Montevideo which bears his name, but that one of world football's great leaders grew old in relative poverty, with no role in developing the sport, suggests he was judged not by the content of his character but by his working-class background and the colour of his skin. If only we could say that was a thing of the past.

14

Alfredo Di Stéfano

ENGLAND MIGHT have fared better at the 1950 World Cup had their best defender not been transferred into football's distant future. Classy centre-half Neil Franklin was earning the maximum wage of £14 a week at Stoke City when he was offered a signing-on fee of £3,400 and £170 a match by Colombia's Independiente Santa Fe.

Forty-five years before the Bosman Ruling, Colombia's *Campeonato Professional* promised to become a money-making machine for the world's best footballers. It started with a familiar fault line: clubs wanted professionalism but the Colombian FA objected. FIFA suspended both in a move that backfired spectacularly. The clubs saw their opportunity: no FIFA membership, no authority to sanction transfers, no transfer fee, even for the likes of Alfredo Di Stéfano. The Argentine was one of the greatest footballers of all time, who went on to shape the destiny of Spanish and European football, but first he had a fortune to make.

Football's establishment hated the Colombian league, or *El Dorado* as it was dubbed, but players saw the chance to finally get what they were worth. Stoke, for example, had turned down a £30,000 bid for Franklin, who was earning around £700 a year: it would have taken him 42 years to make that much. The *Campeonato* kicked off in April 1949 and players soon flooded in: Deportivo Samarios signed eight Hungarians, two Yugoslavs and an Italian. Deportivo Cucuta recruited eight members of the successful Uruguay 1950 World Cup squad. Argentine league bosses chose a bad time to fall out with their players, who first went on strike and then left en masse to *El Dorado*.

Millonarios of Bogotá signed Adolfo Pedernera, who had been part of River Plate's hugely successful side, dubbed *La Màquina*; 5,000 fans turned up to greet him and in turn he helped Millonarios recruit the best players from his old club, who had become South American champions. Amid all that talent, the shining light was Di Stéfano, who walked out on River Plate and inspired Millonarios to the title in 1949, 1951 and 1952.

El Dorado wasn't everyone's idea of paradise. Franklin and his wife were horribly homesick and understandably spooked by the civil unrest in the country, which meant there was a 6.30pm curfew. He returned home after six games, without his signing-on fee. Charlie Mitten, who had left Manchester United, lasted a little longer, but none of the Englishmen thrived and were harshly treated by their old clubs and the FA when they returned. FIFA were forced into a deal in 1950 and Colombia were readmitted on condition that all players' contracts would revert to their old clubs but not until 1954 – a strange compromise, the repercussions of which caused a rift that still runs through the heart of Spanish football.

In March 1952 Real Madrid's ambitious President Santiago Bernebéu invited Millonarios to his club's half-century celebratory tournament. He had thought he might try to buy Pedernera but was instead captivated by the skilful and energetic Di Stéfano. He made an offer and Millonarios were interested. But was he theirs to sell?

FC Barcelona thought not. They also liked Di Stéfano and made their offer to River Plate. At first, the Spanish FA believed Barcelona had it right but Spanish football politics is rarely straightforward. Barça had the better team, champions in 1945, 48, 49 and 52, but Real Madrid had better connections. Bernebéu had been a player and manager of Real Madrid and was also decorated for fighting on the side of General Franco's far-right Nationalists in the Civil War of 1936–39. That was the winning side, and Bernebéu had influential friends who had helped him with access to foreign currency, credit and planning permission to develop the Chamartín stadium. He subsequently built a great team to play in it. The extent to which Franco and his government intervened to help the loyal Bernebéu triumph over the troublesome Catalans is disputed still, and there is a catalogue of claim and counterclaim from all four clubs involved. The player didn't help much, saying he was happy to sign for either Spanish club but complicating matters by refusing to give back his latest signing-on fee from Millonarios; he was a wilier character than Franklin.

The Spanish Federation ruled that Di Stéfano should be shared. In years one and three he would play in Madrid and spend years two and four in Barcelona. Barça initially agreed but more politics happened and their President Marti Carreto was forced to resign and his successors pulled out, asking only for their money back. What a blunder! Barça won the title again in 1952/53, as the row rumbled on, but once Di Stéfano took to the pitch for Real Madrid they were transformed. As Sid Lowe puts it in *Fear and Loathing in La Liga*, '1953 was the turning point, the year that changed everything. Football can be divided into "Before Alfredo Di Stéfano" and "After Alfredo Di Stéfano".' Real Madrid hadn't won La Liga in 20 years, but as soon as they had the 'Blond Arrow' they became champions, and crucially retained the title in 1955, setting them up to dominate the early years of pan-European football.

There had been various cross-border club competitions such as the Mitropa Cup and the Latin Cup, but the claim by Wolves manager Stan Cullis that his team were the best in the world pushed French football journal *L'Équipe*, edited by Gabriel Hanot, into action. UEFA agreed to start a European Cup, with Hanot and his colleagues responsible for choosing the participants. Sporting Club of Lisbon and Partizan Belgrade played in the first game. Hibernian represented Scotland, even though they weren't champions, and reached the semi-finals. To no one's surprise, England refused to send a club even though champions Chelsea were invited. The secretary of the Football League Alan Hardaker told a journalist at *The Times* it would mean dealing with 'too many wogs and Dagoes'.

The rest of Europe went ahead with the new competition in the autumn of 1955. Real Madrid lost away to Partizan and AC Milan but were too strong for everyone at the newly rebranded Bernebéu stadium. In the June 1956 final at the Parc des Princes, they were 2-0 down inside ten minutes to French champions Reims, but Di Stéfano quickly pulled one back and another veteran of Colombia's *Campeonato*, Héctor Rial, got two in a 4-3 win. French international Raymond Kopa impressed for Reims and he was a Real Madrid player at the start of the following season. There was nothing revolutionary about Bernebéu's Real Madrid; he wanted the best and found ways of paying for it. He certainly knew how to use his influence, both at home and with UEFA. Atlético Bilbao won the Spanish title that season, but Real Madrid successfully proposed that the reigning champions be allowed to defend their crown by right.

Against Hardaker's wishes, new English champions Manchester United insisted on taking part in 1956/57 and reached the semi-final. A 19-year-old Bobby Charlton watched from the stand at the Bernebéu, 'high on the rim of that vast concrete bowl'. He wrote, 'I was utterly captivated by the genius of Alfredo Di Stéfano, who masterminded Real's 3-1 win like a general on a battlefield. Before that I had never imagined that one player could influence a game in such an all-embracing fashion. He was everywhere, totally in charge from first whistle to last.' Charlton appeared and scored in the return match, but the 2-2 draw wasn't enough for that great United side, the Busby Babes, whose story ended so tragically ten months later.

Real Madrid beat Fiorentina in the 1957 final, with Di Stéfano among the scorers. They won the first five editions of the European Cup, helping to revitalise Spain's international standing, to the delight of the Franco regime. Di Stéfano scored in all five finals and the run only ended when Barcelona gained some long-awaited revenge, beating them in the first round in 1961. Real Madrid remains the world's most successful football club and Di Stéfano suffered few setbacks. He was crowned champion eight times in Spain, three times in Colombia and twice in Argentina. Take that Matthews and Finney! He succeeded Matthews as the European Footballer of the Year in 1957 and succeeded Kopa in 1959.

He also inspired a future Ballon d'Or winner, George Best, who watched those European Cup games on TV in Belfast. 'The most complete player I ever saw and my hero was Di Stéfano, the centre-forward, who I thought could do everything,' Best wrote. 'He scored goals, he was good in the air, he could defend, he could use both feet.'

But Di Stéfano's international career was a globetrotting non-event. He played for Argentina, the rebel Colombian XI, and, from 1957, Spain. Losing in Glasgow meant they failed to qualify for the 1958 World Cup, General Franco refused to let the squad go to communist USSR for the first European Nations' Cup in 1960 and, though they qualified for the 1962 World Cup in Chile, 36-year-old Di Stéfano was injured and didn't play.

He played until he was 40, spending his last two seasons at Español after falling out with Bernebéu, who wanted him to retire and join Real Madrid's coaching staff. He had success as a coach – when he was ready – winning La Liga and the European Cup Winners' Cup with Valencia and the Argentine title with Boca Juniors. He was appointed as Real Madrid's honorary president in 2000. He died in 2014 at the age of 88.

15

Ferenc Puskás

A FOOTBALL team doesn't have to reinvent the game to become great. Real Madrid won the first five European Cups by targeting the best players and finding a way to make best use of them. Success came first; the system was secondary. Pioneers often have to settle for historical kudos. So let it be with Hungary's Golden Team, variously known as the Mighty, Magical, Marvellous or Magnificent Magyars. The fabulous Ferenc Puskás had the best of both worlds.

His early story has a familiar ring. He was born into an ethnic German family in 1927 and grew up in a poor neighbourhood of Budapest playing street football with homemade rag balls. His father was a semi-professional player who later became a coach. Their family name was Purczeld until his father changed it when Ferenc was ten. He used a false name when he signed for Kispest, because he was too young to be registered.

Puskás made his international debut aged 18 for a Hungary side that would revolutionise football. The coach, Gusztáv Sebes, had a notion of 'football socialism', soon to be advocated by Bill Shankly, who became Liverpool manager in 1959. Rather than players performing a role in a rigid formation, they would work together as a moving unit. By contrast to the authoritarian regime that ruled Hungary, Sebes encouraged his players to express themselves and share opinions.

Most of the players came from two clubs. Kispest was renamed Honvéd and became the army team, while MTK Budapest was linked with the secret police. Puskás was given an army rank – hence his nickname: The Galloping Major. In truth they were professional footballers, although expected to keep military discipline. They beat another team of Eastern European 'shamateurs' from Yugoslavia in the Olympic final of 1952, but when they arrived in England for a friendly in 1953 they were greeted with scepticism. Bobby Robson, then a young winger with Fulham, recalled, 'We didn't know anything about Puskás and all these wonderful players. They were men from Mars as far as we were concerned.'

The match at Wembley dispelled the lingering myth of English superiority. The Magyars looked so modern. Movement was the main difference but their technique and fitness were better too. Number-nine Nándor Hidegkuti dropping into midfield was hailed as revolutionary – but watch Puskás and you see him doing the same: drop off, find space and use your technique to pick out runners. Or often, in his case, lash the ball into the goal with his wicked left foot. He scored 84 times for Hungary; I can't imagine many were with his right foot. His drag-back left England captain Billy Wright on the seat of his pants: this was new stuff to the founders of the football. You could watch five minutes of the game and not realise Stanley Matthews was playing. England's best player was stuck out on the right wing, out of camera shot, while Hungary swarmed all over the midfield.

'They were almost too good for words, brilliant both individually and collectively,' wrote Tom Finney, who watched from the stand. 'Their brand of football was revolutionary and I will never forget the thrill of being present to see it for myself. I came away from Wembley wondering to myself what we had been doing all these years. Yes, the Hungarians were so much better in technique it was untrue.'

FERENC PUSKÁS

Finney played in Budapest the following year, where Hungary's winning margin was 7-1 and the Olympic champions went to the 1954 World Cup in Switzerland as favourites. In a baffling quirk, FIFA opted for four-team groups but each side only played two opponents: Hungary crushed South Korea 9-0 and West Germany 8-3. German coach Sepp Herberger held back some of his stronger players, probably because he expected to finish level on points with Turkey and would therefore play them again in a play-off. He was right, and West Germany faced Turkey twice but didn't play South Korea!

Perhaps crucially, Puskás suffered an injury against the Germans. Despite his family's origins, he didn't speak good German and had asked for help translating the trash-talk he wanted to aim at Werner Liebrich. The West Germany centre-back responded by stamping on Puskás's ankle in a challenge, and a hairline fracture forced him to miss the knockout ties against Brazil and Uruguay. Hungary won anyway and going into the final they had 25 goals from four games: Honvéd's Sándor Kocsis had scored 11.

Then came the 'Miracle of Bern', where Hungary lost or maybe West Germany won. There was a blazing row within the Magyars squad about Puskás's inclusion. No one knew whether he was really fit, but he scored in the sixth minute of the final. Almost immediately, German keeper Toni Turek fumbled the ball like it was covered in grease and Zoltán Czibor got Hungary's second. It looked like the 62,500 in the Wankdorf Stadium were there for a coronation. But a lucky break allowed Max Morlock to pull a goal back, before West Germany equalised from a corner in the 18th minute. Turek made amends for his error and the German radio commentator upset religious conservatives by calling him a 'Football God'.

It was 2-2 for over an hour. For half of the lifespan of organised football, there were no substitutions and frequently games were decided by who had most fit players. Maybe it was Puskás's injury, maybe it was the lack of sleep caused by the town fair outside their hotel the night before, or maybe it was the walk to the stadium after their bus had got stuck, but Hungary couldn't overwhelm the Germans this time. Helmut Rahn scored his second of the game with six minutes to play, and when Puskás hit the net again Welsh linesman Sandy Griffiths flagged for offside.

Puskás blamed darker forces than oom-pah bands for West Germany's victory and, after a number of the victorious squad contracted jaundice, it was admitted they had received pre-match injections. Team officials insisted they contained nothing more sinister than vitamins, but a recent investigation suggested it could have been a methamphetamine that was regularly given to German soldiers in the war. In a way, it didn't matter because performance-enhancing drug use wasn't yet against the laws of football.

The outcome was politically significant in both countries. West Germany was only five years old as a nation and this was the first time they had been welcomed back into the football community. It was a nation ravaged by war and wracked by confusion and guilt: can you be proud of your country when it has caused such horror? The shock success of their semi-professional footballers against the Mighty Magyars gave West Germans a reason to be proudly and positively patriotic.

Hungary's players were smuggled back into their country, old privileges were removed and goalkeeper Gyula Grosics was arrested and accused of espionage and treason. He believed the game led eventually to revolution.

'The reaction in Hungary was terrible,' he said. 'Hundreds and thousands of people poured into the streets in the hours after the match. On the pretext of football they demonstrated against the regime ... in those demonstrations, I believe, lay the seeds of the 1956 uprising.'

The team went on another unbeaten run, which only ended early in 1956. In October that year there was a student-led popular uprising against Hungary's communist regime.

The Soviet army rolled in to crush the revolutionaries, 2,500 Hungarians were killed and an estimated 200,000 became refugees, including some of the world's best footballers.

One newspaper incorrectly reported that Puskás had been killed but he was safe and Honvéd's players realised the European Cup could be their way out of Hungary. They were drawn to play against Atlético Bilbao in Spain that November. Striker Lajos Tichy recalled, 'We hadn't even had time to unpack our suitcases and we were surrounded by agents. There wasn't a single player who didn't get some sort of offer.' The players refused to return into the chaos of the uprising, and their families travelled to Brussels where the second leg was played a month later.

Sebes was sent to bring his national team players back but only three returned with him, including Tichy, who scored a half-century of international goals. The Honvéd players went on a money-raising tour of Europe and South America and then dispersed. The defectors were banned at the insistence of the Hungarian FA and most of them didn't play competitively in 1957. Kocsis and Czibor later joined Barcelona's Budapest-born László Kubala, who had fled on the back of a truck in 1949 and was by then playing for Spain.

Puskás was in Italy for much of his suspension, but when it finished he was 30 and overweight and the big clubs weren't interested. He offered to play for free for Manchester United, who had been devastated by the Munich Air Disaster of February 1958. The club said no, because he would have to become a British citizen and they felt his offer to play for free was unsustainable. They had a point. The English maximum wage was £20 a week. When he later signed for Real Madrid he was given a four-year contract worth, by my calculations, roughly £45 a week (Sources: the contract is on Puskas.com and I used FXsauber.ubc.ca for the currency values).

His welcome in Madrid was lukewarm at best; Di Stéfano apparently referred to him as 'Big Belly, Little Cannon'. The

Hungarian worked hard to get fit and lost 18kg, training with plastic wrapped around his ample midriff in the Spanish summer. He made his La Liga debut, aged 31, in September 1958, and in his first game at the Bernebéu he scored a hat-trick in a 5-1 win over Sporting Gijón. He scored four hat-tricks that season, including in a 10-1 win over Las Palmas, in which Di Stéfano also got three. The Hungarian scored the decisive penalty as Real beat Atlético Madrid in a European Cup semi-final replay but was injured before the final.

His second season was even better. He scored 47 goals and appeared in the 1960 European Cup Final against Eintracht Frankfurt in front of 127,621 at Hampden Park. The game was widely watched on television and is regarded as the pinnacle of that great Real Madrid era, but it nearly didn't happen. The West German FA had banned its clubs from playing against Puskás because of his accusations of drug use. Only a written apology persuaded the Germans to back down. Madrid were mesmerising. Puskás scored four and Di Stéfano three in a 7-3 victory.

Puskás scored another hat-trick in the 1962 final, although Eusébio's Benfica won 5-3. That summer, 35-year-old Puskás had another crack at the World Cup, as a naturalised Spaniard, but they were knocked out after losing their last group game to Brazil, and their mercurial winger Garrincha. Puskás outlasted Di Stéfano at Madrid and was part of the squad that won the club's sixth European Cup in 1966, although he missed the final and retired that summer. He had played 262 times for Real Madrid and scored 242 goals, adding five La Liga titles to the three European Cups: not bad for an overweight ageing refugee.

He became a globetrotting manager, visiting Hungary in 1981 for the first time in decades. Hungarian people knew hardly anything of his achievements at Real Madrid, such was the government's control of the media. He moved back home after the collapse of the regime. As a young footballer he had spent an afternoon helping to build the Népstadion in a public relations exercise: in 2002 they renamed it in his honour. He died in 2006, and in 2009 FIFA created the Puskás Award for the most beautiful goal of each calendar year.

Puskás scored 622 goals in 629 club games, and 84 goals in 85 games for Hungary, but I wonder whether the unfortunate legacy of his great national team is the era of negative football that followed. In one obvious way the 1954 World Cup was a high point. There were only 26 games but 140 goals, 5.38 per game, including Austria 7 Switzerland 5 in the quarter-finals. Teams got wise to the downside of having players spread out in fixed positions, while their opponents moved as a unit dominating key areas. Scoring dried up and in 1958 there were 3.6 goals per World Cup game. With more sophisticated offside traps and increasingly brutal tackling, defences became dominant. No World Cup since has had as many as three goals per game. No wonder the old men of my childhood harked back to the glory days.

16

Pelé

WHEN URUGUAY broke Brazil's hearts at the 1950 World Cup, it wasn't only the 200,000 plus who were rammed inside the Maracaña who wept; 600 kilometres inland in Bauru, nine-year-old Edson Arantes do Nascimento was shocked to see his father, a footballer known as Dondinho, cry for the first time. His father's friends sobbed too. Edson had never seen men show such emotion.

Edson's home was crammed with family and friends gathered around a huge, crackling radio, and they heard fireworks shooting off prematurely when it seemed Brazil were about to fulfil destiny. He and his friends drifted outside to play football, occasionally popping inside for updates. The last time they went out, Brazil still seemed certain to be champions, but when they returned at the end of the game they were struck by the silence broken only by tears. Edson prayed to Jesus, asking why Brazil had been punished and vowed to win the World Cup for his father.

There is no meaningful story behind the nickname, but Edson became Pelé, and Pelé became a football phenomenon. Dondinho was an injury-prone semi-pro, which meant Pelé grew up in poverty; he and his friends played barefoot with improvised footballs. It was a local coach, Waldemar de Brito, who saw the boy's potential and persuaded directors at Santos, 350km away, to give him a trial. Pelé was instantly brilliant. He scored on his Santos debut, aged 15, and in 1957, his first full season, he was top scorer in the league. In 1958 he scored 58 goals in 38 games. There is some scepticism about Pelé's goalscoring claims, but these were real numbers in a real competition. Santos won the Sao Paulo state championship ten times in Pelé's career and five of the first seven editions of the nationwide championship that started in 1959.

He made his Brazil debut against Argentina, aged 16, and scored. The teenage sensation was a certainty for the 1958 World Cup until he was clattered in a warm-up game against Corinthians. The doctors didn't think he would be fit in time, but he was taken to Sweden anyway. After the calamity of 1950 and a quarter-final elimination in 1954, Brazil were better prepared than ever. The team doctor visited Sweden a year earlier to make arrangements, including asking for their hotel to be staffed exclusively by men. The squad was gathered together months before. A team of medics descended and discovered the grim state of health of Brazilians from rural and poor urban backgrounds, even if they were footballers; 470 bad teeth were removed, players had intestinal parasites, digestive and circulatory problems and sexually transmitted infections. A psychologist declared Pelé 'infantile' and 'lacking fighting spirit'. Thankfully, he was ignored.

With Pelé still recovering, Brazil beat Austria and drew 0-0 with England, so they needed a positive result in their final group game against a highly rated USSR team. Pelé came in up front and Garrincha on the right wing. *L'Équipe*'s Gabriel Hanot claimed they played the best three minutes of football ever. Pelé hit the bar, Garrincha turned defenders inside out and Vavá scored as the Soviets were overrun. They eased up but still won 2-0.

They played Wales in the quarter-finals. Pelé scored after flicking the ball past Mel Charles (brother of John, Wales's best player who was injured). Pelé dived into the back of the net to celebrate and photographers swarmed onto the pitch to get their shot.

Another European side awaited in the semi-finals: France had Real Madrid's Kopa and the prolific Just Fontaine, who scored a record 13 goals in that tournament. But Brazil were improving. Vavá scored early again, midfield playmaker Didi got the second but Pelé was sensational and hit a hat-trick in a 5-2 win.

It was the same score in the final against the host nation. This time Pelé scored twice. For his first he chested the ball past one defender, flicked it over another and volleyed past the keeper. 'No one had seen a goal quite like that before,' he reflected in his autobiography. He also headed Brazil's fifth, prompting Sweden defender Sigge Parling to say, 'Even I wanted to cheer for him.'

The World Cup made Pelé a global superstar. In 1959 he scored 100 goals in 83 club matches including friendlies. Santos cashed in with a seemingly never-ending world tour. He also scored nine international goals that year, as Brazil finished second in the Copa America.

Europe's biggest clubs were desperate to tempt football's hottest property across the ocean, but under threat of riots and political pressure from the Brazilian government Santos refused all offers. There was huge anticipation ahead of the 1962 World Cup and, although Brazil retained their title, a groin injury restricted Pelé to two games and one goal, while Garrincha was the hero.

Santos won the Copa Libertadores twice and perhaps the peak of Pelé's club career was the 1962 Intercontinental Cup against European champions Benfica and a clash with the great Eusébio. Pelé scored twice in a first-leg 3-2 win, then went to Lisbon and got a hat-trick in a 5-2 victory. A year later he scored again in Milan as Santos retained their title. Pelé was a world champion for club and country.

The 1966 World Cup was a bitter experience for Pelé, who thought the tournament was ruined by brutal tackling and lax refereeing. He was kicked by the Bulgarians, missed a defeat against Hungary and returned half-fit to face Portugal. One lunge laid him low and, with no substitutes allowed, he limped through the rest of the game as Brazil went out. He vowed never to return to the World Cup. He had a point about the tackling – it wouldn't be allowed now – but there were even more barbaric times to come.

Pelé was coaxed back for Mexico 1970 and won his third World Cup. Brazil had a military dictatorship but a communist coach in João Sandanha. President Emilio Medici publicly advocated for striker Dario to be called up but Sandanha refused. The coach also told foreign journalists that political prisoners were being killed by the regime. Shortly before the tournament, he gave the authorities the perfect opportunity to sack him when he threatened a critic with a revolver. Pelé's team-mate from 1958 and 1962, Mario Zagallo, took over. Brazil's players trained in a military base before leaving for Mexico; a team renowned for flair and flamboyance were underpinned by fitness. Dario was picked for the squad but stayed on the bench.

It is a fondly remembered tournament, partly because of that Brazil side but also because of colour TV and because teams could finally substitute injured players. Brazil faced Czechoslovakia first and Pelé missed a sitter at 0-0. The Czechoslovaks scored, then Rivelino lashed in a free kick before Pelé chested down a long pass and made it 2-1. Jairzinho got the last two. But it was another Pelé miss from this game that you might remember – a shot from inside his own half that beat the keeper but dropped just wide. He scored plenty of brilliant goals but the power of the World Cup is such that his shot in this game and his outrageous dummy on the Uruguay keeper in the semi-final are among his most famous moments.

Their second group game was a classic – a 1-0 victory over England with another Jairzinho goal. Pelé's memorable contribution was another failure to score! This time his powerful downward header was brilliantly flipped over the bar by Gordon Banks: the so-called 'Save of the Century'.

He scored twice against Romania and was influential in victories over Peru and Uruguay in the knockout phase. Brazil met Italy in the final at Mexico City's Azteca Stadium and Pelé scored first with a goal that showed off his athleticism – a tremendous leap and thumping header. England captain Bobby Moore said in the TV commentary, Pelé leapt 'like an eagle'. Shambolic defending allowed Italy to equalise but this time the era-defining team turned on the style when it mattered. Gérson ripped one into the bottom corner before another Pelé header teed up Jairzinho, who had scored in every match.

Brazil's fourth goal is one of the most famous of all time. Centre-forward Tostao tracked back to recover possession and the nine-pass move took 30 seconds to complete, with Pelé rolling the ball to the right-back and skipper Carlos Alberto to lash home. Pelé had become the first player to win the World Cup for the third time and he was lauded as the greatest-ever footballer.

So was he? There is now a stream of opinion keen to downgrade Pelé, comparing him unfavourably with Messi, Ronaldo, Maradona and even his contemporaries. When I typed 'Pelé' into YouTube, item five was an idiotic video proclaiming him as 'the most OVERRATED footballer ever'. It is very effective click-baiting judging by the millions of views.

Okay, his much-vaunted 1,283 goals include plenty scored in Santos's endless tour matches and friendlies. So maybe he didn't score 1,000 official goals, but that is hardly damning. He played 763 official club matches for Santos and New York Cosmos and got 707 goals. He scored 77 goals in 92 matches for Brazil. He was no goal poacher but a massively influential free-ranging, attacking midfielder.

Okay, he did play for one club in his peak years – but they were world champions and Brazilian footballers weren't the globetrotters they later became. His critics argue injuries reduced his role in two of his three World Cup victories. Again this is acclaiming with faint condemnation. He played in four World Cups in an era when gifted stars received little protection from referees. To have played so long, so successfully, is a sign of a remarkable man. The main thrust of the criticism is that football was different then from now. Italy were bedraggled when Brazil sliced through them for the famous fourth goal which wouldn't happen now. Fair enough, times have changed, but if you want to downgrade Pelé because his opponents weren't running 13km a game, then Galileo was an idiot because he didn't know how to use a sandwich toaster.

If you are not convinced, judge by Pelé's contemporaries.

Johan Cruyff: 'Pelé was the only footballer who surpassed the boundaries of logic.'

Franz Beckenbauer: 'Pelé is the greatest player of all time. He reigned supreme for 20 years. There's no one to compare with him.'

Bobby Charlton: 'I sometimes feel as though football was invented for this magical player.'

Bobby Moore: 'Pelé was the most complete player I've ever seen. He had everything: two good feet, magic in the air, quick, powerful, could beat people with skill, could outrun people. Only 5ft 8in tall, yet he seemed a giant of an athlete on the pitch; perfect balance and impossible vision. He was the greatest because he could do anything and everything on a football pitch.'

Pelé quit international football in 1971 but that wasn't the end. Santos kept milking their cash cow and his 1,000th game was a friendly against Transvaal in Suriname, which I doubt you would have guessed. He scored a hat-trick against

Newcastle United in 1972, and in 1973 Santos lost to both Fulham and Plymouth on yet another European visit, before he eventually escaped.

One thing Pelé was rubbish at was investing money, and one of his disastrous ventures resulted in him being tempted out of retirement to the North American Soccer League and New York Cosmos. Never mind 'no player is bigger than the club', Pelé was bigger than the league. He drew crowds and media attention the round-ball game had never known in the USA.

A crowd of 77,691 watched The Cosmos beat Fort Lauderdale Strikers on their way to the Soccerbowl in 1977. Franz Beckenbauer was a team-mate. Johan Cruyff, Eusébio and George Best all chased the US dollars but the NASL was unsustainable and declined after Pelé's departure. He remained a global icon, if at times a controversial one, because of his political career and affiliations.

There was also his social impact. As he said of the 1958 World Cup Final: 'There must have been a fair few of the 50,000 spectators who were taken aback to see a little black kid with the teams. I asked my team-mates, "Is it only in Brazil that there are blacks?"'

There were no black African sides in the competition, and even though José Andrade and Obdulio Varela had won the World Cup, and Jesse Owens and Joe Louis had been world-famous sportsmen, there was no black icon to match Pelé. He was subjected to racism in Brazil, where people felt free to publicly disapprove of his marriage to a white woman. This was a country where slavery had only been abolished in 1888 and Pelé's great-grandparents had been slaves. He became aware of his importance when he visited Africa.

'Being in Africa was a simultaneous humbling and gratifying experience for me. I could sense the hope that Africans derived from seeing a black man who had been so successful in the world. I could also sense their pride at my own pride that this was the land of my forefathers. It was a realisation for me that

I had become famous on several different levels – I was now known as a footballer even by people who didn't really follow football. And here in Africa, as well as that, I was a world famous *black* man, and that meant something different still.'

17

Lev Yashin

THE RUSSIANS have interesting heroes: fewer soldiers and politicians than you find elsewhere and more writers, composers and spacemen. They also love a goalkeeper. The poster boy for the 2018 World Cup was long dead but an obvious choice: Lev Yashin, the inventor of modern goalkeeping.

The veneration of Russian goalkeepers predates Yashin, although it was reinforced by having the best-ever practitioner of the art. He grew up with books and films about great fictional goalkeepers, a metaphor for the heroic defender of the Russian state. Young Lev wanted to be a striker but he knew his size and athleticism meant he was destined to be a keeper. Only in Russia is that a promotion.

I have been watching lots of early televised football and, good heavens, the goalkeepers were awful. Obviously, the outfield play lacks intensity to the modern eye but the keepers look like park players. There had been earlier pioneers such as Wales's Dick Roose and Spain's Ricardo Zamora who starred for Español, Real Madrid and Barcelona, but Yashin was the first to be filmed playing something like a modern goalkeeper.

He would rush out towards strikers closing in on goal, distribute the ball accurately to team-mates rather than always punt it, and compete for crosses by punching or catching. Many of Dixie Dean's goals were close-range headers; post-Yashin keepers sought to dominate that space. England's World Cup-winning keeper Gordon Banks, eight years Yashin's junior, described him as 'the model for goalkeeping for the next ten to 15 years.' The Russian remains the only goalkeeper to have won the Ballon d'Or.

He only had one club, Dynamo Moscow, but he played two sports. He made his football debut in a 1950 friendly against Traktor Stalingrad, and conceded from the other keeper after colliding with a defender. After two more calamitous performances, he didn't play first-team football until 1953 but instead turned out for Dynamo's ice hockey team.

After returning to football, he won the Soviet Top League five times, and three Soviet Cups. He made his international debut in 1954, and was man of the match when the USSR won the gold medal at the 1956 Melbourne Olympics. He came fifth in the inaugural Ballon d'Or; between then and 1962 only one other goalkeeper, Harry Gregg, hero of the Munich air crash, finished above him in 1958.

In 1960 the USSR won the first-ever European Nations' Cup, remarkable progress for a federation that only came out of international isolation for the 1952 Olympics. In fact, most of the USSR's best achievements in football were in Yashin's era.

The French first proposed a European competition for international teams in the 1920s, but it only got going in 1958. There were home and away knockout qualifiers, and a four-team final tournament. The draw for the last qualifying round paired the USSR with Spain, sparking a diplomatic incident. After clashing over flags and anthems, General Franco ordered Spain's withdrawal. Yashin and his team went to the tournament, where they beat Czechoslovakia in the semi-final and Yugoslavia in the final. Much to Franco's delight, Spain beat the USSR in the 1964 final at the Bernebéu.

The 1962 World Cup was regarded as a blot on Yashin's career, although I think that is unfair. The tournament wasn't shown on Soviet TV so a single travelling reporter shaped the nation's perception. Yashin was blamed for two bad results. In a group game against Colombia, they were 4-1 up midway through the second half when a corner, taken by Marco Coll, went straight into the goal – the only such instance in World Cup matches. I've watched it and it was 100 per cent the fault of the near-post defender Givi Chokeli, who pulled away at the last second leaving Yashin helpless. By modern standards Yashin was to blame for Colombia's fourth, when he stormed out and, instead of diving at the attacker's feet, tried to tackle him and lost out. But even that match shows he was ahead of the game. Colombia's Efraím Sánchez moved barely three yards from his goal line, even when forwards were running deep into the box. Yashin was perhaps at fault for conceding a free kick against Chile in the quarter-final defeat, but it is hard to say because of the camera work. He took so much abuse when he got back to Russia that he considered quitting. A death threat was written into the dirt on his car – the Twitter of its day, I guess. He bounced back in style – 1963 was his Ballon d'Or-winning year.

The USSR's best-ever World Cup was 1966, and 36-year-old Yashin was hailed as a maestro, although the weakest thing I have seen from him was his attempt to save Franz Beckenbauer's decisive shot in the semi-final. He saved 150 penalties in his career, but not Eusébio's, as Portugal won the third-place play-off. The great striker expressed the admiration Yashin inspired. 'He was a master in goal and he was also a great gentleman. It was because he was so respectful towards opponents that he had so many friends. Yashin will always be the number-one goalkeeper in the world.'

At 40, Yashin was a non-playing squad member as the USSR reached the quarter-finals at Mexico 1970, but that was the last season he donned his trademark dark blue-top (somewhat inaccurately, he was known as the Black Panther or Black Spider, the misunderstanding was probably down to black-and-white TV).

He had a farewell match at the Lenin Stadium, in which Pelé, Eusébio, Bobby Charlton and Gerd Müller played. His relationship with other great players survived the language barrier. Yashin's wife, Valentina, recalled him grabbing a slightly mystified Pelé in a hotel at the 1958 World Cup and saying to her, 'Look at this boy, he will be the greatest footballer in the world soon.'

USSR internationals were accompanied abroad by thinly disguised KGB officers, but there is no suggestion Yashin ever wanted to leave. His grandson Vasily Frolov said, 'He was indifferent to fame. He was an ordinary Soviet man.' Commentator Denis Kazansky told BBC Sport, 'He was like a rock star in a closed society where everybody had the same style, same haircut, same way of thinking. We have two colossuses here: Yuri Gagarin in space, and Lev Yashin in football.'

Even at the height of his fame, Yashin would take his kit home and wash it himself. He had various jobs in sport after retirement but apparently wasn't skilled in the dark art of politics needed to get on in the Soviet Union, despite being held in great affection by the public. He was awarded the Order of Lenin and there are Yashin statues and tributes scattered around Moscow.

He is a near universal choice as the best goalkeeper in history. Outside of Russia, it remains an underrated position, and so few keepers have gone close to emulating his Ballon d'Or victory that *France Football* started a new award and called it the Yachine. The first trophy in 2019 was won by Alisson of Liverpool and Brazil.

Yashin had a leg amputated in 1986 and died of stomach cancer, aged 60. He had been a heavy smoker, as he put it 'to calm the nerves', and drank vodka 'to tone the muscles'. Dubious sports scientist, revolutionary goalkeeper.

18

Jimmy Hill

IF YOU are much younger than I am, or not from the UK, you won't understand just how famous, or infamous, Jimmy Hill was when I was a child. He had been a bang average footballer with Brentford and Fulham, but he used his quicksilver mind and lead-lined ego to change football in England and the world.

England's footballers were significantly underpaid. After the defeat of Billy Meredith and his union comrades, there was one more concerted attempt to get a fair deal with a threatened strike in 1920, but again it failed. The maximum wage actually reduced and left a chasm between the likes of England's Stanley Matthews and Italy's Giuseppe Meazza. There were ways around it, some of which were above board. Tom Finney had his plumbing business and Hill supplemented his Brentford wage by working as a chimney sweep. There were other, less honest solutions. Wilf Mannion wrote in the *Sunday People* that a club had offered him £3,000 cash and a job in sales on £25 a week on top of his £12-a-week maximum salary if he persuaded Middlesbrough to sell him. Boro refused, as they did when Juventus later came calling.

Up the road at Sunderland, Len Shackleton wrote in *The Clown Prince of Soccer* in 1955, 'The professional footballer's contract is an evil document of that I am certain. I am quite amazed that such a hopelessly one-sided document has survived the tremendous amount of criticism hurled at it by so many people in these enlightened times.'

Clubs could terminate a player's contract whenever they wanted but such freedom didn't cut both ways. As long as a club had offered the maximum wage, they could hold on to players' registrations, even after their contracts ended. Shackleton only transferred twice: from Bradford Park Avenue to Newcastle for £13,000 and to Sunderland, known as the Bank of England club, for £20,000. He was paid the maximum wage, which was £15 a week, when he wrote his book.

Some Brits tried their luck abroad. The most obvious success was John Charles, who went from Leeds to Juventus for a British-record £65,000 and won the *scudetto* three times, finishing third behind Di Stéfano and Kopa in the 1959 Ballon d'Or poll. More common were the likes of Neil Franklin and Charlie Mitten, working-class Englishmen, who came back from Colombia with their tails between their legs.

The fight back began when Hill became secretary of the players' union in 1956, and chairman the year after, and changed its name to the Professional Footballers' Association. He was an inside-right of limited ability, as his Fulham team-mate, future England manager Bobby Robson said, 'With respect, he wasn't a great player but he was very hard-working and tremendously fit.'

Hill was just the character the players needed as their advocate. As David Goldblatt put it in *The Ball is Round*, 'Hill did not see riveters as the reference point for himself or professional footballers. The new, often working-class stars and entrepreneurs of the TV, film and music industries were his models.'

The PFA demanded an end to the maximum wage, changes to the retention system that held players in virtual serfdom, a new draft contract and a share of transfer income. He organised a strike and this time the authorities blinked. Three days before the action was due to begin, the maximum wage was scrapped. Another Fulham player, Johnny Haynes, soon became the UK's first £100-a-week footballer, a fivefold pay rise. Haynes was injured in a car crash a year later and was never the same player again. By the time he left the club in 1970, Fulham had dropped to the Third Division.

In the time-honoured tradition of the British ruling class, football's bosses retreated only as far as they had to so the PFA fought a legal battle on behalf of George Eastham, who had gone on strike at Newcastle. The club had refused to let Eastham join Arsenal when his contract had finished in 1959. It took years, but eventually the High Court ruled against Newcastle for 'restraint of trade', and a fairer transfer system was introduced. It underwent minor reforms until football finance was turned upside down by the 1995 Bosman Ruling.

Hill didn't directly benefit from his victory. He retired in 1961 because of a knee injury and that November became the manager of Coventry City. This is the history of football through players, but Hill's post-playing career was so impactful it is hard to ignore. He boasted that he did everything in the game and he had a point.

Coventry rose from the Third Division to the First in his six years. One of his players, John Sillett, recalled: 'He had wonderful ideas that people called gimmicks but they weren't. He was a dream, he worked on our weaknesses and there was a lot of emotion in his work.'

Hill had a remarkable eye for publicity and co-wrote a club anthem, the 'Sky Blue Song'. When Coventry were promoted to the top division for the first time in the club's history, he asked for a ten-year contract and when the chairman refused, promptly resigned. Within weeks he joined London Weekend Television and didn't manage again. At LWT he was partly responsible for inventing football punditry as we know it, helping recruit the colourful, controversial World Cup panel of 1970. Always a lover of the limelight, he volunteered to replace an injured linesman when Arsenal hosted Liverpool in a league match at Highbury in 1972.

He was lured to the BBC where he combined being an expert with presenting the highlights programme *Match of the Day*. My first memories of the programme were the opening credits in which the crowd turned over cards to make pictures, one of which was Hill's face.

His punditry was forthright, outspoken, and, to my young mind, endlessly negative. He is Grumpy Pundit No. 3 at the beginning of *Football's Coming Home* by Baddiel, Skinner and the Lightning Seeds: 'We'll go on getting bad results ... getting bad results, getting bad results ...'

Former England manager Terry Venables worked on a Merseyside derby for TV and recalled walking around the pitch with Hill when a chant started: 'Jim-my Hill ... is a wanker ... is a wanker!' Hill turned to Venables and said, 'That's fame for you! They love me here.'

Hill revelled in his reputation and didn't lack a sense of humour, being regularly lampooned on comedy shows such as *Mrs Merton*, where Caroline Aherne played the eponymous host. She said to Hill, 'You weren't, if you don't mind me saying, the greatest player in the world, but you don't mind slagging everybody else off, do you?'

His iron-cast ego helped him continue innovating. He returned to Coventry, first as managing director and then as chairman, during which time Highfield Road was converted to England's first all-seater football stadium. Incidents of hooliganism were all too common and Hill would often call for the reintroduction of National Service, a familiar refrain of men of his generation.

Perhaps most significantly, he inspired the introduction of three points for a win. He used his platform to push the FA into making the change in 1981, years before it was adopted by FIFA. Derrick Robins, who had been Coventry chairman in the 1960s, said, 'He's got a hell of a brain; he bubbles the whole time. That's half the trouble. He had so many ideas; some of them were quite crazy. We had to dampen those down a little bit.'

Unfortunately, not all of Hill's crazy ideas were successfully doused and he led a rebel football tour of apartheid South Africa in defiance of the sporting boycott. Protests forced the tour to be cut short, but Hill was given only a ticking off by the BBC.

He ignited another row in 2004 when he defended manager-turned-pundit Ron Atkinson's use of extreme racial language, comparing use of the N-word to people calling him 'chinny'.

'It was a load of fuss about nothing,' he said of Atkinson's outburst that had been picked up by microphones at half-time. 'In the culture of football calling a black man a n***** is just a bit of fun.' A mark of how attitudes to racism in the media have changed is that Sky ignored calls for Hill to be sacked and he presented *Sunday Supplement* for three more years. Sky, the BBC and other major broadcasters are now actively anti-racist.

Also fun for Hill was fox hunting. He deployed his remarkable growth mindset to learning to ride in less than a year and joined his local hunt. He lamented the decline of the British Empire. He was perhaps football's most curious paradox: the reactionary innovator, a chimney-sweeping, union-leading, fox hunter. Imagine Jimmy Hill in the social media age.

I know Sunderland fans who call him a cheat because of the last day of the 1976/77 season, when he contrived to delay Coventry's game against fellow relegation candidates Bristol City so it finished later than Sunderland's match at Everton. After full time at Goodison Park, Coventry and Bristol City knew both would stay up if they played out a draw. That's just what they did.

JIMMY HILL

In 1991 he was diagnosed with bowel cancer. His attitude was that you had to 'trust the doctors and get on with it'. He lived another 24 years. I met him when I was a reporter with Sky Sports and we filmed an interview at the All England club at Wimbledon where he had just played tennis. He was charming and funny; my childhood anxiety about him bringing back National Service seemed silly: the Jimmy Hill paradox.

19
Garrincha

NOT EVERY Brazilian thought losing to Uruguay at the 1950 World Cup was a tragedy. A 16-year-old Manuel Francisco dos Santos, Garrincha to his family and friends, heard the commentary on the loudspeakers in his local town square but couldn't see what the fuss was about: why get upset because somebody else lost a football match? Garrincha couldn't understand worrying about lots of things: money, fidelity and tactics to name but three. He did care about playing football, having sex and drinking alcohol and took all three to extremes.

He is the only one of *The Fifty* with a disability. An abnormality of the spine gave him bent legs: his right knee went inwards and his left knee outwards. His left leg was an inch or two shorter than his right. He had breathtaking acceleration but knee problems were a factor in his later decline, along with his staggering alcohol intake.

Garrincha was of black and Fulniô Indian heritage and came from Pau Grande in the state of Rio de Janeiro. His father was an alcoholic and passed the curse to Garrincha, who as a child regularly drank cachaça, a spirit distilled from sugar cane juice. They were poor, although it is hard to describe young Garrincha's poverty as grinding because he wasn't ground down by anything. He did what he liked. He went to school occasionally but more often skipped off. He got a job in the local factory but did hardly any work, preferring to sleep. He was desperate to lose his virginity so he did, with a goat.

He signed a semi-professional contract with a club but stopped turning up because he preferred the factory team. His first few trials with professional clubs were failures and Garrincha felt he wasn't taken seriously because of his legs. He eventually signed for Rio club Botafogo when he was 19 and, as he didn't like thinking about money, signed a blank contract that the directors would fill in later. He continued doing this as he inspired the club to state championships in 1957, 1961 and 1962. In one way it is obvious Garrincha was being ripped off: Botafogo played in front of mammoth crowds, and when they toured they could demand more money if their great winger was playing. But the lavish contracts of modern footballers bring strict limitations on lifestyle and nothing could restrict Garrincha. He would take the train back to Pau Grande for drinking sessions with his old friends and could persuade some engine drivers to slow down near his house so he could jump off the moving locomotive. He married Nair, the first woman he got pregnant, and went on to have eight daughters with her and a total of 14 kids with five women. He drank all the time and yet became an amazingly talented and successful footballer: the 'Angel with the Bent Legs'.

He wasn't picked for the 1954 World Cup. Brazil's squad was chosen for its ability to graft and follow orders. They lost to Hungary in the quarter-finals in the 'Battle of Berne', which finished with a brawl, during which the injured Puskás hit Brazil's Pinheiro on the head with a bottle. English referee Arthur Ellis said the players behaved like animals. Brazil's delegation accused him of being part of a communist plot.

While Pelé's introduction at the 1958 World Cup had been delayed by injury, the doubts about Garrincha focussed on his extreme individualism. In a warm-up game against

Fiorentina, he dribbled past four defenders and the keeper, but rather than roll the ball into the empty net he dragged it back and beat one more man before finally scoring. After Brazil's meticulous preparations, they weren't prepared to risk Garrincha on the biggest stage – at least not until they needed the sort of inspiration he and Pelé could provide. When they got to the final, Garrincha didn't realise it was the end of the competition because he was expecting to play all the teams in a league competition.

When they returned to Brazil as heroes, Pelé had a street named in his honour and was given a car he was too young to drive; Garrincha sent money ahead to keep the bars in Pau Grande open all night. He stayed out drinking until 8am, before going home to see his wife and family, having a quick sleep and hitting the bars again at noon. He missed an official reception held in his honour and was found in the street in a drunken stupor.

In 1959 Pelé played 103 matches for Brazil, Santos and Sao Paulo while doing his military service. In 1959 Garrincha had his fifth daughter with his wife, got a Swedish woman pregnant on a summer tour, got his mistress in Rio pregnant and ran over his own father in a drunken hit and run. As he tried to flee, he was chased by a crowd who told him who the victim was. His father wanted no legal action taken. He survived the accident but died of liver disease within a year. Real Madrid made a massive bid for Garrincha that Botafogo rejected. Somehow his best was yet to come.

The 1962 World Cup in Chile was Garrincha's time, or, as Pelé put it, 'I think an angel was watching over him.' Brazil beat Mexico with a goal by Pelé, who was hiding a groin injury that caught up with him in the second game against Czechoslovakia. Sportingly, the Czechoslovaks went easy on the great man in a 0-0 draw, but that was the end of his tournament. His replacement Amarildo scored twice as Brazil came from behind to beat Spain and qualify for the quarter-finals.

Against England, Garrincha was magnificent, scoring an unlikely opener when he jumped to meet a corner from Mario Zagallo. England equalised but a Garrincha free kick forced the second. Ron Springett fumbled and Vavá poached the rebound. The third was the best: England backed off and Garrincha picked out the top corner. 'England were a good team,' said Amarildo, 'but to have stopped Garrincha that day they would have needed a machine gun.'

His goals in the semi-final against Chile were remarkably similar, only this time the long-range shot was with his left. He also set up one of Vavá's double as the hosts were beaten 4-2. Garrincha's tournament nearly ended after he lost his usually cheery demeanour following a series of fouls by the Chileans, who had been involved in the notorious 'Battle of Santiago' against Italy earlier in the tournament, a match described rather pompously by David Coleman on British TV as 'the most stupid, appalling, disgusting and disgraceful exhibition of football possibly in the history of the game'.

Peruvian referee Arturo Yamasaki turned a blind eye to Chilean aggression until Garrincha lashed out at left-half Eladio Rojas and was sent off. As he left the pitch he was hit by a stone thrown from the crowd. The diplomatic might of the Brazilian federation was mobilised and the tournament disciplinary committee voted to allow him to play in the final, although come the big day he was ill and below his best. They faced the Czechoslovaks again, and Garrincha had to be reminded that it was the same team they had played in the group. Two bad goalkeeping mistakes allowed Brazil to win 3-1. Garrincha won the Golden Ball and returned home a hero.

Amarildo summed up his popularity: 'He is the only player who is loved by every single fan from every single club in Brazil. When Garrincha played he entertained even the opposition. I don't think you could have another player like Garrincha.'

But the reverence was about to be tested. As Ruy Castro put it in his moving biography, 'What had once been looked upon with good humour, as simply part of the Garrincha legend, was now being called indiscretion.'

It emerged that Garrincha was having an affair with a famous singer, Elza Soares, and while they were living it up, touring Europe making money, his wife Nair and their daughters lived in a squalid house in Pau Grande. Elza received more abuse than he did, along with racially abusive threats. She had political connections and after a military coup in 1964 the couple were held at gunpoint in their flat by a gang, who stripped them naked and killed a mynah bird Garrincha had been given after the World Cup.

His knee problems were slowing him down and his alcoholism soon had deadly consequences. He was drunk again when he crashed into a lorry and Elza's mother was thrown from the car and killed. Remarkably he was recalled for the 1966 World Cup in England. He scored with a free kick against Bulgaria, but Brazil's defeat at Goodison Park against Hungary in their second group game was his last international match and, remarkably, his first-ever defeat.

In 1973 a Brazil XI took on a FIFA XI in a money-raising match for Garrincha in front of 131,000 at the Maracaña. It made a fortune but he wasted or gave away his share. Depressed and ill, he became violent towards Elza and even her remarkable forbearance ran out, although there was always somebody somewhere who would buy Garrincha a drink. He died of multiple organ failure at the age of 49. Reports of his funeral procession said millions turned out to pay their respects.

20

Bobby Charlton

BOBBY CHARLTON won the World Cup, European Cup, three Football League titles, the FA Cup and the Ballon d'Or. He broke the appearance and goalscoring records for both England and Manchester United. For all that, his memories of a brilliant career were clouded by one day: 6 February 1958.

When football resumed in 1945, Manchester United appointed former Liverpool and Manchester City player Matt Busby as manager. After three second-place finishes, in 1951 he guided United to a first league title in 41 years. Busby then rebuilt the team and won the league twice more, in 1956 and 1957. The average age of the players was 21, then 22: the famous Busby Babes.

Charlton grew up in a miner's cottage in Ashington, Northumberland. His mother was a cousin of Jackie Milburn, who won the FA Cup three times as Newcastle's centre-forward. Charlton became an England schoolboy international before doing National Service in Shrewsbury, while playing for Manchester United at weekends. He made his debut in 1956, scoring ten goals in 14 games but, with characteristic modesty, he said he didn't feel part of the team and considered himself fortunate to get a medal.

United defied the authorities to become the first English team to compete in the European Cup. They beat Anderlecht 10-0 at Old Trafford, but fell to Di Stéfano and Real Madrid in the semi-final. English champions again the following season, they believed they could go all the way, knocking out Shamrock Rovers and Dukla Prague to set up a quarter-final with Partizan Belgrade. Charlton and Eddie Colman scored in the first-leg, 2-1 win before United flew to Yugoslavia for the return game on a pitch of slush and mud. Charlton scored twice in a 3-3 draw, good enough for Busby's side to go through. The return flight stopped to refuel in Munich. Take off was twice aborted and Charlton's friend and team-mate Duncan Edwards sent a telegram to his landlady: 'All flights cancelled. Flying tomorrow. Duncan.'

Pilot James Thain tried for a third time but the plane hit a fence and then a house. The fuselage crashed into a hut and a truck inside exploded, and 20 people were killed immediately. Three died of their injuries later, including Edwards. Eight United players died: Edwards, Colman, Geoff Bent, Roger Byrne, David Pegg, Billy Whelan, Mark Jones and Tommy Taylor. Charlton had been a housemate of Edwards, Jones, Taylor and Jackie Blanchflower, who lived, but, along with Johnny Berry, didn't play again. Thain helped his crew to safety but couldn't save co-pilot Ken Rayment. Three Manchester United staff members and former Manchester City goalkeeper Frank Swift, there as a journalist, were also killed. United's goalkeeper Harry Gregg dragged Charlton, Blanchflower, Violett and Busby from the burning wreckage and also saved a Yugoslav diplomat and her daughter.

It wasn't the first or last aircraft tragedy involving a football club. Nine years earlier, the great Torino side that made up most of Italy's national team were all killed when their plane crashed into the basilica of Superga on their return from a match in Lisbon. A total of 31 people died. Vittorio Pozzo, the World Cup-winning manager from the 1930s, had to identify the bodies of the players. In 1993 18 players from Zambia's national team were among 30 killed when their plane crashed into the Atlantic Ocean. In 2016 19 players from Brazilian club Chapecoense were among 71 dead after a crash near Medellín, Colombia.

Charlton suffered cuts, concussion and deeper emotional scars. He described walking around 'in some impenetrably dark fog'. Byrne and Taylor were England regulars but Charlton was hit hardest by the loss of Edwards, his strapping teammate from the FA Youth Cup win three years earlier, who had already won 18 England caps. Charlton rated Edwards as the best footballer he played alongside.

Without Busby, who spent two months in hospital, United still played the semi-final but lost to AC Milan, and even reached the FA Cup Final. Bolton Wanderers made sure there was no fairytale, yet. Nat Lofthouse scored twice. His second is the archetypal goal of the era as he barged into Gregg's back, as the keeper was about to catch the ball, dumping both in the net.

Charlton made his England debut less than three months after the crash and volleyed in a Tom Finney cross in a 4-0 win over Scotland, but the selection committee decided against taking him to the World Cup in Sweden so he had to wait until he was 24 to play on the biggest stage.

In Chile, in 1962, England lost to Hungary and beat Argentina, with a goal and an assist from left-winger Charlton. A draw against Bulgaria would be enough and they settled for a drab 0-0. Charlton argued that a team with ambitions of winning the tournament should play with more style. Johnny Haynes told him to stop moaning. They went out to Brazil in the quarters, thanks to Garrincha's wizardry.

Meanwhile, Busby was rebuilding United. Charlton scored 29 goals as they finished second in the first season post-Munich. But Charlton insisted it was Denis Law who provided the impetus that took the club into its next great phase. The Scotland striker had one season with Torino, but his frustration with Italian football and the abolition of England's maximum wage meant he was keen to return. United paid a record £115,000 and, despite a lacklustre 19th place in the league, they won the FA Cup. Law and Charlton were joined by Northern Irish teenage sensation George Best and United finished second to Bill Shankly's Liverpool in 1963/64.

Charlton played 59 games the following season. United lost the semi-finals of both the FA and Fairs Cup (forerunner to UEFA Cup/Europa League) but won the title on goal difference from newly promoted Leeds, who had Bobby's brother Jack in defence. In 1966 Manchester United finished fourth and again suffered double semi-final disappointment, but that summer all eyes turned to England's home World Cup.

Alf Ramsey had played right-back for Tottenham when they won the Second Division in 1950 and the Football League a year later, using groundbreaking tactics, by English standards. 'Push and Run' saw Spurs play with short passes and fluid movement, not unlike the Hungary side that overwhelmed England at Wembley in 1953, Ramsey's last international as a player. In contrast to most observers, he refused to accept England had been outclassed. He became a manager with Ipswich Town, winning promotion from Division Three (South) and then replicating his experience with Spurs by winning promotion to the top division in 1961, and winning the league in 1962. He was the obvious choice to lead England into the World Cup.

Ramsey saw that playing with two wingers could leave a side shorthanded in midfield and England started the tournament with a 'loose 4-3-3'. They played poorly in a 0-0 draw with a negative Uruguay side. At full time commentator Kenneth Wolstenholme declared, 'The Uruguayans are as happy as sand boys with that … you'd think Uruguay had won 5-0.'

Some magic from England's best player got them going against Mexico, Charlton ripping in a trademark long-range shot. 'Everyone backed away so I hit it in the general direction,' was his typically understated assessment.

Two goals from Liverpool's Roger Hunt saw off France in the last group game. After a controversial foul by Nobby Stiles on Jacques Simon, the FA asked Ramsey to drop the Manchester United midfielder, but he threatened to resign if he was forced to do so. The rough stuff wasn't one-sided; Jimmy Greaves finished the match with a blood-stained sock from a gashed shin.

England's quarter-final was an infamous culture clash with Argentina. England complained about the sly, underhand tactics of their opponents; the South Americans were convinced they were victims of a conspiracy by Europeans, keen for their robust tackling game to prevail. All hell broke loose when the West German referee Rudolf Kreitlein sent off Argentina skipper Antonio Rattín, or at least tried to. The towering Rattín refused to go and his team-mates surrounded and jostled the referee. It took eight minutes and two policemen to get Rattín off. He claimed he was asking for an interpreter.

Hurst glanced in a late header and Argentina claimed offside. It is hard to be sure because of the limited camera angles but I don't think it was. After the full-time whistle, peace was about to break out and George Cohen was swapping shirts with an opponent when Ramsey ran across and grabbed it, firing off a foul-mouthed volley. The England manager later branded the Argentina players 'animals'.

That match led to a change in the law. Both Charlton brothers were booked (one of only two occasions for Bobby) but Ken Aston, the head of FIFA's referees committee who was at Wembley, didn't realise, and nor did Jack. Aston drove home wondering how everyone involved in a match could be made aware when a player is cautioned. He stopped at traffic lights and had the idea for red and yellow cards, which were introduced for the 1970 competition.

Bobby scored both England goals in the semi-final against Portugal, first-time finishes benefitting from the hard running of Hunt and Hurst, who were partnered up front, keeping Greaves out. The tournament's top scorer, Eusébio, was closely marked by Stiles and in reply Portugal only managed a penalty, given for a blatant Jack Charlton handball.

In the final, both managers played their trump card defensively. Charlton and West Germany's brilliant 20-year-old midfielder Franz Beckenbauer were each instructed to mark the other and played out an anticlimactic truce. Helmut Haller gave the Germans the lead. England's elegant captain Bobby Moore then strode into midfield and was fouled. He got up, spotted his West Ham club-mate Hurst running unmarked in the box and picked him out with a floated pass. Hurst headed in for 1-1. England went in front in the 79th minute. A Hurst shot was blocked and the ball bounced kindly for another Hammer, Martin Peters, to smash it in. West Germany's equaliser came in the last minute, from a softly awarded free kick and a subsequent penalty-box scramble before Wolfgang Weber scored from four yards. Ramsey told his tired players to get off the ground as they waited for extra time: 'You've won this trophy once, now win it again!'

Hurst then scored the most controversial World Cup Final goal of all. Alan Ball crossed and Hurst controlled and smashed a shot against the bar. The ball bounced down and out. The onrushing Hunt turned away and claimed a goal, but West Germany were adamant it hadn't crossed the line. Swiss referee Gottfried Dienst passed the buck to linesman Tofiq Bahramov, who seized his moment and indicated it was a goal. They named a stadium after him back in Azerbaijan.

England's players did a good job of convincing themselves the ball crossed the line, and, to be fair, some of it did. Hawkeye technology can now show the whole of the ball wasn't over but we've always sort of known that. Hurst smashed in another anyway and it really was all over. Moore wiped his hands before he collected the Jules Rimet Trophy from the Queen. She told Bobby Charlton he seemed to be sweating a lot. That sweat earned him the World Cup Golden Ball and the Ballon d'Or. Charlton and England were on top of the world.

Ramsey's formations set the template for English football for years to come. Charlton observed, 'The following year everyone was playing 4-3-3 even if they didn't have the players for it.' In time the 4-4-2 used (loosely) in the latter stages came to dominate English football. Cohen described it as a rough 4-4-2 because Stiles played deeper and more defensively than Charlton. The wide midfielders Peters and Ball were grafters, as were the front two. Unimaginative coaches seized on it, and by the time I was learning football it was a default formation.

Charlton won 106 England caps and scored 49 goals. He was hoping for the half-century at the 1970 World Cup but Mexico was a struggle for England. They beat Romania and Czechoslovakia 1-0 and lost to Pelé's Brazil by the same score, in a match that kicked off at noon to accommodate European television schedules. The quarter-final brought sweet revenge for West Germany. Ramsey's side were 2-0 up early in the second half until Beckenbauer beat England's stand-in keeper Peter Bonetti. Charlton was taken off with 21 minutes to play, unaware it was the end of his brilliant international career. Uwe Seeler's freakish header forced extra time and the extraordinarily prolific Gerd Müller poached the winner.

I was born a year later, but I grew up with the received wisdom that Ramsey messed up by substituting Charlton. Only watching the game recently did I realise his replacement Colin Bell was denied a blatant penalty after an awful challenge by Beckenbauer; I don't know why so little is made of that in English football folklore. Ramsey continued as manager but was sacked after England lost out to Poland in the qualifiers for the 1974 finals.

Charlton's club career was crowned in 1968. United had won the league again in 1967 and they completed an emotional journey to the top of the European game ten years after Munich. Two-time European champions Benfica were the opponents at Wembley, another showdown with Eusébio.

Charlton opened the scoring with what looks like a brilliant header but according to the man himself was intended as a flick on. He got the fourth after Best and Brian Kidd had both scored early in extra time. Charlton, a reluctant captain, lifted the trophy. He was a European champion with Manchester United and world champion with England, surely his nation's greatest footballer.

21

Eusébio

MODERN FOOTBALL reached Africa at the same time and in the same manner as most other places, from the wandering Brits. The earliest mention seems to be in Cape Town in 1862. The most famous of Victorian missionaries Dr David Livingstone reportedly turned up in Zambia with three things: his medical bag, a bible and a football. The oldest African clubs were formed at similar times to their European counterparts. Egypt competed in Olympic football in the 1920s and at the 1934 World Cup, but after that no African country competed at a World Cup until 1970. The route to qualification for African nations changed, but places were few and the barriers high. For example, Morocco won the African qualifiers in 1961 but then had to play-off against the Spain side of Di Stéfano, Puskás and Paco Gento. They lost both games by a single goal. African sides weren't hopeless, they were unwanted.

Individual Africans did shine. The French were never as keen as the English to take football to their colonies but they were happy to acquire players; Morocco-born Just Fontaine's 13-goal haul at the 1958 World Cup has never been surpassed. By 1966 the African federation had had enough and refused FIFA's offer of a single place to be shared with Asia and boycotted the whole thing. But an African-born player followed in Fontaine's footsteps and claimed the Golden Boot.

Eusébio da Silva Ferreira was a special talent. When I started watching old films, I realised he was left-footed. Then I realised he wasn't. He was so comfortable with his technique he would take set pieces with either foot. There is a danger of white commentators overstressing the physicality of black sportspeople but, with that caveat, allow me to point out that Eusébio ran the 100m in 11 seconds at the age of 16. He was good young and became a great through a long, successful career that started in Mozambique, then a colony known as Portuguese East Africa, and finished in the USA over two decades later.

He joined Benfica when they were champions of Europe. They had beaten Barcelona in the 1961 final, the first time anyone but Real Madrid had lifted the European Cup. The scorer of the clinching goal was another East African, Mário Coluna. Benfica weren't forging a new path when they snapped up Eusébio from Sporting Lourenço Marques.

Benfica were led by the legendary globetrotting coach Béla Guttman, a Jewish former-Hungarian international who survived the holocaust after escaping from a Nazi labour camp. He met an old contact from his Sao Paulo days in a Lisbon barber shop, who told him about the sensational player he had seen on a recent tour.

Guttman wanted Eusébio immediately but Benfica's Lisbon rivals Sporting objected because they had an arrangement with his club, Lourenço Marques. Months of legal wrangling followed and the player spent some time hidden in an Algarve seaside village, using the codename Ruth Malosso. He was worth the trouble. He scored a hat-trick in his first friendly match and made his official debut in a cup game, scheduled for the day after the European Cup Final. Still in June, Benfica faced Pelé's Santos in a tournament in Paris and were 0-4 down. Guttman sent on his new striker who scored a hat-trick. Benfica lost but Eusébio's picture made the front cover of *L'Équipe*. He scored a total of 29 goals in his first season, as Benfica reached the European Cup Final again.

In the semi-final they beat English double winners Tottenham and faced Real Madrid in the final. Puskás scored a first-half hat-trick in Amsterdam's Olympic Stadium, but the men from Mozambique won it for the Portuguese. Coluna got Benfica's third before Eusébio scored twice. He was only 20 and would go on to get 473 official goals for the club, win the Primeira Liga 11 times and the Ballon d'Or – but that final was arguably his peak in club football.

Guttman asked for a pay rise and quit when he was turned down, cursing the club as he left, saying Benfica wouldn't be European champions for 100 years. It is nonsense, of course, but in Eusébio's day Benfica lost the final to AC Milan in 1963, to Inter Milan in 1965 and Manchester United in 1968. They have since lost two more European Cup finals (PSV in 1988, and AC Milan again in 1990) and two Europa League finals.

Mozambique had no international football team until the day of its independence from Portugal in 1975, after the end of a bloody conflict, so there was never a question about which country Eusébio would represent. He made a scoring debut for Portugal in 1961 – in a defeat against Luxembourg in a World Cup qualifier. The 1966 qualification was the first time Portugal ever succeeded. Eusébio's seven goals made him the top scorer in the whole process.

Portugal was no one-man team, with Benfica, Sporting and Porto players making up most of the squad. They beat Hungary and Bulgaria before the much-anticipated showdown between Eusébio and Pelé proved to be an anticlimax, with the great Brazilian limping badly after being hacked down by João Morais. Eusébio defended his team-mate, saying Pelé hadn't been fit to play. In the quarter-finals they faced the sensations of the tournament. North Korea had benefitted from the African boycott and got to the tournament beating only

Australia. They qualified from their group after drawing with Chile and then upsetting Italy at Middlesbrough's Ayresome Park with a goal from army corporal Pak Doo-ik.

Sensationally, North Korea scored inside a minute and were 3-0 up before Portugal knew what had hit them. But Eusébio bit back and got two before half-time. He equalised and then won a penalty at the end of a run in which he looks speeded up compared to everyone else; four goals in a 5-3 win. Portugal left Goodison Park for Wembley to face the hosts in the semi-final, and despite Eusébio's penalty it was England's and Bobby Charlton's day. Eusébio put another penalty past Lev Yashin, as Portugal claimed third place before leaving the big stage for the next two decades.

Benfica got lots of offers for Eusébio. Juventus had tried to buy him, and after the World Cup Inter made a bid, only for Portugal's dictator, Antonio Salazar, to personally intervene and stop the deal, to Eusébio's fury. He said, 'Inter made a big offer which would have made me the highest-paid player in the world. And yet I was not allowed to move. Why? Salazar was not my father and certainly not my mother. What gave him the right? The truth was he was my slave master, just as he was the slave master of the entire country.'

Eusébio didn't leave until after the Carnation Revolution, when the military finally abandoned Salazar's regime. The NASL was the destination for ageing stars seeking cash, and in his first stint Eusébio played for Boston Minutemen, before returning with the unfashionable Toronto Metros-Croatia. The Canadian club won the 1976 Soccerbowl to the frustration of the NASL bosses, who wanted Pelé's New York Cosmos to prevail. Only the Brazilian could cut through to the American public in an era when a match commentator literally explained that the teams were trying to kick the ball into their opponents' goal. Toronto Metros-Croatia were a solid team based, as the name suggests, around a core of Croatians. Eusébio scored 16 goals in 22 games. In the final game they beat Minnesota

Kicks, a team dominated by English journeymen, in an 11am kick-off. It was Eusébio's last game for the club, who then slipped back to obscurity. The NASL was soon in terminal decline and the great Eusébio finished his career playing in the rival Major Indoor Soccer League.

So was Eusébio Africa's greatest footballer? Writer Ayo Akinfe doesn't even believe Eusébio is African, having been closely connected with Portugal and not becoming a notable advocate for Africa or Mozambique. Plenty of others think differently and I'm not qualified to arbitrate. Eusébio died and was buried in Lisbon but was mourned in Mozambique, where the President Armando Guebuza said, 'He's a figure who has contributed to the deep and rich history of Mozambique. Eusébio came here from time to time. He always maintained a link with Mozambique. He is a very well known and respected figure in our country.'

It doesn't make him sound like a national treasure does it? His brilliance helped highlight the ludicrously low regard for African football in the 1960s, although progress was painfully slow after that. The truth is Eusébio was an early example of a great player who couldn't be pinned to a particular place: the great European and African footballer.

22

Billy McNeill

WHEN BILLY McNeill stood at the head of his Celtic team-mates in the tunnel of Lisbon's Estádio Nacional, he wondered whether their opponents, the mighty Italians, Inter Milan, would think they were facing a pub team.

'Directly behind me stood this collection of freckle-faced, white-legged individuals. Opposite I could see a group of handsome Latins with bronze faces and limbs shimmering under a coating of oil.'

It was 1967 and the 11 previous European Cup finals had been won by 'Latins'. McNeill and his team-mates all came from the city of Glasgow or nearby, but there was more at stake than civic or national pride. They were playing for the soul of football, or so it was portrayed.

Catenaccio changed football forever, not for better. It helped the two-teamed city of Milan disrupt the Real Madrid–Benfica duopoly but it also hastened football's transition to a low-scoring game. The word itself means a bolt you find on a gate or door. It started as a tactic and became a mindset. The Italians imported it from the Swiss, where it developed, basically, as a means of having defenders outnumber attackers. The obvious downside was that teams employing it were left shorthanded up front, so the system was popularised by small clubs: 'the right of the weak'.

The mighty AC Milan turned to *catenaccio* after recruiting Nereo Rocco, whose success at Padova had come from keeping the bolt firmly shut. Milan won Serie A and then took on Europe, knocking out Alf Ramsey's Ipswich Town and Dundee en route to the 1963 final at Wembley. They trailed to a Eusébio goal but won thanks to a double from their Brazilian, José Altafini. To be fair to Rocco's Milan, they scored goals and the talented Gianni Rivera had licence to roam. It was the response from their San Siro co-habitants that sealed *catenaccio*'s dreaded reputation.

Inter had appointed Helenio Herrera, a four-time winner of La Liga: twice with Atlético Madrid and twice with Barcelona. The Buenos Aires-born, former France international initially doubled up as Spain's national team boss, but once his focus was purely on Inter he took *catenaccio* to new heights, or depths. Herrera hadn't always been miserly: in his two La Liga-winning seasons at Barcelona in 1958/59 and 1959/60 they played 60 games, scoring 184 goals.

Petroleum magnate Angelo Moratti bought Inter excellent players and Herrera fitted them into an ultra-defensive system. In their first European Cup tie in September 1963, they faced Harry Catterick's Everton, another side put together at great expense that had the strongest defence in England. The two-leg aggregate score was 1-0 to the Italians.

On their way to the final, Inter had scored 13 to Real Madrid's 27, but two goals from Sandro Mazzola helped them win 3-1. Then in 1964/65 they knocked out Rangers and Liverpool before slamming the bolt on Eusébio, who had scored nine times in the competition: one goal was enough to beat Benfica. To stop the narrative being too neat, Real Madrid beat Inter in the 1965/66 semi-finals, and won the final against Partizan, one last flash of European glory for Santiago Bernebéu.

After Italy's embarrassment at the 1966 World Cup had been pinned on them being too open, the advocates of defensive football doubled down. Juventus won Serie A in 1966/67, scoring 44 goals in 34 games and conceding 19. Serie A matches were down to an average of two goals per game. The low point was to come in 1972/73, with an average of 1.87 per game. Not until the 1990s did that figure rise back above 2.5.

In *Calcio*, John Foot argues that Italians aren't especially defensive-minded, just very good at defending – but the most influential football writer of the *catenaccio* generation, Gianni Brera of *Gazzetta dello Sport*, believed with passion that the perfect score in a football match was a 0-0. *Catenaccio* was more than a formation, it was a philosophy. That is what Celtic faced in Lisbon in May 1967.

McNeill was nicknamed Cesar, not after Julius Caesar but Cesar Romero who played a getaway driver in the 1960 film *Ocean's 11*. He was the only one of his friends who had a car, so that served as a nickname. He never drove far: of all the Lisbon Lions, Bobby Lennox came from farthest afield – Saltcoats, 30-odd miles away from Glasgow, on the coast.

McNeill made his debut in 1958 but grew disillusioned by Celtic's struggles and the poor pay in Scotland compared to England. He won nothing until Jock Stein arrived as manager. Stein had been Celtic's reserve coach before leaving for Dunfermline and Hibs. He returned in March 1965 and won the Scottish Cup, beating Dunfermline 3-2, clinched by McNeill's towering header. Celtic finished eighth that season, but Stein rapidly transformed the club and in his first full campaign they won the title, scoring 106 goals. He believed fans who paid hard-earned money deserved to watch attacking football.

It was the start of a nine-year reign as Scottish champions which ended a period of six seasons in which four clubs won the league, the most open the competition has ever been. In their first attempt at becoming European champions, Celtic defeated Zurich and then Nantes, where McNeill was praised for addressing local journalists in French. In the quarter-final second leg against Yugoslavia's Vojvodina in March 1967 he scored the winning goal in the 90th minute at Celtic Park. They dug in when they had to, seeing off Dukla Prague with a goalless second leg in the semi-finals. Inter's journey to the final involved aggregate wins over Torpedo Moscow (1-0) and Real Madrid (3-0).

Stein had met Herrera a few years earlier. When he was Dunfermline manager, the *Daily Express* paid for him and future Rangers coach Willie Waddell to travel to Milan to watch Inter train. Thoroughbred shyster that he was, Herrera refused to even talk about his tactics, but Waddell said that Stein saw the Argentine as more than a tactician: 'Jock saw a wee man with the burning ambition to be top of the heap. He saw a man absolutely dedicated to the game with a single-mindedness and driving urge to get the best out of the players at his disposal.'

Despite their superficial physical disadvantages, McNeill believed Celtic could win. 'While the Inter players looked the part, we didn't suffer an inferiority complex. There was a cockiness about our team and a real self-belief.'

It was a good job because Sandro Mazzola scored an early penalty, which could have been the death knell for Celtic against a team that counter-attacked ruthlessly. McNeill thought Inter should have looked for a second but that wasn't their style: 'Strangely they didn't press home their advantage and allowed us to take the play to them.'

Tommy Gemmell was Celtic's left-back, but Inter sat so deep he pushed into midfield and just after the hour smashed in an equaliser from the edge of the box. Inter had no answer and six minutes from the end Stevie Chalmers hit the winner. 'They were a spent force,' McNeill wrote in his autobiography, 'unable to readjust their game and we won easily in the end.' He collected the European Cup alone, perched precariously on a ledge in front of the paranoid Portuguese dictator, Antonio Salazar, Eusébio's 'slave master'.

It would be nice if the story ended with plucky, sun-starved Glaswegians liberating football from the grip of *catenaccio*, but that is not what happened. The European Cup was back in Italy two years later, after Rocco returned to AC Milan. They beat Celtic 1-0 on aggregate, ended Manchester United's defence and knocked out an Ajax side containing a young Johan Cruyff. That was more of an ending because no Italian club became European champions again until 1985. Herrera won only one more trophy, the Italian Cup, after moving to Roma to become the world's highest-paid coach.

In Scotland, Celtic were finally toppled by Rangers in 1975, McNeill's last season as a player. He was frustrated that a generation of Scots were allowed to move to England for money. 'They weren't bigger clubs in England,' he wrote. 'They were clubs prepared to pay decent money. There aren't many clubs anywhere bigger than Celtic and its problem is that it plays in a smaller league.' McNeill won the Scottish title four times as Celtic's coach, either side of a stint in England with Manchester City and Aston Villa.

Celtic and McNeill reached another European Cup Final in 1970 when they were outplayed by Feyenoord. The rise of the Dutch in the early 1970s felt like more of a new era, but *catenaccio* didn't really die, it mutated; 99.9 per cent of teams play with more defenders than attackers now. Inter's long wait to become European champions again ended when Jose Mourinho was the coach. Former Inter midfielder Diego Simeone masterminded Atlético's toppling of Real Madrid and Barça. Both coaches deployed superb players in defensive structures. The battle for the soul of football is never-ending, but the game is more tactically cautious than in innocent pre-*catenaccio* times.

Underdogs win football matches and competitions from time to time, but McNeill and the Lisbon Lions deserve their place in history for doing so in style. A club that couldn't match the resources of their competitors from the richer leagues became European champions, not by invoking the 'right of the weak' but by playing attacking, entertaining football. They were rare but not unique; we will get to Cruyff and Ajax soon.

23

George Best

IT WAS a good tale for the after-dinner speaking circuit that gave George Best an income long after his football career had finished and he had blown more than one fortune. He and Mary Stävin, Bond actress and former Miss World, had ordered champagne on room service. It was delivered by an Irish waiter who looked at Best, his beautiful girlfriend and the pile of cash on the bed from a successful night at a casino and asked, 'George, where did it all go wrong?'

You are supposed to laugh but the sad fact is that it did go wrong. I suppose 'all' is the crucial word because plenty went right. He won the European Cup, the Football League (twice), the Ballon d'Or, got rich, slept with beautiful women, partied with stars and became a terrace song: 'Georgie Best, Superstar, wears frilly knickers and a Playtex bra.' He flew close to the sun and plummeted to earth.

But what a journey. As a 15-year-old, Best sailed from Belfast to join Manchester United, only to bolt home a day later, overawed. He was welcomed back and given an office job with the Manchester Ship Canal to get around restrictions on Northern Irish and Scottish youngsters signing with English clubs. He threatened to do another runner so the club got him a different job that meant he could train full time before he was 17. It was not the last time the rules were bent for George Best.

He quickly broke into United's first team and played 59 matches in the 1964/65 title-winning season. His speed and incredible skill had already wowed dedicated football fans but his status went stratospheric on United's return to the European big time. They were drawn against Benfica in the quarter-finals in March 1966 and won 3-2 at Old Trafford. Nineteen-year-old Best was a sensation in the return game at the Stadium of Light, scoring the first two in United's 5-1 victory. Commentator Kenneth Wolstenholme called him a 'supreme cheeky chappy'. The Portuguese press dubbed him 'El Beatle'. Their English counterparts changed it to the 'Fifth Beatle' and he was photographed wearing a huge sombrero when the squad arrived back from Lisbon.

There had never been a phenomenona like George Best. Stanley Matthews had got the turnstiles clicking and been paid to advertise cigarettes, but while Best was still a teenager he was getting thousands of letters a week. He signed with an agent who was soon overrun with commercial offers. He was young, handsome and talented when the Beatles were spearheading an explosion of pop culture that made Brylcreemed figures like Matthews seem like shadows from the distant past. As Best put it, 'It was inevitable the world would latch onto the footballer eventually and I just happened to be the first.'

A couple of years after the abolition of the maximum wage, Best was earning £1,000 a week including bonuses and Manchester United allowed him leeway that seems extraordinary now. Commercials for products ranging from eggs and sausages to bras bolstered his earnings and he enjoyed spending his money. The shy boy from Belfast found it easy to attract women once he was famous, and easier to deal with the madness when he was drunk.

In his 2001 autobiography he wrote, 'Just a few years earlier I had been kicking a ball about in the streets of Belfast. Now

THE FIFTY

I was being paid fortunes to do it. It would have been difficult for anyone to keep their feet completely on the ground under such circumstances. I felt like I was living a fantasy world and could act accordingly.'

At first he swam fast enough to keep up with the raging torrent. He and Bobby Charlton were ever-present as United won another title in 1966/67, staying unbeaten after Boxing Day. The following season was his Ballon d'Or year. He missed just one league match in 1967/68 and scored a total of 32 goals, as Matt Busby finally conquered Europe.

After narrow victories in the second round and quarter-finals, Best scored the only goal of the semi-final, first leg against Real Madrid. Successive league defeats between the European games allowed Manchester City to snatch the Football League title, so the pressure was on when United went to Spain. They were 2-0 and 3-1 down at the Bernebéu, before David Sadler made it 3-3 on aggregate. Best then set up the winner for Bill Foulkes, a 36-year-old centre-half and survivor of Munich. It was Foulkes's ninth and final goal in almost 700 games.

In their long-awaited final, United faced Benfica at Wembley. Eusébio hit the bar, Charlton headed the first and Jaime Graça equalised. In extra time, Best rounded the keeper and scored. Brian Kidd and Charlton made it 4-1.

It was the pinnacle for Busby. It should have been a springboard for Best but instead it was the beginning of the end. 'It seemed like everyone was saying, "that's it, we've done what we set out to do", but I was 22 and I wasn't going to reach my peak for another seven or eight years. I felt they should have been saying, "this is the first of many".'

Busby stayed as first-team manager for another year before switching to 'general manager', while reserve-team coach Wilf McGuinness was promoted. Busby frequently undermined his successor, including in his attempts to discipline Best, whose behaviour was becoming increasingly outrageous.

Best was scathing about United's signings and became depressed about the team's rapid decline. He spent more time drinking and gambling and was a regular on the front and back pages of the tabloid newspapers. Given his drink-fuelled lifestyle, it was remarkable that he scored over 20 goals for four successive seasons after the European Cup win.

English football had long had a damaging drinking culture. Best's antics were splashed over the front pages of ostensibly outraged newspapers, but the indulgent nudge-nudge attitude egged on a rich, confused young man to seek answers to his problems in liquor. He wasn't alone: Jimmy Greaves, Jim Baxter, Bobby Moore, Alan Hudson, Howard Kendall, Brian Clough and many more succeeded in football despite dangerous hard-drinking. The press and public could never decide whether Best's story was a triumph or a tragedy, which is part of his fascination. 'I spent a lot of money on booze, birds and fast cars,' he quipped, 'the rest I just squandered.'

Squandered like the second half of his football career. The former European Footballer of the Year became an itinerant, playing for, among others, Stockport County, Cork Celtic, Dunstable Town, Hong Kong Rangers and Brisbane Lions: a shadow of his former self, never reliable, never fulfilled. America and the NASL distracted him for a while but chiefly because the money and the weather were good and the football bad enough for him to shine, despite his declining physicality.

He was Northern Ireland's best-ever player by a distance but won only 37 caps. At his lowest, he stole money, fought with girlfriends, was declared bankrupt, had 57 stitches after drunkenly crashing a car and was sent to prison for headbutting a policeman. Eventually he accepted he was an alcoholic but side-stepped all attempts to reform him as skilfully as he had once side-stepped bewildered defenders. He died aged 59.

It took a lot of wasted talent but football is now much better at helping its young stars deal with fame and fortune. Best was rich by the standards of the day, but not sufficiently to detach himself from the public. He moved into a luxury, futuristic house but people sat in his garden, watching him through the windows. We complain about a lack of characters in modern football, but at least the players reliably turn up for matches; Best once spent days holed up with an actress hiding from paparazzi. The current generation might be over-protected but Best was often humiliated, once appearing drunk on BBC primetime chat show *Wogan*, slurring to the host: 'Terry, I like to screw.'

He invited the intrusion into his life and never escaped it. He had a liver transplant and was snapped drinking in a pub soon afterwards. On his deathbed he was photographed by the *News of the World*.

Despite his occasional bluster, he regretted blowing his football career. 'It went wrong with the thing I loved most of all, my football, and from there the rest of my life unravelled … United had never had to deal with a star football player before and Sir Matt had little idea of how to handle me or what was happening around me,' he reflected. 'Willingly or not, I represented a generation that was alien to him.'

His friend Michael Parkinson summed it up, 'I don't think any of us really knew what made George tick. I don't think any of us got that close to him. He was never going to be pinned down by anyone, defender or concerned friend alike. It was his ball, his life and he was going to keep it to himself.'

24

Johan Cruyff

WHEN JOHAN Cruyff was promoted to Ajax's first team in 1965, he became the club's second-ever full-time professional player. In 1971 they won the first of three consecutive European Cups. In 1974 the Netherlands reached the World Cup Final, with stylish play that inspired football romantics like Eric Cantona. 'Cruyff was my childhood hero,' the Frenchman said. 'I had a poster of him on my bedroom wall. He was a creator. He was at the heart of a revolution with his football. Ajax changed football and he was the leader of it all.'

The Dutch had made little impact on European football before Cruyff. Its conservative hierarchy stuck doggedly to amateurism, even banning Dutch players from the national team if they moved to professional clubs abroad. Pop culture and modern football hit the Netherlands in the 1960s, with Cruyff at the heart of both.

Cruyff was 12 when his father died, having given young Johan an appreciation of football and a reverence for Alfredo Di Stéfano's use of space. Johan's mother was a cleaner for Ajax coach Vic Buckingham and it is only a slight exaggeration to say the club itself adopted the boy. He formed a particularly close bond with Rinus Michels, who took over as coach in 1965, and they became the twin powers behind Ajax winning the Dutch league in 1966, 1967, 1968 and 1970.

'Because I subconsciously absorbed everything – always watching, listening – I developed really quickly as a footballer,' Cruyff recalled.

They were ahead of their time: long hours of dedicated practice and marginal gains, familiar concepts now, helped make Ajax the strongest team in the world, transforming the Netherlands from a football backwater into a major power.

After Ajax beat Liverpool 5-1 in thick Amsterdam fog in the 1966 European Cup, Bill Shankly complained, 'We never play well against defensive teams. Ajax got lucky. In Liverpool we'll beat them 7-0.'

The return finished 2-2 in the Anfield mud; 19-year-old Cruyff scored twice. The Anfield Wrap blog argues that for all of Shankly's bluster, he learned from that defeat and Liverpool's transition into a possession-based team can be traced to this tie. It took time for word to spread. The following season Nurnberg's Max Merkel said he thought Ajax was a cleaning product, not a football club. He knew better after a 4-0 thrashing, as the Dutch side reached the final, which they lost to AC Milan.

Rotterdam's Feyenoord beat them to become the first Dutch champions of Europe in 1970, but Ajax were getting stronger. In 1970/71 they beat Basel, Celtic and Atlético Madrid 3-0 at the Olympic Stadium, before clinching the trophy against Greek side Panathinaikos, who were managed by Ferenc Puskás.

In common with Puskás's Hungarian team of the 1950s, Michels encouraged discussion and dissent among his players and in Cruyff there was a clear on-field leader. The style was dubbed Total Football. When they lost possession, rather than retreating into defensive positions, they pressed opponents to quickly win back the ball. Players had to be able to swap positions to fill gaps wherever they appeared. Cruyff would pop up all over the pitch. It allowed players to thrive through technique rather than physicality. To the modern eye it looks more normal than the rigid 4-4-2 usually seen in England at the time; a sign of how the Dutch revolutionised football. It worked as long as the players were good enough.

Michels was tempted away to Barcelona but Ajax's success continued under the easy-going Romanian Ștefan Kovács. Cruyff scored both goals in the 1972 European Cup Final against Inter and the hat-trick was completed against Juventus in 1973. Cruyff won his second Ballon d'Or that year but was stripped of the Ajax captaincy after his team-mates took a vote. He quit the club for the first, but not the last, time that August and signed for Barcelona for a world-record fee.

Cruyff's influence in Spain ran deeper than football. Barcelona hadn't won La Liga since 1960 when he joined for 6m guilders, 60m pesetas, roughly £920,000 (the English record at the time was £225,000). Ajax and the Dutch authorities made the process difficult and it was late October before he made his debut, with his new club struggling in 14th place. He scored twice and Barça soared through the rest of the season. They beat Real Madrid, winners of nine championships since Barça's last, 5-0 in El Clásico, and won La Liga by ten points.

Those were the latter days of the Franco dictatorship that had suppressed the identity of Spain's regions, banning the use of the Catalan language and the naming of children with traditional Catalan names. Cruyff defied the authorities, registering his son as Jordi when local officials insisted he be called Jorge. Barcelona's Camp Nou and Bilbao's San Mames had become focal points for dissension against Franco, as did Cruyff – the long-haired super-cool foreigner arriving in a country ground down by decades of autocracy.

With Spain seemingly conquered, the world was next. The Netherlands hadn't played at the World Cup since 1938 and had never won a game, but this generation, mainly made up of Ajax and Feyenoord players, was sensational.

THE FIFTY

The 1974 World Cup in West Germany had two group phases and the Netherlands won five of six games, scoring 14 and conceding only a Rudi Krol own goal, when 3-0 up against Bulgaria. In the only group game they failed to win, Cruyff produced the flash of skill that bears his name. He hadn't practised the move. In fact, it came from a slight mis-control of a diagonal pass he received on the left flank, just outside the penalty area, which forced him to turn his back on Sweden right-back Jan Olsson. Cruyff shaped as if he was going to either go back away from the byline or pass the ball with his right foot. Instead he clipped it behind himself and chased it. Olsson was literally facing 180 degrees in the wrong direction. The Cruyff Turn was born. Holland didn't score from the cross or win the tournament, but Cruyff insisted it is missing the point to dwell on the negatives.

It wasn't all clever passing and rotating positions. The Dutch played long balls when it suited and against Brazil in Dortmund, in what was effectively a semi-final, they rose to the physical challenge. Bluntly, the sides hacked one another to bits while the referee flashed cards on what looked like an entirely random basis.

The pinnacle of that Dutch team was the first minute of the final against West Germany at Munich's Olympic Stadium. Cruyff was the deepest outfield player when he collected the ball. He glided through the German defence and was hacked down just inside the box. Johan Neeskens scuffed the penalty into the net and the world expected the Dutch masters to turn on the style. But, as in 1954, everyone had underestimated West Germany.

Midfielder Willem van Hanegem said, 'One half of your team decided to keep playing as we had for the whole tournament. The other half wanted to humiliate them.'

That assessment doesn't account for the excellence of Franz Beckenbauer and his team-mates who soaked up pressure, hit hard on the break and won the game 2-1. Cruyff shrugged off the defeat.

'I got over it quickly enough. In fact, it wasn't that much of a blow. Much more important was the vast amount of positivity and admiration for our performances that our play had generated all over the world. Pretty much everyone who wasn't German thought we should have won. We weren't on top form in the final, but we had set an example for billions of people. We had also given hope to all the players who, like me, weren't big or strong. The whole philosophy of how football should be played was adjusted during that tournament.'

Barça didn't win La Liga again until 1985, and didn't become European champions until Cruyff returned as manager, but one of his leading disciples, Pep Guardiola, doesn't mind. 'As a player and as a manager he won a lot of titles but that's not his legacy. The titles only help. Johan has changed two clubs. Not only did he change Ajax but also Barcelona and then the Dutch and Spanish national teams, too. Forget the titles. I've won more titles than him. Messi, for example, is someone who runs less, and in that, he's the best of Cruyff's alumni.'

Cruyff was a curmudgeon. His autobiography is full of tales of other people creating awkward situations in which he was forced to stand his ground. He was proudly ahead of his time in the field of dissent to match officials. He was sent off by an East German referee when playing against Czechoslovakia in 1967 and banned from internationals for a year. Cruyff was adamant he acted for the good of the game; this time I disagree.

He didn't play in the 1978 World Cup, later explaining he was nervous about leaving his family after they were victims of an attempted kidnapping in Barcelona, in which he was tied up by a man with a gun before his wife was able to raise the alarm. He first retired in 1978 before being forced to play again having lost a fortune in pig farming.

He played for NASL sides LA Aztecs and Washington Diplomats before going back to the Netherlands and playing three more seasons, winning the league in each – two with Ajax and, after falling out over money, one with Feyenoord.

His coaching career took a familiar path: Ajax to Barcelona with lots of success and lots of arguments. He won the Cup Winners' Cup with his boyhood club before creating Barça's Dream Team that won La Liga in four successive years, and the 1992 European Cup at Wembley.

He smoked heavily throughout his career and had a heart bypass operation in 1991. Another heart scare influenced his decision to quit coaching after he left Barça. He was diagnosed with lung cancer in October 2015 and died five months later, aged 68. The Amsterdam Arena was renamed in his honour but Cruyff's true legacy is the football of Guardiola, Xavi, Frenkie de Jong and Messi.

25

Franz Beckenbauer

THERE WAS no nationwide professional football league in West Germany until 1963, and even then there were maximum transfer fees and wages. The egalitarian Bundesliga was won by seven different clubs in its first seven seasons. Unfortunately, the restrictions cultivated a culture of corruption with tax havens, disreputable agents, secret payments and direct bribery of players. When this was laid bare, the solution was to create a free market for wages and transfers, which triggered a period of dominance for two clubs: Bayern Munich and Borussia Mönchengladbach.

Bayern weren't included in the first Bundesliga. They had won the German national play-offs back in 1932, but senior club figures were Jewish and it was impossible to thrive under Nazi rule. So in 1964 Munich-born Franz Beckenbauer made his debut for a southern regional league club. They were promoted in his first full season, with the youngster contributing 17 of 146 league goals; *catenaccio* had clearly not conquered the Regionalliga Süd.

He made his West Germany debut in 1965 and was excellent at the following year's World Cup in England. He scored twice in his first game against Switzerland after quick, skilful runs from central midfield. Only Eusébio and Helmut Haller outscored him, despite his negative role in the final, tracking Bobby Charlton. The Englishman was impressed by Beckenbauer's fitness, saying he had 'the lungs of a horse'.

Bayern won the German Cup that summer, followed by the 1967 European Cup Winners' Cup, when they beat Rangers in the final. They won their first Bundesliga in 1969 with starring roles for Beckenbauer, goalkeeper Sepp Maier and Gerd Müller, who scored 30 goals in as many games. The short, stocky Müller hit an extraordinary 652 in 707 club games, despite playing in an era of largely defensive football and tough tackling.

West Germany knocked England out of the 1970 World Cup on their way to a third-place finish. In their semi-final defeat against Italy, dubbed 'The Game of the Century', Beckenbauer dislocated his shoulder after the Germans had used both substitutes and played on with his arm strapped to his side.

Bayern won the first of three successive Bundesliga titles in 1972. That summer six of their players and four from Mönchengladbach were in the West Germany team that beat the USSR 3-0 in the final of the European Championships at Brussels' Heysel Stadium. Müller scored two. Beckenbauer, now the captain and nicknamed Der Kaiser, lifted the trophy.

Beckenbauer was now reinventing the role of the sweeper. The *libero* of the early *catenaccio* had a purely negative task: sweep behind two markers and clear the ball. By switching one of the world's best midfielders into the position, Bayern and West Germany released its attacking potential. Beckenbauer was good enough to provide defensive stability and talented enough to start attacks from defence. In truth, it took a law change for 'ball-playing' defenders to become the norm. Until goalkeepers were banned from handling back passes in 1992, there was always an easy way out for the 'no-nonsense' defender.

FRANZ BECKENBAUER

In 1974 those same six players – Beckenbauer, Müller, Maier, Paul Breitner, Uli Hoeness and Hans-Georg Schwarzenbeck – were the core of the Bayern side that conquered European club football. In the final, they fell behind to Atlético Madrid in extra time, thanks to a goal from future Spain coach Luis Aragonés, but centre-back Schwarzenbeck beat Miguel Reina from 30 yards in the 120th minute and Bayern cruised through the replay two days later.

West Germany hosted the 1974 World Cup but Beckenbauer had to use his diplomatic skills to even get a team on the pitch. The players revolted over the size of bonuses compared to their rivals, and coach Helmut Schön was prepared to call up an entirely new squad. After a fractious meeting that went on into the not-so-early hours, a compromise was struck. Schön obviously wasn't happy and later sulked throughout a press conference in which Beckenbauer was left to analyse the team's performance after victories over Chile and Australia. More pressure followed a defeat to East Germany, the only senior international between the two Germanys. It worked out well for the West, setting up an easier second phase, and they had found form by the time they faced the much-loved Netherlands in the final.

Bertie Vogts man-marked Cruyff and, despite the early penalty, he kept the best Dutch player relatively subdued. However, Beckenbauer's role was crucial. Dutch post-mortems focussed on attitude but their high press was much less effective than it had been. Fatigue no doubt contributed, but Beckenbauer's ability to play from deep stopped the Netherlands from building pressure. They dropped back quicker and were generally more passive, allowing the Germans to expose their defensive frailty. Breitner equalised with a penalty after Bernd Holzenbein took a tumble in the box; I doubt that gets mentioned in Germany as often as Geoff Hurst's goal from 1966. Müller scored the winner, his 68th goal in his 62nd and final international.

THE FIFTY

Bayern's 1975 European Cup win marked the end of an era for Leeds United. Under Don Revie, Leeds had won almost everything, and lost almost everything. They were Football League champions twice but finished second on five occasions. They won the FA Cup once but lost three finals. They won the Fairs Cup twice but lost the final once, and were beaten in a play-off against Barcelona for the right to keep the trophy when the competition was replaced by the UEFA Cup. Revie became England manager in the summer of 1974 and was replaced by Brian Clough, who lasted only 44 stormy days. The easy-going Jimmy Armfield guided Leeds to the European Cup Final in Paris.

Leeds were convinced they were cheated by French referee Michel Kitabdjian. They pointed to a rejected penalty claim for a Beckenbauer foul on Allan Clarke, and a disallowed Peter Lorimer goal. The Scottish midfielder volleyed into the net and initially the referee gave the goal, only to change his mind after Beckenbauer complained that Billy Bremner had been offside. It is not obvious from the pictures whether the flag had gone up, but Bremner was offside, although he was purposefully getting out of the way of the shot. Franz Roth put Bayern in front, before the prolific Müller got the second. Not every key decision went Bayern's way: in the third minute Terry Yorath stamped on Björn Andersson, who was stretchered off. The night ended in shame for Leeds, and for English football, which was gripped by hooliganism. Leeds fans rampaged around Paris and the club was banned from Europe, but they were in decline anyway.

The great Bayern team had one last night of glory – the 1976 European Cup Final, in which they beat St Étienne. West Germany came within a penalty of retaining their European title, losing a shoot-out to Czechoslovakia and Antonin Panenka's Panenka.

Beckenbauer won his second Ballon d'Or in 1976 and a year later joined Pelé at New York Cosmos. He was only 31 and arguably the NASL's most successful import. He didn't draw the crowds like the Brazilian, but no one could. As Beckenbauer put it, 'Reversing the flow of play, building a rhythm, consistency; these are hard things to get excited about.'

One apocryphal tale about Beckenbauer illustrates the lack of understanding of soccer at the heart of the NASL venture. A Cosmos executive is said to have seen the great German playing deep and shouted, 'Tell the Kraut to get his ass up front. We don't pay a million bucks to have a guy hang around in defence.'

Beckenbauer's arrival transformed Cosmos into the victorious team the NASL promoters wanted. They won the Soccerbowl in three of his four seasons but the league was doomed. The mix of players jarred: fading greats, British journeymen and American no-hopers. The owners couldn't decide whether to grow it slowly or throw money at the likes of Pelé, Cruyff, Eusébio, Best and Beckenbauer. Attendances, TV viewing figures and commercial deals didn't come close to paying the bills, and it was scrapped in 1984. Beckenbauer won his last Bundesliga title with Hamburg in 1982 but left before their subsequent European Cup-winning campaign.

Beckenbauer was national team coach from 1984 to 1990, losing one World Cup Final and winning another. He, Mario Zagallo and Didier Deschamps have been world champions as both players and coaches, although, as there have been only 21 tournaments, that seems a lot. Between 1972 and 1996, there were 13 World or European finals and the Germans won five and were runners-up in another four. They invented little, not even anything as negative but groundbreaking as *catenaccio*; they just found ways to win. It was a remarkably successful era, but the team remained unloved, only begrudgingly respected.

26

Viv Anderson

ENGLISH FOOTBALL in the late 1970s and early 1980s was a whirl of paradoxes. England dominated club football but made barely a ripple in the international game. The best English teams played possession football, but the long-ball game was on the rise. Black players were given unprecedented opportunities and then abused by racist mobs. Great sportsmen refuelled on meat pudding and pale ale. The glory days of English club football were stained by hooliganism. It was the best of times; it was the worst of times.

As a young player, Viv Anderson once told Nottingham Forest manager Brian Clough that he didn't want to warm up because he was being racially abused and pelted with fruit. Clough told him to 'fetch me two pears and a banana'. The message was clear: ignore the racists or forget about your football career.

Anderson had recently broken into the Forest team when Clough arrived in January 1975. The charismatic and bombastic Teessider had turned Derby County into champions but left when his feud with the chairman became unsustainable. After a notorious month and a half at Leeds, he was unemployed and tempted to Second Division Forest, a club that seemed to be going nowhere, despite having future European champions Anderson, Martin O'Neill, Tony Woodcock and John Robertson in its ranks. Forest's fortunes really took off when Clough's old assistant Peter Taylor joined him at the City Ground in July 1976.

Clough had a unique genius for motivation. Taylor was the master of spotting potential. They signed the likes of Larry Lloyd, who had won the title and UEFA Cup with Liverpool but was on a downward trajectory, and journeyman centre-forward Peter Withe, who went on to win the league with two clubs, and score in a European Cup Final. Forest crept up in third place in 1976/77 and, while the football world was expecting them to battle against relegation, they stormed the First Division. They signed Stoke's Peter Shilton, who Clough described as the best goalkeeper in the world. It wasn't hyperbole. Scotland midfielder Archie Gemmill came from Derby and Kenny Burns was transformed from a hothead Birmingham City striker into a central defender and the Football Writers' Player of the Year. Anderson was a tall and quick right-back, attack-minded by the standards of the day — although Clough made it clear his responsibility was to defend first and foremost. Ipswich's Mick Mills described them as a 'crowd of has-beens'. They didn't lose a league game after November and finished as 1977/78 champions, seven points clear of Liverpool, who they also beat in the League Cup Final.

The sequel was even more spectacular. Withe was sold and replaced by teenager Garry Birtles, who had been bought from non-league Long Eaton but not used in the 1977/78 season. The Nottingham-born striker scored his first senior goal in the first round of the European Cup as Forest knocked out holders Liverpool. They beat AEK Athens, Grasshoppers and Köln before meeting Swedish champions Malmö in the final at Munich's Olympic Stadium.

The English transfer record had been broken in January 1979 when David Mills moved from Middlesbrough to West

Brom for £516,000. A month later, Clough made Trevor Francis the first £1m English footballer, turning up at his unveiling an hour late carrying a squash racket. 'I bought this in case he made a balls-up of it,' he said, in typical style.

Francis scored six goals in the rest of the league campaign, as Forest finished second, but he was ineligible in Europe until three months after his transfer, which meant the final. It wasn't a great game but Francis settled it, diving to meet a Robertson cross and heading the ball into the roof of the net. Forest had gone from the Second Division to European champions in two years.

In November 1978 Anderson made history when he became England's first black international footballer. He was born in Nottingham, the son of Jamaican immigrants, and had grown up aware of only two black players: Leeds's South African winger Albert Johanneson and West Ham's Bermudan striker Clyde Best.

There is an argument that Leeds full-back Paul Reaney actually became the first black or mixed-heritage England international in 1968 but, as far as I know, he has never identified as such. It was big news when Anderson was called up even though he pushed the historical significance aside to concentrate on his performance: 'Clearly it was a landmark, but I was focussed on trying to win a football match,' he wrote in 2010.

It was only a friendly against Czechoslovakia but it was a hugely significant moment. Black players from that era changed football in a way that outliers like Andrew Watson, Arthur Wharton and Walter Tull never had. Anderson wasn't alone. West Brom had an exciting team containing Cyrille Regis, Laurie Cunningham and Brendan Batson. Manager Ron Atkinson nicknamed the trio 'The Three Degrees' after the black American vocal trio, who were having hit songs at the time. The players and singers even posed together for the newspapers. It seems incredible now, but in the days of

VIV ANDERSON

The Black and White Minstrel Show and Jim Davidson on TV, anything in the media that celebrated black success seemed progressive. Ricky Hill, Luther Blissett, Mark Chamberlain, Danny Thomas and John Barnes followed Anderson into the England team.

As doors opened for black footballers, racists tried to slam them shut. Someone posted a bullet and a threatening note to Regis after he was first called up by England. I remember standing at Middlesbrough's Ayresome Park in the mid-1980s, with hundreds of people around me chanting racist abuse at Aston Villa's Gary Thompson. It was rife: a significant hardcore were vocal, the majority said nothing. Anderson feels his generation of black players had no option but to accept the racism they suffered, or look for a new job.

Hooliganism was also poisoning football. There was an ever-present threat of violence, and notorious incidents in Europe involving Leeds in Paris, Manchester United in Ostend and Tottenham in Rotterdam were far from unusual. Fan violence became a depressingly familiar feature of England games, starting significantly in the ill-fated Euro 80 campaign and sticking around like a bad smell for years. The newspapers loved to hate the hooligans and the establishment treated the national game as a pariah. In 1985 the *Sunday Times* described football as, 'a slum game played in slum stadiums watched by slum people'. It was heading for tragedy, but the season of darkness was also the season of light, and there was plenty of success for English football fans to savour.

Anderson and Forest won the European Cup again in 1979. They beat West German champions Hamburg, who had European Footballer of the Year Kevin Keegan in their side. Francis was missing with an Achilles tendon injury and the superbly skilful Robertson scored the only goal. Liverpool reclaimed the trophy a year later, and arguably the pinnacle of English club football came in 1982 when Aston Villa beat Bayern Munich, thanks to a goal from Clough-reject Withe.

THE FIFTY

As a child, I thought it was entirely natural that English clubs would win the European Cup every year.

Clough broke up the Forest squad, too quickly for Anderson's liking. Francis moved on quickly, having sparked a spate of million-pound moves for players with much less talent. Ian Wallace and Justin Fashanu both cost Forest a million. Manchester City made Steve Daley and Kevin Reeves into million-pound players, even Wolves were at it, paying nearly a million and a half for Andy Gray, who would have great success after being offloaded to Everton. It was unsustainable as hooliganism and crumbling stadiums combined to scare away supporters, no matter how well English clubs performed in Europe. The 1985 Heysel Stadium disaster ended the English dominance overnight, but fans had already been turning their backs: between 1977 and 1984 average crowds in the top division had fallen from 29,405 to 18,834.

After his early promise, Anderson became something of a nearly-man. He won 30 caps, but although he went to two World Cups he didn't get onto the pitch in either. Ron Greenwood's 1982 side should have been contenders. They won their first group but were eliminated after goalless draws with West Germany and Spain in the second phase.

He signed for Arsenal where Don Howe was soon sacked for George Graham. Under Graham, the defenders trained literally roped together, perfecting the offside trap that would propel them to the title – but only after Anderson had become Alex Ferguson's first signing at Manchester United. He was part of the heavy-drinking side that finished second, 11th and 13th. United's board showed patience almost unknown now. Ferguson initially tolerated the culture of alcohol abuse, but in time he cracked down.

Anderson signed for Sheffield Wednesday who were promoted and won the League Cup in his first season, although he was cup-tied and couldn't play. They finished third in the last season before the launch of the Premier League, and in

1993 lost both domestic cup finals to Arsenal. Anderson's last matches were as a 39-year-old assistant manager in Middlesbrough's promotion campaign of 1994/95.

He managed Barnsley in 1993/94 and thought he might be a trailblazer for a second time: 'I thought when I became a manager I was at the start of a generation like I was by playing for England,' he said, 'but in terms of black managers it's absolutely embarrassing.'

As I write, 19 out of 20 Premier League managers are white and there are only four black or mixed-heritage managers out of 92 in the English league. There have been a number of incidents of racist abuse of players in domestic, international and European games. It would be stupid to think racism has gone, though thankfully players are no longer told to suck it up and get on with it. Anderson is a hero, but a reluctant one: 'I don't want to be remembered as the first black footballer who played for England. I want to be remembered as Viv Anderson the footballer.'

27

Kenny Dalglish

AMID THE success of English clubs in the late 1970s and early 1980s, there was one dominant force: Liverpool. And of all the wonderful players in Liverpool's glory years, one was outstanding: Kenny Dalglish.

Admittedly, they were European champions and had won back-to-back English titles when he arrived in the summer of 1977. He replaced Kevin Keegan after the England striker moved to Hamburg for £500,000. Dalglish, who had won the Scottish title four times under Jock Stein at Celtic, cost £440,000. Ian St John, another Scot and part of Bill Shankly's Liverpool sides of the 1960s, felt it was an obvious upgrade: 'Dalglish had the football brain, the thing that Shanks always talked about: a bit of craft, of cunning, the old Scottish inside-forward. You can't give that to people. It's an inherent talent.'

Shankly built the foundation of Liverpool's success after taking over a Second Division club in 1959. He won the Football League three times and the UEFA Cup before his surprise retirement in 1974, when his deputy Bob Paisley was promoted. A character like Paisley would never get a job managing a major club now, more's the pity. Unkempt and overweight, he had a strong working-class County Durham accent, and none of Shankly's media-friendly charisma. But he had his own charm; as Dalglish put it, 'Everyone loved old Bob.'

Paisley was manager for nine seasons. He won the English title six times, the European Cup three times and the League Cup three times. He had a genius for managing change. Keegan and his big strike partner John Toshack moved on, so Paisley adapted the style for Dalglish, who found the transition straightforward: 'It was easy to play for Liverpool because their philosophy of football was simple. The guiding principles were always the same: players had to make themselves available so moves could continue. There was no star treatment; Liverpool did things properly, not extravagantly.'

Dalglish wrote in his autobiography that no one begrudged Liverpool their success. Who was he kidding? They were the motivation for Alex Ferguson's relentless pursuit of excellence at Manchester United. Ferguson admitted to *The Guardian* in 2002: 'My greatest challenge was knocking Liverpool off their fucking perch.' There was something about Liverpool that drew the invective of their rivals. Brian Clough geed up his Nottingham Forest players: 'You know the sign when you run out says, "This is Anfield", well, so fucking what!'

No club recruited better. Keegan and goalkeeper Ray Clemence came from Scunthorpe. Phil Neal won eight English titles and four European Cups after signing from Fourth Division Northampton Town. Alan Hansen won 17 major trophies after signing from Partick Thistle. Steve Nicol was bought from Ayr United. Ian Rush cost £300,000 from Third Division Chester and was sold to Juventus for £3.2m. Graeme Souness was signed from another First Division club, Middlesbrough, for a comparatively substantial £352,000, but he was a bargain. And, of course, there was Dalglish.

They retained the European Cup at Wembley, with Dalglish scoring the only goal against Club Brugge. Forest challenged their dominance for a while, but Paisley's side were soon back on top. Between 1978/79 and 1983/84 they won the league in five out of six seasons. Their fifth place in 1980/81 was the only time in 19 years they finished below the top two. Regaining the European Cup was consolation enough when left-back Alan Kennedy's late goal beat Real Madrid.

When Aston Villa won the 1982 European Cup, Bayern Munich's Paul Breitner took a swipe at the rest of the English sides, describing the Midlanders as the only ones playing 'European-style football'. It was a strange complaint because Liverpool weren't a long-ball side and, although Dalglish had many strengths, he wasn't big or lightning fast. He was perfectly formed for the club and the era: clever and skilful but strong enough to relish physical battles.

Hamburg interrupted the English success in 1983 but Liverpool were back again in 1984, beating Roma at their own Stadio Olimpico. Bruce Grobbelaar's 'spaghetti legs' in the shoot-out might have been the reason Francesco Graziani missed the Italians' final penalty. The seven English winners in eight years played a total of 61 matches and conceded only 33 goals. Six consecutive finals finished 1-0 (including Hamburg's). Defending wasn't a purely Italian art.

Scots were at the heart of the English success. From 1978 to 1985 every English team in the European Cup Final played at least three Scots. Ipswich, Tottenham, Arsenal and Everton all played in either the UEFA or Cup Winners' Cup Final with at least one Scot in their starting XI. In the 1984 European Cup Final, Liverpool had Dalglish, Souness, Hansen, Nicol and Gary Gillespie in the 16.

Scotland qualified for both the 1974 and 1978 World Cups when England didn't. Dalglish won a record 102 caps and equalled Denis Law's 30 goals, but Scotland failed to make it out of the group at any of the World Cups in which he played. In 1974 they went out without losing a game. In 1982 they lost to a much-loved Brazil side before drawing with the USSR and going out on goal difference – creditable but frustrating. By contrast, the 1978 World Cup was an embarrassment.

Scotland had finished above Wales and European champions Czechoslovakia in qualifying and took a squad to Argentina containing European Cup winners Dalglish and Souness, three players from English champions Nottingham Forest, three from Scottish treble winners Rangers and four from Manchester United. All 22 were top-flight players in England or Scotland. When manager Ally MacLeod talked openly about winning the World Cup, plenty of people bought into his optimism; 25,000 turned up at Hampden Park to send them off. They drove to the airport in an open-top bus and 'Ally's Tartan Army' was number six in the UK charts.

If only MacLeod's attention to detail matched his showmanship. He hadn't watched Scotland's opponents, despite being offered a paid trip to Peru by a TV company. He brushed questions aside, saying his team were prepared to perfection. He was wrong. There was no water in the hotel pool, training facilities were dilapidated and the bus broke down.

Joe Jordan scored first against Peru but it was downhill from there. The South Americans were no mugs: they had reached the quarter-finals in 1970 and had a genuine star in Teófilo Cubillas, who scored twice in the 3-1 win. West Brom winger Willie Johnston then failed a drug test after taking Reactivan, which he had used before, not knowing it was banned. Scandal turned to farce in a 1-1 draw with Iran, in which Scotland benefitted from a bizarre own goal. MacLeod wilted visibly on the bench, head in hands, seemingly choking back tears.

To survive they had to beat the Netherlands by three. The Dutch scored a penalty, Dalglish equalised, before Archie Gemmill scored a penalty and a famous weaving wonder goal but it wasn't enough. Johnny Rep smashed one in from long range and Scotland's team of enormous potential was on the early flight home.

We make a great fuss of football matches lost and won, but Dalglish was present at three of football's worst disasters. As a young Celtic player, he was in the crowd at Ibrox Park for the

Old Firm game in January 1971 when 66 Rangers supporters were killed in a crush on a staircase. Two people had been killed on the same staircase ten years earlier and there had been two subsequent incidents in which spectators were injured.

He was at Heysel Stadium in May 1985 when years of English football hooliganism reached a sickening low. A mob of Liverpool fans charged through a flimsy wire fence into a section of the stadium supposedly reserved for neutrals. Lots of Juventus fans had bought tickets for that area, including families hoping to stay clear of their club's Ultras. In the desperate retreat from the Liverpool fans' charge, a wall collapsed and 39 people were killed: 32 Italians, four Belgians, two French and one from Northern Ireland. Fourteen Liverpool fans were convicted of manslaughter. The BBC's Barry Davies said on the night, 'Those of us in the commentary box felt once again an embarrassment to be British.' He added that English fans were 'despised around the football grounds of Europe'.

They were held in equally low regard at home. As Conservative politician David Mellor reflected later, 'Football looked like yesterday's sport being attended by yesterday's people, a sort of sub-race of really unpleasant and unattractive individuals who, certainly in the eyes of people like Mrs Thatcher, summed up everything that was most awful about the English nation.'

The Prime Minister wanted English clubs out of European competition and UEFA agreed, banning them for five years (Liverpool eventually served six). Families of the victims fought for years to get UEFA and the Belgian authorities to take their share of responsibility: English fans rioting abroad was depressingly familiar, but Heysel Stadium was a death trap and the policing and stewarding disastrously unprepared.

It is a mistake to try to draw a straight line between the disasters of Heysel and Hillsborough, which happened four years later. On that day, 96 Liverpool fans were killed as a result of a crush at the 1989 FA Cup semi-final against Nottingham

Forest, staged at Sheffield Wednesday's stadium. South Yorkshire Police's incompetence was the decisive factor, along with a poorly prepared ambulance response but the nature of the stadium itself was also deadly. Years of hooliganism the length and breadth of the country had contributed to the perception that football fans were, as Mellor put it, a 'sub-race', in the minds of many in the police, media and establishment. Put less emotively, football matches were viewed as matters of public order rather than of public safety. Hillsborough's solid metal fences designed to keep fans off the pitch, and from roaming around, crushed them to death. Dalglish's family were there supporting Liverpool; his 12-year-old son Paul was watching with the fans and was missing for more than half an hour.

Decades of police and establishment denial compounded the fatal errors of the day. Dalglish, as the manager of Liverpool, was deeply affected, attending as many of the victims' funerals as he could. A couple of years later he resigned from his job, emotionally exhausted. The citation for his knighthood started with how he made himself available to the Hillsborough families. In the moving documentary *Kenny* he spoke of his own inability to engage with the emotional trauma of the day. 'My only thought was to help somebody else. If it means you cut yourself out of the deal that was no problem for me,' he said.

Dalglish played 824 games and scored 336 goals for Celtic and Liverpool. He became Liverpool's player-manager in 1985 and won three more league titles with the club. The one that got away provided English football with one of its two most exciting moments. The final league game of 1988/89 had been delayed to the end of May, after Liverpool had won an emotional FA Cup Final. Arsenal went to Anfield three points behind Liverpool and had to win by two goals to steal the title. Alan Smith headed a goal for the Gunners early in the second half, before midfielder Michael Thomas charged through to win the game and the championship in the 91st minute. It was amazing drama, matched only by Sergio Agüero 23 years later.

Dalglish won another league title – his 13th all told – as Blackburn's manager in 1995. Liverpool's glory faded when the magic touch in the transfer market deserted them, but the trophy cabinet was packed by then and Dalglish will be remembered as the greatest player of the greatest team of his generation.

28

Mario Kempes

ARGENTINA 1978 was the darkest of all the World Cups. Its legacy isn't Archie Gemmill weaving past Dutch defenders, Arie Haan beating Dino Zoff from 35 yards, or even Clive Thomas making the maddest decision in the history of refereeing. It was a football tournament played under the shadow of state-organised mass murder. It was won by a player who epitomised what Argentina had lost, and by a coach who was philosophically hostile to the regime but fixed his gaze steadfastly away from the truth.

In 1976 a coup installed the bloodthirsty General Jorge Videla as Argentina's president at the head of a military junta. Estimates of how many people they killed vary but it could have been as high as 30,000, including teachers, trade unionists, left-wing politicians and artists. Babies were taken from political prisoners and given to friends of the regime. Victims were drugged and thrown from military planes into the River Plate.

The football context was humiliation at the previous World Cup, where Argentina vowed to take on the Europeans at their own muscular game. There had been room for the talented 19-year-old Mario Kempes but he didn't shine. Argentina beat only Haiti. They lost 4-0 to a Dutch side that was physically and technically superior.

A philosophical flip led to the managerial appointment of football romantic César Luis Menotti, who had won a league title with a free-flowing Huracán side. Menotti styled himself as a left-wing football philosopher, reviving the stylish, joyous traditions of Argentine football. The World Cup would only be won with attacking, risk-taking football, he said. Anti-football needed players who were useful idiots. Menotti craved intelligence. 'Right-wing football,' argued the chain-smoking former striker, 'wants to suggest that life is a struggle. It demands sacrifices ... that we have to be made of steel and win by any method.'

Scratch the surface of bohemian idealism and you see a modern football coach. Argentina's players had been used to taking the field with stomachs full of steak and fries; Menotti's squad ate sensibly and trained hard. He persuaded the football authorities to ban players from being sold abroad, allowing him a squad of home-based players and a long pre-tournament camp. There was one exception: Kempes was with Valencia and had won the *Pichichi*, awarded to La Liga's top scorer, for the previous two seasons. An attacking midfielder of grace and pace with 63 goals in 80 games in two years in Spain was too good to ignore. There were other talents: René Houseman, Osvaldo Ardiles and Leopoldo Luque, but Menotti's romanticism didn't extend as far as picking the new sensation of Argentine football, 17-year-old Diego Maradona. Ardiles articulated Menotti's deadly dilemma, dealing with a junta desperate to parade Argentina's brilliance before the world: 'Menotti was a left-winger and for him survival meant winning.'

Menotti wrote a book titled *Football without Tricks*, but if he believed there was no skulduggery behind Argentina's victory he was kidding himself. Their first-round group was tough. One member of the junta told Luque it might prove to be his 'Group of Death'. The player wasn't sure whether he was joking; after all the dead body of a friend of his brother had been found on the banks of the River Plate with concrete covering his legs.

They beat Hungary, who had two men sent off, late in the game and justifiably, but following prolonged provocation. Kempes was superb against France, repeatedly running from midfield. He created a chance for Luque that led to a disputed penalty, awarded by the Swiss referee. I'm departing from the accepted narrative to say it was a reasonable call – Marius Trésor had his arms spread wide and it would definitely be given as handball now.

Argentina's defeat against Italy meant they finished second in their group, as did Brazil, who were denied a win over Sweden because Welsh referee Clive Thomas blew his whistle for full time with the ball heading into the goal. It beggared belief. It was 1-1 when a corner was awarded in the 90th minute. After some fussing by the linesman, the kick was taken and Zico glanced a header into the net, seven seconds past 90 minutes. It would be part of the litany of suspicious decisions, but Thomas had previous form in bizarre decision-making.

Poland and Peru had won their first-phase groups but Argentina and Brazil came good. Such is the importance of the World Cup that Kempes built his legend in 12 days. The Poland game was his 11th in World Cups and he finally scored his first goal, a header on the run. He then made a diving save Lev Yashin would be proud of – 22 years later Luis Suárez was sent off and treated like a monster for doing the same. Kazimierz Deyna's penalty was saved by Ubaldo Fillol, before Ardiles set up Kempes for a fine second.

Brazil and Argentina then kicked lumps out of each other in a goalless draw, setting up one of the most controversial days in football history. Brazil played Poland first and won 3-1. So Argentina kicked off that evening knowing they had to beat Peru by a margin of three, scoring at least four. Peru had lost their momentum, losing 3-0 to Brazil and 1-0 to Poland, so a big Argentina win wasn't out of the question.

Was it a fix?

The case for 'no' is that Peru played well early on. They hit the post at 0-0 and were a threat on the counter-attack. Winger Juan Carlos Oblitas also told FIFA TV they had struggled for motivation after winning their first group: 'We were totally deflated. It was like we felt that by finishing first in the group we already felt we were world champions.' Kempes dismisses talk of cheating as 'a farce and a lie'.

The prosecution case is busy. Peru also had a military dictatorship under General Francisco Morales-Bermudez, and future senator Genaro Ledesma alleged a secret deal was struck between the regimes. He told a human rights hearing in Argentina that he and other trade unionists were kidnapped by the Peruvian regime and sent to Argentina to be tortured. In 1986, the *Sunday Times* claimed Peruvian assets had been unfrozen by the Argentine regime and a shipment of grain was made as part of the deal.

That much is perhaps unproved, but there is no doubt the Peru players were taken by a roundabout route to the stadium and had their security withdrawn. The limited amount of time left in the dressing room was interrupted by a visit from President Videla himself, accompanied, bizarrely, by former US Secretary of State Henry Kissinger. Videla addressed the players, saying something about Latin American brothers before reading out a letter from the president of Peru.

Kissinger later claimed to have 'no recollection' of visiting the dressing room, although as he left Argentina he gave the junta the affirmation they wanted: 'The World Cup has projected an excellent image of Argentina towards the world. It is obvious the country has made notable progress in a short timeframe.'

Peru started well but what does that prove? With 90 minutes available why not play competitively for a while to distract observers looking for signs of a fix? Kempes scored another good goal. Alberto Tarantini headed a second late in the first half, and in the fourth and fifth minutes of the second half Kempes and Luque made it 3-0 and 4-0. Peru's defensive midfielder Jose Velasquez was then substituted in the 52nd minute. He spoke to *Channel 4 News* in 2012: 'Were we pressured? Yes. What kind of pressure? From the government to the management of the team and to the coaches.'

It was 6-0 by the 72nd minute and Argentina were in the final.

Football without tricks? Hardly. Argentina objected to the appointment of Israel's Avraham Klein, who had refereed their defeat against Italy. The coach detour trick was reprised for the Dutch, who were also left standing on the Monumental pitch, soaking up the boos and whistles of 76,000 fans. Argentina then objected to a cast on the arm of Netherlands midfielder René van de Kerkhof, even though he had worn it for weeks. Only when the Dutch threatened not to play was the issue left alone. FIFA gave Argentina the Fair Play award.

Let's be fair, Menotti's team were great to watch and it was an entertaining final. Fillol saved brilliantly from Johnny Rep before Kempes opened the scoring. His deft first touch and rapid acceleration allowed him to squeeze the ball under Jan Jongbloed. Dutch substitute Dirk Nanninga headed an equaliser and in the 90th minute Rob Rensenbrink hit the post. It was a difficult chance and it is harsh to remember him as the man who lost the World Cup.

Instead Kempes won it. In extra time he beat two defenders and poked the ball at Jongbloed. Luck played its part, as it often does. The ball deflected off the keeper and span kindly for Kempes to poke home. His sixth goal won him the Golden Boot. His sublime run of form won him the Golden Ball. He dribbled at the heart of the defence in search of a hat-trick but this time a ricochet allowed Ricardo Bertoni to make it 3-1.

It was a victory for Argentina, the players, the fans and the murderous junta. The players did their best to block out the grim truth. Is it fair to expect them to have made a stand? Tarantini did, in his own way, supposedly rubbing his sweaty genitals before shaking hands with Videla. Anything more was potentially fatal: when Fillol asked for a transfer away from River Plate, a member of the junta casually threatened him with a gun.

Kempes was soon back scoring goals in Valencia. 'I was practically never in Argentina during the military regime,' he reflected. 'Within the camp we were playing for ourselves, then the people and then Argentine football as a whole.'

Ardiles and Ricky Villa joined Tottenham and became hugely popular figures in England, despite the 1982 Falklands War, which was the beginning of the end for the junta. Videla died in prison. The world champions of 1978 have a complex legacy, sometimes abused and denounced as collaborators, sometimes hailed as the greatest players of their generation.

29

Justin Fashanu

TAKE A minute to look up Justin Fashanu's goal for Norwich City against Liverpool in February 1980. He flicks the ball up with the outside of his right boot, swivels and volleys it left-footed into the top corner: bold and brilliant. It was the BBC's goal of the season and is accompanied by Barry Davies's iconic commentary: 'Fashanu! Oh, oooooh what a goal! Oh, that's a magnificent goal!' It was a few days before Fashanu's 20th birthday, a year after his league debut.

Fashanu was born in London in 1961, the son of a Nigerian barrister and a Guyanese nurse. When his parents split up, Justin and his younger brother John went into a Barnardo's care home, and were later adopted by a stridently Christian white couple from Norfolk, while maintaining contact with their mother.

Justin scored 40 goals in 103 senior games for Norwich, and played regularly for England under-21s. He signed for Brian Clough's Nottingham Forest in 1981, becoming the first million-pound black footballer. His career began to unravel after his manager discovered he was gay. Clough claimed Fashanu's homosexuality 'didn't bother me too much' but he didn't like him or consider him to be 'one of us'. In his 1995 autobiography Clough revealed how he confronted Fashanu, who had been seen in Nottingham's gay bars.

'I asked him, "Where do you go if you want a loaf of bread?"

"A baker's, I suppose."

"Where do you go if you want a leg of lamb?"

"A butcher's."

"So why do you keep going to that bloody poofs' club?"'

Viv Anderson witnessed Fashanu's night terrors when they were roommates on an away trip. Anderson was woken by Fashanu punching the inside of the hotel room door until his hands bled. Clough effectively sacked a supremely talented young striker, for whom he had just paid a huge transfer fee. Fashanu was banished from the first team but turned up to train anyway, so Clough had him escorted away by the police. Homosexuality had been made legal in the UK in 1967 but attitudes were inconsistent; some entertainers were well known for being gay, while others kept it secret. The first MP didn't come out until 1984. Clough's attitudes were old-fashioned but not unusual.

Fashanu was loaned to Southampton and then sold to Notts County in December 1982, accepting a 50 per cent pay cut. He later played for a dizzying array of clubs including Manchester City, West Ham, Los Angeles Heat, Toronto Blizzard and Hearts but never rediscovered his Norwich form, not helped by an infected knee injury.

Fashanu came out publicly in 1990 with a series of attention-grabbing headlines in a tabloid newspaper. He was well paid for stories he later said were untrue. Attitudes to homosexuality were more liberal by then: Culture Club, the Communards and the Pet Shop Boys had all had successful pop careers, but sections of society were still openly, steadfastly hostile. Fashanu got attention as much for the reaction of his brother John as for the revelation itself.

John had signed for a Wimbledon team that enjoyed great success with muscular, direct football. Their journey from non-league to the top flight, and a victory over Liverpool in the 1988 FA Cup Final, was down to smart transfers, hard graft and raw aggression. John carefully cultivated his tough-guy image and paid Justin to keep his homosexuality a secret.

After Justin came out, John denounced him in a TV interview: 'He'll have to suffer the consequences but I wouldn't want to play or even get changed in the vicinity of him – that's just the way I feel, so if I'm like that I'm sure the rest of the footballers are like that.'

Justin responded: 'It's disappointed me because I thought he had more depth, more tolerance, that he was better than that. We've been through so much together, especially as kids; it's disappointing to me because I thought he was better than that.'

It might seem obvious that being gay in the macho culture of 1990s football made Justin's life a misery, but that wasn't how *The Independent* newspaper reported it in 1994.

'Oddly, coming out did not make Justin the pariah in football that John had predicted. He returned from Canada, a gold stud in each ear, and began to play again for whoever would take him: Newcastle, Manchester City, Bournemouth. Crowds were not rude to him, they loved him: he got a particularly good hand when he played once at Wigan. He received more hate mail when he urged *Guardian* readers to vote Tory at the last election than he ever has about his sexuality.'

But the end of Justin's life made it hard to see his story as anything but a tragedy. Homosexual acts were still illegal in the US State of Maryland in March 1998, when a 17-year-old man told police he had been sexually assaulted by Justin Fashanu. Police questioned Justin but didn't arrest him. On 3 May he was found dead in a garage in London. He had broken in and hanged himself, leaving a suicide note, saying the sex with the teenager had been consensual but he felt he would not receive a fair hearing.

'I realised I had been presumed guilty. I did not want to give any more embarrassment to my friends and family,' he wrote.

There was no other openly gay male footballer until Robbie Rogers came out in 2013. Rogers was a USA international who won the MLS Cup with Columbus Crew before an injury-blighted spell at Leeds and a loan at Stevenage. He was injured and without a club when he decided to reveal the truth in a blog post that would change his life. He was only 25 years old but announced his retirement as his post exploded into the world.

He later reflected, 'I had been in locker rooms and guys would have discussions and I'd be, "Oh gosh, I'm never coming out while I'm in the sports world." But later the same guys called me and encouraged me to come back. They're not homophobic but there's a weird pack mentality; they say things they don't mean. They're just insensitive.'

The positive reaction encouraged Rogers to change his mind about retiring and he signed for LA Galaxy. Just in case you thought British sport was uniquely old-fashioned, Rogers became the first openly gay male athlete to join MLS or any of the five major North American sports leagues. His experience as a gay male footballer was a world away from Fashanu's.

'Team-mates were supportive and I got messages from all around the world. It's very different when you have experience with someone close to you, it changes very quickly. We shower together and guys ask me about my relationships and ask me about marriage equality and normal things.' He played for LA Galaxy until 2017 when he quit because of injury.

Another gay footballer, Thomas Hitzlsperger, won 52 caps for Germany and played in the Premier League, Bundesliga and Serie A. He didn't come out until after he stopped playing but is still active in the game, currently head of sport at VFB Stuttgart. There are probably other gay male footballers who have chosen not to tell their story: that is up to them. I am certain there would be a largely positive reaction from clubs, mainstream media and commercial sponsors, but that would not be the end of the story.

If footballers were gay in the same ratio as men in wider society, there would be dozens in the Premier League alone. I don't think there are. If I am right then something in the deep culture of football drives away gay teenage boys.

Young people are generally much more tolerant than past generations, as is mainstream culture – but the sort of attitudes that once saw heterosexual footballers such as Graeme le Saux and Sol Campbell receive homophobic abuse haven't disappeared entirely. It is a deeply macho sport down to its grassroots. That is the motivation for campaigns such as 'rainbow laces'.

It is impossible to unpick the effect of homophobia from his injury problems, but Justin Fashanu had tremendous talent for football that went largely unfulfilled. How many gay footballers hid their sexuality after his experience? Who knows. He was 37 at the time of his suicide. Rogers and Hitzlsperger's stories were happier but it would be nice to write about a gay man who came through the ranks and had a great football career without hiding anything.

30

Paolo Rossi

THE PAOLO Rossi Story: How to become a living legend in less than one week.

Mario Kempes took 12 days to achieve greatness; Paolo Rossi made that look positively ponderous. The Juventus striker woke on the morning of 5 July 1982 a notorious cheat and the beneficiary of inexplicable loyalty from Italy's coach. He went to bed – eventually – after the final on 11 July as a national hero.

Like Kempes, Rossi was not exactly flash-in-the-pan. He was once a young Juventus winger with bad knees who was sent to Serie B side Vicenza in a co-ownership deal. There he became a striker and top scorer in Vicenza's promotion campaign. Far from a traditional centre-forward, Rossi was all about skill, speed and timing.

Player and club improved again and he was Serie A's top scorer as Vicenza finished second in 1977/78. That summer, Rossi became football's most expensive player. Juve wanted him back and made various offers for Vicenza's half of his contract. Eventually it was sorted by sealed envelope bids, a process that seems normal only to followers of Italian football.

To widespread astonishment, Vicenza outbid Juve and smashed the two billion lire fee that Napoli had paid for

Giuseppe Savoldi in 1975. Rossi transferred for 2.6 billion, around £1.5m – months before Trevor Francis joined Nottingham Forest. It was an extraordinary price. Rossi flew to the World Cup in Argentina and shone, scoring three goals and winning the Silver Ball (second to Kempes) as Italy finished fourth.

Vicenza had not spent wisely and were relegated in 1979, despite 15 goals from Rossi, who was subsequently loaned to Perugia. They finished mid-table a year later and Rossi was Serie A's third-highest scorer behind Roberto Bettega and Alessandro Altobelli, as Italian football was hit by scandal.

Betting was only legal on a pools system, but a black market had grown allowing punts on single games. This was exploited, somewhat incompetently, by two Roman businessmen who started paying players and coaches to fix matches. The scam, known as *Totonero* (black-market betting), was uncovered in 1980. Eight Serie A clubs were implicated and AC Milan and Lazio were demoted. A host of top players were banned, including Rossi and Savoldi, the two latest holders of the world transfer record.

Conveniently for Italy coach Enzo Bearzot, Rossi's three-year ban was commuted to two, making him available for the World Cup in Spain. Juventus signed him during his ban and gave him three matches at the end of their 1981/82 campaign. Giovanni Trapattoni's side contained six future World Cup winners and the great Irish midfielder Liam Brady, who scored the penalty that clinched the title amid furious accusations of malpractice from second-place Fiorentina.

At the tournament, Bearzot's faith in Rossi seems remarkable, although a serious knee injury to Bettega contributed. Rossi struggled and Italy failed to win any of their first-phase games, drawing with Poland, Peru and Cameroon, finishing second because they scored one more goal than the West Africans.

In the second group phase they beat defending champions Argentina in a game best remembered for Claudio Gentile's man-marking of Diego Maradona. Rossi still hadn't scored and Altobelli had played only ten minutes. Brazil had beaten Argentina by more goals, so a draw in the last group game against them would send the South Americans to the semis.

Brazil's '82 squad is one of football's most loved sides for good reason. It is worth watching some videos. In a tournament of great goals, they were the master entertainers. The full flair of Zico, Socrates, Falcao and Eder was unleashed by coach Telê Santana. They trailed against both USSR and Scotland but didn't panic. They scored 13 goals in four games before meeting Italy in one of the great World Cup games. Zico dubbed it 'the day football died', but that is harsh. Italy dropped back when Brazil had possession but kept looking for attacking opportunities, which the South Americans' defensive naivety delivered.

Rossi came good, justifying Bearzot's angelic patience. Amid the maddening buzz of air horns, decades before the vuvuzela, he headed the *Azzurri* into an early lead. Some Zico magic set up Socrates to beat Italy keeper Dino Zoff, but a bad mistake by defensive midfielder Cerezo allowed Rossi to put Italy in front again. After Zoff had made two good interventions, Rossi missed a chance to grab his hat-trick. Brazil levelled again in the 68th minute when Roma's Falcao smashed a shot past Zoff. Should Brazil have tightened up, given that they needed only a draw? Perhaps, but it would have been like telling a nightingale not to sing. Following a disputed corner, Marco Tardelli's shot fell to Italy's centre-forward, who scored on the turn. It was 3-2, and redemption for Rossi. People mourned for Brazil 82, one of the great unfulfilled teams, along with Hungary 54 and Netherlands 74. But Santana's side were outliers, not innovators, a team of talents playing almost off the hoof.

The 1982 World Cup was largely excellent. Along with spectacular goals there were shock results, such as Northern Ireland's victory over Spain, thanks to Gerry Armstrong's goal, and Algeria beating eventual finalists West Germany. The Germans were involved in the two most controversial incidents. Results in their first group phase meant they and Austria would both qualify with a narrow West Germany win. It didn't need a grand conspiracy: both sets of players ambled to the required 1-0. FIFA eventually cottoned on and four years later introduced simultaneous kick-offs for the final group games. West Germany won their semi-final after an infamous challenge by keeper Harald Schumacher left France's Patrick Battiston unconscious and missing three teeth.

Italy won the other semi-final with two goals from Rossi: easy finishes for a striker with impeccable timing. He also scored the first goal in the final, meeting a cross from Gentile. Until the Brazil game, he hadn't scored an international goal in 11 games since 1979. Now he had six in three, in the most important week in football. Given the huge value we place on major tournaments – played by shattered stars after a long season – it is worth noting that Rossi's seminal week came after his lengthy lay-off.

Tardelli scored the second and set off on Italian football's most famous celebration, eyes bulging, sinews straining as the enormity of the moment hit him. When Altobelli made it three, Italy were on top of the world. Detractors should note that Tardelli's famous strike was set up by sweeper Gaetano Scirea, a converted midfielder. This was not *catenaccio*.

Rossi was a world champion and winner of both the Golden Boot and Golden Ball, emulating Garrincha and Kempes. He was also awarded the 1982 Ballon d'Or. It was a good week's work.

Juventus signed two of the stars of the tournament: France's Michel Platini and Poland's Zbigniew Boniek. They finished second to Roma in Serie A and lost the European Cup Final to Hamburg; some revenge for West German World Cup stars Manfred Kaltz, Horst Hrubesch and Felix Magath. A first-minute goal from Rossi in Birmingham had helped end Aston

Villa's reign as European champions and he finished as the tournament's top scorer, but those suspect knees limited his time at the top.

He scored 13 as Juventus reclaimed the *scudetto* in 1983/84 but only two in the following campaign. His last European Cup match was the listless, haunting final played in the grim aftermath of 39 deaths at Heysel Stadium.

He had one season at Milan, alongside England's Ray Wilkins and Mark Hateley, and finished his career with a short stay at Hellas Verona. He retired aged 31, after only 251 league games. Including all cups and internationals, he played 386 times and scored 154. It compares unfavourably to Kenny Dalglish, for example, with over 900 appearances and 366 goals, but Rossi's greatness was always in the timing: cometh the hour, cometh the man.

31

Michel Platini

MICHEL PLATINI was an elegant attacking midfielder, with a goalscoring record most top strikers would be proud of. He conquered European football with a unique hat-trick, but his attempts to rule the world were thwarted by German defenders and Swiss investigators.

It took a long time for Platini to make any money out of football at all. France was remarkably late to commercialise and fully professionalise the game. He didn't turn professional until he was 21, after playing at the 1976 Olympics. By then he was already well known, having scored 62 goals for Nancy.

He'd added another 50 before going to the 1978 World Cup, where Les Bleus failed to survive the group of death. Inter approached him about a transfer. Nancy responded by cutting his wages. He joined St Étienne a year later but, despite scoring 82 goals in three seasons, couldn't stem a decline in the mismanaged former doyennes of French football.

The 1982 World Cup could not have started worse for France. Terry Butcher flicked on a throw-in and an untracked Bryan Robson scored for England, 27 seconds in. Beating Kuwait became crucial for France and they did, despite an Alain Giresse goal being ruled out at the insistence of a Kuwaiti

FA official. Platini's pass sent Giresse through on goal, clearly onside, but a loud whistle from the crowd caused a moment's hesitation in Kuwait's defence, sparking the diplomatic incident. As the argument raged on the pitch side, Sheikh Fahad Al-Sabah came down from the stands and called Kuwait's players off. The Soviet referee Miroslav Stupar disallowed the goal and didn't referee again at the tournament.

France were in luck: finishing behind England gave them an easier second phase. They beat Austria and then faced Northern Ireland. At 0-0, Martin O'Neill had a good goal ruled offside – maybe the Northern Irish should have learned from the Kuwaitis – before France ran away with it.

So it was on to Seville for a semi-final with West Germany, where Platini and his team-mates lost the game but won the sympathy of every neutral. The skipper's penalty equalised a Pierre Littbarski opener before France coach Michel Hidalgo sent on Patrick Battiston. It was Platini's perfect through ball that sent the substitute into the path of the human juggernaut Harald Schumacher. Battiston was no striker and his shot was going wide when the keeper demolished him. Battiston woke up in the dressing room and had to be told where he was. Dutch referee Charles Corver awarded a goal kick to widespread fury and astonishment, although, to this day, keepers get away with grievous bodily harm after an attacker has had an attempt on goal.

France went 3-1 up in extra time, with Giresse pre-empting Marco Tardelli's famously manic celebration by three days. But insult was added to injury because, while the tiring French had used their second substitution to replace Battiston, West Germany had the reigning Ballon d'Or winner Karl-Heinz Rummenigge easing his way back to fitness. He came on and scored before Klaus Fischer equalised acrobatically; another brilliant goal from the Spain World Cup. Adding insult to insult to injury, Schumacher decisively saved twice in the shoot-out and Platini's team were thwarted.

Platini and Zibi Boniek had already been recruited by Juventus, the two-foreigner rule forcing out Liam Brady. Roma, inspired by Falcao and Carlo Ancelotti, won the *scudetto* but Platini was Serie A's top scorer from midfield. He retained the *Capocannoniere* (head gunner), as Juve recaptured the title in 1983/84.

France hosted the 1984 European Championships. A February friendly with England, who failed to qualify under Bobby Robson, was the first time Hidalgo put together the *Carré Magique*: the midfield magic square of Luis Fernández, Jean Tigana, Giresse and Platini. Fernández was the most defensive-minded, Tigana the grafter, Giresse a midfield linkman. They were adaptable and talented but Platini lit the flame. 'French football needed a leader like him,' Fernández said. 'When he arrived was when French football began to show its potential.'

Platini was incredible at Euro 84. He scored against Denmark in the opener then hit back-to-back hat-tricks against Belgium and Yugoslavia. He got the 119th-minute winner in a thrilling semi-final against Portugal, and opened the scoring in the final after a mistake by Spain keeper Luis Arconada. The 2-0 victory was France's finest footballing moment, their first tournament win. Platini played in the Euros only once, but his nine-goal total wasn't levelled until Cristiano Ronaldo played in his fourth tournament 32 years later.

Juve's 1984 league title set them on the fateful path to Heysel, and a hugely anticipated European Cup Final between two great teams. Juve had never been European champions, despite a dominant record in Italy, and Liverpool were the reigning champions. By kick-off none of that mattered, with the death toll on its way to 39. The police said playing the game was the best way to curtail further violence, though accounts from the players vary as to how much they knew. Dalglish, Rossi and Platini all said they had no idea of the scale of the disaster. Antonio Cabrini said he and other players had spoken to fans and been told directly by UEFA officials that there were multiple fatalities.

It was the worst game ever. German TV didn't show it, choosing to focus on the unfolding tragedy. Gary Gillespie fouled Boniek clearly outside the area, but Swiss referee Andre Daina decided a penalty was the best idea. Platini beat Grobbelaar and celebrated ecstatically. At full time Juventus fans invaded the pitch and most of their players later took a 'lap of honour'. Juve fans partied in the streets of Turin. Opposition supporters taunted Juve about Heysel for years. Juventus supremo Gianni Agnelli described the English as a 'race of incorrigible hooligans' and Italian football continued to regard violence at matches as somebody else's problem, an attitude that would see them fall behind other major leagues.

Platini had won three consecutive Ballons d'Or when he led France and the *Carré Magique* to the 1986 Mexico World Cup. They played a classic quarter-final against Brazil on his 31st birthday. He scored an equaliser, his 41st goal for France, a tally only bettered by Thierry Henry 21 years later. Zico came off the bench and missed a penalty in what proved to be his and Socrates's last internationals. In the shoot-out, Platini sent his penalty skywards but was bailed out by his team-mates.

Once again it was West Germany who ended the dream, this time without controversy. France looked dog tired, particularly when Schumacher's prodigious throw set up a late second goal. Fitness never was Platini's strong point. Apparently, Agnelli once saw him smoking in the Juventus dressing room and said, 'That worries me.' Platini pointed at midfield workhorse Massimo Bonini and said, 'You only need to worry if he starts to smoke.'

Platini's illustrious playing career finished a year later, just short of his 32nd birthday, but he was far from done with football. He was appointed as France's coach and led a team containing Laurent Blanc, Didier Deschamps and Eric Cantona into Euro 92, with a 100 per cent qualifying record.

After two draws they faced tournament outsiders Denmark, who had been given a place with less than a week's notice, after Yugoslavia were banned. The Danes had started with a defeat and a draw but they beat Platini's side, knocked out the Dutch on penalties and won a famous victory in the final against Germany.

His brief coaching career over, Platini was appointed joint head of the organising committee for the 1998 World Cup. He made powerful friends in FIFA president João Havelange and general secretary Sepp Blatter. Initially, he was Blatter's football advisor but ousted the long-serving Lennart Johansson to become president of UEFA in 2007. His stated aim was to protect football's values from the growing influence of high-finance, but what a world he had entered. US Attorney General Loretta Lynch said, 'At least two generations of soccer officials ... abused their positions of trust to acquire millions of dollars in bribes and kickbacks.' Richard Weber of the US Inland Revenue Service described a 'World Cup of Fraud'.

If you want the grubby details read David Conn's superbly written *The Fall of the House of FIFA*, but I doubt you will enjoy it. Conn starts in 1974, when Havelange, with Pelé at his side, tapped the political power of impoverished nations to snatch the FIFA presidency from 79-year-old Sir Stanley Rous, the stiffest of British blazers, who could not understand why black Africans criticised him for wanting apartheid South Africa in world football.

Havelange, Blatter and Adidas boss Horst Dassler helped make world football rich, but as wealth grew so did corruption. The danger in telling FIFA's story is one of snow blindness. There was so much blatant corruption it is hard to be angry enough. Eventually, US law enforcement agencies blew the racket with the aid of thief-turned-whistleblower Chuck Blazer.

Blatter and Platini were brought down by something both regarded as trivial: back payment for Platini's role as Blatter's football advisor. Amid the wide-ranging investigations in

2015, Blatter said he would resign the FIFA presidency and a month later Platini entered the race to replace him. But FIFA's new ethics committee found both men guilty, saying of Platini he 'didn't show commitment to an ethical attitude'. The Frenchman insisted he was at peace with his conscience but was banned from the game he had graced so magnificently as a player.

32

Diego Maradona

DIEGO MARADONA grew up in a Buenos Aires slum with no electricity, running water or sewers. He fell into a cesspit and heard his uncle's voice cry out, 'Diegito, keep your head above the shit!' It became Maradona's mantra as he became the best, the most loved and the most hated footballer of his generation.

At the age of nine, Diego was ball-juggling at half-time at Argentinos Juniors matches. By ten he was on TV and, aged 11, he was in Argentinos Juniors' youth team. His first contract allowed his family to move out of the slum, a daunting responsibility for a child. He made his senior debut at 15 and was capped at 16. It was a shock when he was left out of the 1978 World Cup squad.

Maradona helped pave the road to today's agent-dominated world of football finance. In *Barça: A People's Passion*, Jimmy Burns met translator-turned-coach-turned-agent José Maria Minguella, who spotted the lucrative potential of funnelling South American footballers to European clubs. Being conscience-free helped. Trying to get Maradona out of Argentina, Minguella negotiated with Admiral Carlos Lacoste at the Navy Mechanics School, the junta's notorious torture centre. Former Argentinos Juniors board member Settimio

Aloisio said, 'Everyone was trying to make money – hundreds of thousands of dollars were played with. It was a very degrading spectacle.'

Barça club secretary Jaume Rossell refused to pay a million dollars, so Maradona moved for less to Boca Juniors, who won the Metropolitano title in 1981. It was his only season with the club he supported as a boy. He had played in 206 Argentine league games and scored 144 goals, having just turned 21.

With Argentina's economy in meltdown in 1982, Barça and Minguella got their man. They bought bonds on the US stock market then took a van full of cash to Buenos Aires to break Paolo Rossi's world transfer record. In a very modern way, it is hard to know exactly how much was paid or to whom.

At the 1982 World Cup, Argentina's players were shocked when they read in Spanish newspapers that their country was losing the Falklands War, such was the junta's media manipulation. The reigning champions disappointed, stumbling into the second phase, where Italy's Claudio Gentile subdued Maradona and Brazil pressed his detonator. He was sent off for a vengeful high kick on Batista at Español's stadium, setting alarm bells ringing at FC Barcelona.

Barça hadn't won La Liga in the eight seasons since Johan Cruyff's initial triumphant arrival. Maradona joined two brilliant Europeans in Bernd Schuster and Allan Simonsen, but they finished fourth in 1983, as the title was claimed by Javier Clemente's cynical Athletic Bilbao. Barça were rattling through big-name coaches and in March 1983 appointed ex-Argentina boss César Luis Menotti. They won the Copa del Rey that summer but the championship wouldn't return until the Terry Venables era. Maradona missed 15 matches with hepatitis and described his time in Catalonia as his most miserable, making enemies in the club's hierarchy and the media. Team-mate Lobo Carrasco said Maradona showed 'humility and humanity' but foresaw trouble: 'He wanted to eat the world and that frightened me. The more I got to know him, the friendlier we became, the more I worried about him, the more I feared it would all end in tears.' Junk food wasn't Maradona's only enemy; this was when he started taking cocaine.

That September, Maradona suffered his most infamous injury playing against Athletic. Basque defender Andoni Goikoetxea had previously badly injured Schuster's knee and sealed his grim reputation with a horrible long-range lunge that broke Maradona's ankle. Menotti branded him an anti-footballer; English journalist Edward Owen dubbed him 'The Butcher of Bilbao'.

Barcelona's surgeon operated on Maradona's ankle but his personal doctor, Ruben Oliva, persuaded him to throw away his crutches and start walking. He was playing again within three months but there the miracles ended. Menotti and Clemente raged at each other about football philosophy and personal conduct. Maradona weighed in claiming the Athletic manager 'hasn't got the balls to look me in the eye and call me stupid'. The spiky Clemente responded: 'Maradona is both stupid and castrated. It's a shame that a player like him who earns so much money has no human qualities whatsoever.'

The feud erupted spectacularly. Athletic retained La Liga and beat Barça in the Copa del Rey Final at the Bernebéu in front of 100,000 fans and King Juan Carlos. Maradona had been kicked and taunted all match and on the full-time whistle a mass brawl started. The running kick was the attack method of choice for both sets of players. Maradona knocked out Athletic's unused substitute Miguel Sola, catching him flush in the head as he was trying to get up. Dozens of people were injured in the ensuing riot. Barcelona's hierarchy were mortified and wanted Maradona out. The only club willing to pay their asking price for an injury-hit firebrand was an outsider from southern Italy.

Napoli had only ever won two Italian Cups, despite twice breaking the world transfer record. They paid over $10m and unveiled their new hope in a packed Sao Paolo stadium. The first question at the press conference was, 'Does Maradona know what the Camorra is, and does he know that Camorra money is everywhere here in Naples, even in football.' Club president Corrado Ferlaino furiously denounced the journalist and had him thrown out, insisting Naples was a law-abiding city with a strong police force. Maradona would soon get to know Naples's organised crime gangs, developing a personal relationship with Camorra bosses. He told the press conference the thing he longed for most was peace.

Napoli improved steadily, building a solid base to give Maradona freedom. He enjoyed the city, on and off the field, and was the club's top scorer for the two seasons leading up to the 1986 World Cup.

Colombia pulled out of hosting the tournament in the midst of civil breakdown caused by a rampant drug trade. Mexico stepped in and Maradona stepped up. He stayed drug-free and went on a frenzied fitness campaign. He was something of a shape-changer throughout his career and in 1986 he was muscular like a bulldog, almost bursting out of his shorts.

Carlos Bilardo was Argentina's new coach, supposedly the latest embodiment of anti-football, but wise enough to recognise Maradona was special. They won their group with Maradona scoring in a draw with Italy. The second round was now a knockout and they beat Uruguay to set up a quarter-final with England. The English tabloids had their bloodlust up: 'IT'S WAR SEÑOR,' shouted *The Sun*.

Argentine officials bought new shirts in a shop three days before the match because they wanted a lightweight kit for the afternoon kick-off in Mexico City's Azteca Stadium. Bilardo's team set up deep and narrow. England had just beaten both Poland and Paraguay 3-0.

His two goals that afternoon epitomised Maradona. The infamous opener came in the 51st minute, after Steve Hodge sliced the ball back into his own box. Maradona jumped with Peter Shilton, flicked out his left arm and punched the ball over the keeper. Neither the Tunisian referee Ali Bin Nasser nor the Bulgarian linesman Bogdan Dochev spotted the handball, and Maradona urged his team-mates to join his celebration before suspicions were raised. In defence of the officials, BBC TV commentators Barry Davies and Jimmy Hill didn't call handball, and I'm told the BBC radio commentary was later re-edited to include a reference to it. For a man who wanted a peaceful life, Maradona had a genius for attracting attention, describing his goal as 'the hand of God'.

The 'goal of the century' came four minutes later. He took possession in his own half, outwitted Peter Reid and Peter Beardsley and headed for goal. He glided past centre-backs Terry Butcher and Terry Fenwick and skipped around Shilton, taking a kick on the ankle from Butcher as he slotted the ball into the net.

Uruguayan commentator Victor Hugo Morales cried, literally, 'Genius, Genius, Genius, Goaaallll, Goaaallll. Sorry I want to cry! Dear God! Long live football! Maradona, you make me cry. Forgive me ... cosmic kite! What planet do you come from to leave so many Englishmen in the dust?'

Davies was more measured: 'You have to say that's magnificent.'

Gary Lineker pulled a goal back but Argentina went to the semi-finals, where Maradona again stole the show with two excellent goals against Belgium.

The opener in the final against West Germany was scored by José Luis Brown, a descendant of the famous Browns of early Argentine football. Jorge Valdano made it 2-0, before Karl-Heinz Rummenigge and Rudi Völler pulled it back to 2-2, but it was another near miss for the Germans. Maradona's pass set up Jorge Burruchaga for a late winner.

Maradona was incomparable. He inspired Napoli to their first-ever *scudetto* and the city partied for a week. Thousands of boys in Naples were christened Diego, including one that he wrongly denied was his. The spotlight was incredibly intense.

THE FIFTY

The child's mother was interviewed in her hospital bed, newborn baby at her side. Maradona was filmed in nightclubs high on drink, drugs and adulation.

The following season saw Napoli four points clear of AC Milan with five games to play. It has never been proved that their late collapse was deliberate, but they took just one more point and finished second. It was rumoured the Camorra had gambled a fortune on Napoli failing to repeat their title triumph.

In a way it worked out well, as they won the UEFA Cup the following season while finishing second in Serie A again. Maradona's last full season in Italy was another triumph, on the pitch at least. They held off the European champions Milan, with Maradona using the hate-filled invective of northern fans as personal motivation and a rallying cry for the Neapolitans.

He misjudged the extent of the alienation between north and south when he called for Napoli fans to support Argentina when they faced Italy at the San Paolo in the semi-final of the 1990 World Cup. The hosts had won all five games, inspired by Toto Schillaci, who only made his international debut that March. The holders, by contrast, had lost to Cameroon, drawn with Romania, and beaten Yugoslavia on penalties.

Maradona appealed to the locals: 'For 364 days of the year you are considered to be foreigners in your own country; today you must do what they want by supporting the national team? I am Neapolitan 365 days of the year.'

His plea failed, but Maradona scored in the penalty shoot-out and set up a rematch with West Germany. Rome's Stadio Olimpico witnessed the worst World Cup Final. Fans of England and Cameroon might disagree but Italia 90 was a poor tournament with 16 red cards and a measly 2.2 goals per game. The Italians booed the Argentina national anthem and Maradona called them 'hijos de puta' – sons of bitches.

Argentina's indiscipline in the game has become legend, but the officials allowed the Germans to persistently foul

Maradona, a tactic that successfully limited his impact. Mexican referee Edgardo Codesal was awful. He refused West Germany a penalty when keeper Sergio Goycochea fouled Klaus Augenthaler but gave one when Völler felt a touch from Roberto Sensini and flung himself down. Argentina substitute Pedro Monzon became the first player to be sent off in a World Cup Final for a foul on Jurgen Klinsmann who, characteristically, got full marks for artistic merit as he fell. It might be a red card by today's standards, but commentator John Motson was stunned. The second red was clear-cut – Gustavo Dezotti floored Jürgen Kohler and Argentina should have lost two or three more players for outrageous dissent. Motson suggested they could be banned from the next tournament. Andy Brehme's penalty settled it and the brilliant West German captain Lothar Matthäus lifted the trophy. Franz Beckenbauer had won the World Cup as player and coach.

Maradona's relationship with Italy was broken. Whereas previously a blind eye had been turned to his drug-taking, he soon tested positive and was banned for 15 months. He signed for Sevilla in 1992 and linked up again with Bilardo. Maradona was overweight and odd flashes of brilliance failed to justify his wages. The two Argentine World Cup winners came to blows after a game against Real Burgos. At half-time Maradona asked to be substituted because of knee pain but was persuaded to have a cortisone injection, only for Bilardo to take him off early in the second half anyway.

He played for Newell's and Boca back in Argentina and even made the squad for USA 94. He scored one last glorious goal for Argentina against Greece and screamed wild-eyed into a TV camera. He failed another drug test, not for cocaine but for performance-enhancing ephedrine that he claimed he had taken by mistake. No one listened.

Maradona's post-playing career has been almost as wild as his glory days. He had a heart attack and nearly died aged 43 but recovered to coach Argentina at the 2010 World Cup. He becomes more popular as he gets older. He has been voted as football's greatest player and Napoli have retired their number-ten shirt. He has met two Popes and various world leaders. The 'Church of Maradona' has over 100,000 members and people are even coming to like him in England. He has had a life of incredible highs, some legal, some not – but one thing he definitely did not do was keep his head above the shit.

33

Hope Powell

HOPE POWELL'S first involvement with the FA was when they banned her from playing football with boys; 20 years later they asked her to almost single-handedly drag English women's football into the modern era.

The home of men's football had wilfully fallen behind in the women's game. The FA stadium ban was still actively enforced when Powell was born in 1966. The independent Women's Football Association was formed in 1969 and, under international pressure, the FA ended the restrictions two years later. England and Scotland met in both countries' first official international in 1972, a century after the men. Official hostility gave way only to indifference and the early pioneers of English women's football survived without FA help, until the WFA was given the status of a county federation in 1983. When she was called up in 1983, aged 16, Powell and Brenda Sempare were the first two black players in England's women's national team.

She had been barred from school matches because FA regulations meant from the age of 11 girls and boys had to play separately, and parents of opposition players had complained. She was lucky to be able to turn to Millwall Lionesses, but after she was late home from her first training session – two bus rides away – her mum banned her from going again. She carried on anyway and made her debut in secret.

Like everyone else in this book, she was football-mad as a kid. She had posters of Kevin Keegan and Ray Wilkins on her wall, was obsessed with *Match of the Day*, and played in mass games with local boys on a caged, concrete pitch. She made excuses to leave the house whenever she had a Millwall Lionesses match or training session and established herself in the team, before she plucked up the courage to tell her mum.

Powell wasn't short of courage. She once put herself between her mum Linever, and her abusive stepfather. She also broke her leg jumping out of her bedroom window to go and play football while she was grounded. That combative streak was central to her success, and later failure, as the premier figure in English women's football.

In a way, Powell's playing career peaked when she was 17 when England reached the final of the 1984 European Competition for Women's Football (UEFA didn't organise official Women's Euros until 1991). The first leg was played at Gothenburg's Ullevi stadium, and Sweden took a 1-0 lead through Pia Sundhage, who would later coach the USA to two Olympic gold medals. The WFA couldn't find a London club willing to stage England's home leg so took it to Kenilworth Road. England made up the deficit but lost on penalties – in that aspect at least, the women's game in England was ahead of the men's. Swedish TV showed highlights of the games and 36 reporters travelled to Luton for the second leg – in England it got almost no media interest.

Players were wholly amateur and Powell juggled playing football with her job coaching kids' sport. She moved to Friends of Fulham FC and played in the 1989 Women's FA Cup Final at Old Trafford. That was one of the periods in which the English women's game almost broke through, with Channel 4 showing match highlights, but progress remained patchy. She won the cup twice: back at Millwall in 1991 and later with Croydon. Powell and some Millwall team-mates broke away and founded Bromley Borough, who later merged with Croydon and won the Women's Premier League/FA Cup double in 1995/96. Croydon were subsequently swallowed by Charlton Athletic but by then Powell had retired from playing.

England's first World Cup appearance came in the second tournament in Sweden in 1995. They travelled by public train, sometimes overnight, and wore kit designed for men. Powell wasn't central to the team by then, only coming on as a substitute in a win over Canada and a group-stage defeat to eventual champions Norway. She didn't play as England lost their first knockout game against Germany. They were no match for the countries where women's football had deeper roots and strong domestic competitions. She described Ted Copeland as a 'long-ball coach' and England's failure to qualify for the next World Cup cost him his job.

In 1998, aged 31, Powell was invited to the FA's London headquarters at Lancaster Gate. She hoped she might be offered a role coaching youngsters and was stunned when asked to replace Copeland as England manager. She had her UEFA 'B' licence coaching qualification but was still an active player with no managerial experience. It was an extraordinary move by the FA – either a courageous show of faith or an abdication of responsibility. She was the England team's first black coach, first female coach and first gay coach. 'It may seem bizarre,' she reflected in her autobiography, 'but everyone just seemed to assume that I knew what I was meant to be doing.'

She fought for funding and respect, and built up a team of coaches, medics and administrators, maintaining a tight grip on the women's game including all age-group teams and the national side. FA technical director Howard Wilkinson encouraged her to study for her UEFA 'A' and pro-licences but largely left her to it: 'He wasn't openly dismissive, just not particularly interested,' Powell wrote. 'I felt a bit like an alien who had been beamed down to Lancaster Gate. I also think a lot of people there were a little scared of me. In truth, at the time, not a lot of them had much experience of working with black people.'

Under Powell, England qualified for the 2001 Euros but finished bottom of their group after being well-beaten by Sweden and Germany. They failed to reach the 2003 World Cup and, despite hosting the Euros in 2005, and winning their opening game against Finland in front of 29,029 fans, they again finished bottom of their group.

In 2000 Fulham became England's first professional women's club, but they were too far ahead of their time. No other clubs followed and chairman Mohamed Al Fayed grew tired of bankrolling it, announcing in 2003, 'The mediocre advances in women's football during this period have made it impossible for me to continue at a professional level.'

Powell was winning battles slowly. When England travelled to the 2007 World Cup, they arrived eight days before their first match to counter the jet lag and took a chef and a video analyst. Again their involvement ended when they faced a top side, this time the USA.

At Euro 2009 England were the best-ranked third-placed team in the groups, but narrow wins over Finland and the Netherlands saw them reach the final, where they lost 6-2 to world champions Germany. Powell persuaded the FA to introduce central contracts for women internationals (£16,000 a year) but progress towards a reconstituted national league was delayed.

At the 2011 World Cup in Germany, England stayed at the Ritz-Carlton hotel, with its 3-star Michelin restaurant, a world of difference from Powell's playing days sleeping in dodgy hotels and travelling by minibus. But international women's football was also moving on and England were racing to keep up. They beat eventual champions Japan to make it through the group but agonisingly lost out to France in the quarter-finals.

Jill Scott put England in front, but France's Élise Bussaglia scored a brilliant 88th-minute equaliser. Powell asked three times for players to take penalties and was furious that no senior players volunteered before the inexperienced substitute left-back Claire Rafferty spoke up. Karen Bardsley saved France's first penalty and England led until Rafferty dragged hers horribly wide. When captain Faye White's shot hit the bar, England were out.

Losing on penalties in the last eight was no cause for shame, but Powell let off a media hand grenade and upset her senior players by telling a journalist they had shown 'cowardice' by not volunteering to take penalties.

Powell's management style had already alienated some players. Her autobiography makes constant references such as, 'Anyone who's a manager and wants to be liked is on to a loser,' and 'If I was a bit of a sergeant major it was for good reason.' She admits to being a control freak and surely that is incompatible with developing creative football. Powell's England sides were dull compared to their direct rivals.

It was a largely English side who represented Great Britain at the 2012 London Olympics, winning their group after beating Brazil in front of 70,584 at Wembley but going out in the quarter-final against Canada in Coventry.

Powell's last major tournament was the 2013 Euros in Sweden. They lost to Spain, drew with Russia and lost 3-0 to France. She was shocked when the FA sacked her, but regular observers of the team weren't. She had been in charge of almost all aspects of women's football in England for 15 years.

Her many duties were divided up, with the national team coach's job going to Welshman Mark Sampson, who guided the side to the 2015 World Cup semi-final but was sacked in 2017. The FA made a hash of dealing with alleged racist remarks made by the coach: they held three investigations, apologised to the women concerned but paid Sampson a 'significant' sum after he brought a claim for unfair dismissal.

Sampson was replaced by another man, Phil Neville, who had 59 caps but no managerial experience. It is hard to measure progress in a rapidly evolving game, but another semi-final appearance in 2019 seemed about par, given the draw. England's big clubs now had professional women's teams and international players no longer travelled to games on public transport, so expectations were higher.

Powell currently manages Brighton, one of eight women managing WSL teams. There is a valid question about whether women's clubs should be gender-blind when appointing coaches. If an excellent man wants to coach women's football it seems a waste to turn him away but until women regularly get jobs coaching men's teams then there is a case for keeping pathways open for female coaches to get experience. I don't have the answer.

Powell fought hard for women's football in England, at times in the face of apathy from powerbrokers, public and media. Did she stay around too long? Should she have shared the power? Probably, but don't let that detract from what she achieved.

34

Marco van Basten

OCCASIONALLY OLD blokes lament the days when men were men and tackles were tackles. But before you get too nostalgic, remember Marco van Basten and the lost years of the best centre-forward of a generation.

After the English dominance of European club football ended horrifically at Heysel, the cash-rich Italian clubs seemed set to take over – instead there was an interregnum. English champions Everton felt particularly aggrieved, but I can't imagine anyone on the continent missed England's hooligans.

The 1986 European Cup was won by an all-Romanian Steaua Bucharest side. After a goalless final, they beat Terry Venables's Barcelona 2-0 on penalties. Steaua's Helmuth Duckadam saved all four spot-kicks. Porto won it in 1987 and were succeeded by PSV Eindhoven, who beat Benfica on penalties after another goalless final. These were not the glory days.

Finally, a great team emerged, made of Dutch mastery and Italian steel. Van Basten, Ruud Gullit and Frank Rijkaard became European champions with club and country. At AC Milan, they were protected by a legendary back four: Mauro Tassotti, Paolo Maldini, Franco Baresi and Alessandro

Costacurta. Carlo Ancelotti added industry and experience to the midfield. The coach was Arrigo Sacchi, a surprise recruit from Serie B side Parma, whose high-pressing game and compact but flexible 4-4-2 was considered groundbreaking in Italy.

The individual most responsible for the rise of AC Milan was Silvio Berlusconi, a cable TV entrepreneur, who grasped the potential of offering top-level football alongside low-brow programming that was novel to Italy. The club had been disgraced, twice relegated and become debt-ridden since last winning Serie A. Berlusconi pumped in millions, not for love but, as he admitted, because he saw AC Milan as a 'product'. Club and owner thrived. Milan became serial European Champions and Berlusconi became prime minister, but this is not a history of football told through sex-partying tycoon politicians.

Van Basten was the striker who had everything: he was tall, fast enough, intelligent, skilful and an excellent finisher. He scored on his league debut for Ajax, aged 17, and soon became a regular, getting 152 goals in 172 games. He won the Eredivisie three times (1982, 83 and 85) and, under Johan Cruyff, added the Cup Winners' Cup in 1987. Cruyff was furious that Ajax's policy of limiting fees meant Milan got Van Basten for around £1m. What a bargain! Gullit's move from PSV broke the world record for around £6m that same summer.

The Dutch duo won Serie A at the first attempt, benefitting from Napoli's questionable collapse. Van Basten had signed with an ankle injury and had a frustrating campaign, but Gullit believes it helped the Netherlands that Van Basten had been unavailable to the notoriously demanding Sacchi ahead of Euro 88.

'I was exhausted, broken after that first season at AC Milan. I was too tired to play with the energy I had shown at AC Milan, however badly I wanted to … but happily Van Basten recovered his form for the tournament following months of injury ... Marco was so fresh I was constantly passing to him.'

Rinus Michels, back for his third spell as Dutch manager, left Van Basten out of the first game against the USSR and they lost to a single counter-attack goal. The Milan striker returned to face England, who wished he hadn't. For his first goal he received a pass from Gullit 12 yards out and turned Tony Adams inside out. Bryan Robson equalised but Gullit set up Van Basten again. He completed his hat-trick with a close-range shot from a corner. Adams blamed England's naivety on three years without European club football. 'We used to chase them around the pitch and they just sat back and counter-attacked us. We didn't understand this stuff. Then we would get the ball, kick it long and give it back to them.'

The Netherlands still had to beat Ireland, who were at their first major tournament and had beaten England with a Ray Houghton header. Manager Jack Charlton had recruited wisely from the Irish diaspora; nine of 13 players used against the Dutch were British-born.

With nine minutes left, it was goalless, and Ireland were headed for the semis but then Ronald Koeman hit a shot, powerfully, but into the ground and off target. The ball bounced to sub Wim Kieft, who flicked it on. His header seemed to be going yards wide until it bounced and spun freakishly into the goal. Michels thanked his lucky stars: 'In this sort of tournament you had to be lucky at the right time. You need to play well, give everything, and the team needs to give the impression they know they can win it, and you need luck. We had luck against Ireland.'

They also had a brilliant, bright-orange army of supporters who followed them to Hamburg for the semi-final against the hosts. It is not only the English who invoke war imagery when playing the Germans at football, and there was Dutch delight when Van Basten hit a late winner to take them to the final and a rematch with the USSR.

Like Michels, Valeriy Lobanovskyi was a visionary coach. He won the Soviet League nine times with Dnipro and Dynamo Kyiv, playing a style similar to the Dutch and with an emphasis on nutrition and fitness. But the trophy was won by great players. Van Basten crossed to Gullit, whose rocket header is one of the great forgotten goals. That is because the second was possibly the best-ever first-time finish. Arnold Muhren slung over a tired cross, so heavy that the Soviet left-back let it go. But Van Basten had pulled away to within a couple of yards of the right edge of the box, six yards from the byline. The volley was perfect. Van Basten said he was exhausted and thought 'why not?' and so the Dutch were champions of Europe.

Contrastingly, the only mark they left on the 1990 World Cup was the gross image of Rijkaard spitting into Rudi Völler's curly hair as both were sent off. At Euro 92, Van Basten cost them a place in the final when his side-footed penalty was the only one saved in the shoot-out against Denmark. Fine margins decide tournaments: contrast that with Kieft's freakish header four years earlier.

Rijkaard joined his Dutch team-mates at Milan in 1988 as the club chased a third European Cup. They beat Red Star Belgrade on penalties and Werder Bremen 1-0 on aggregate before really coming good in their last two games. Five players scored in a 5-0 win over Real Madrid in the semi-final, second leg. *Los Blancos* were on a sequence of five straight La Liga titles and the result was seen by some as symbolic of Italian pre-eminence. Milan were stunning in the final as well: two goals each from Gullit and Van Basten brushed aside Steaua.

Sacchi's Milan only won Serie A once, but his side retained the European Cup in 1990, knocking out Real Madrid and Bayern Munich en route to a final with Benfica, where Van Basten set up Rijkaard for the only goal. Their bid for a third successive title failed when they were thrown out of the tournament. In the second leg of the 1991 quarter-final at Marseilles, they were trailing 2-1 on aggregate when a combination of floodlight failure and pitch invasions led to the game being paused. Milan refused to restart and demanded a replay but the referee said no. UEFA backed him and awarded the tie to Marseilles, who went on to lose a penalty shoot-out against Red Star after another goalless final.

Sacchi was sacked that summer after falling out with Van Basten about work rate and playing time. Maldini later claimed that the players were exhausted and Sacchi's demands could only be met for a couple of seasons. Former Milan, Juve and Italy midfielder Fabio Capello was his replacement. He largely kept Sacchi's plans in place but allowed the creative players more freedom and Milan went through the Serie A season undefeated, finishing eight points clear. Van Basten won the *Capocannoniere* with 25 goals, seven more than second-placed Roberto Baggio. Between May 1991 and March 1993 Milan went 58 games unbeaten. They won the *scudetto* in Capello's first three seasons and in four from five.

Van Basten had been out for four months before returning for the controversial 1993 European Cup Final defeat against Marseilles. The French club had been taken over by businessman Bernard Tapie in the same year Berlusconi arrived at AC Milan. They won four consecutive French titles with players such as Marcel Desailly, Didier Deschamps, Chris Waddle, Jean Pierre Papin and Völler. Tapie had been annoyed that his players were tired when they lost the 1991 European Cup Final and it was later discovered that Marseilles officials had bribed Valenciennes players to throw a league game six days before they faced Milan. They coasted to victory and clinched the league before beating Milan 1-0 with a header from Basile Boli.

Marseilles were stripped of their French League title and relegated but incredibly were allowed to keep their European Cup win and it has never been revoked. Don't worry about Tapie: his business career flourished and he became a politician.

That was Van Basten's last-ever game. A vicious tackle from behind by Boli inflicted his last injury and he never regained fitness. Milan struggled to replace him, but despite scoring only 36 goals they won the *scudetto* anyway, as the legendary defence conceded only 15. They regained the Champions League beating Barcelona 4-0 with goals from Dejan Savicevic, Desailly, who had signed from Marseilles, and two from Daniele Massaro.

Van Basten won the Ballon d'Or in 1988, 1989 and 1992. He, Gullit and Rijkaard were archetypal top-level, 1990s players: big, strong but technically excellent. Van Basten scored freely with both feet, headers and overhead kicks. He played only 373 club matches yet scored 277 goals, only 20 of which came after the 1992 change to the back-pass rule that put football onto a more positive path.

It was the tackling that defeated him. Boli's assault was typical of the era. It would be a red card now, which is the chief reason Lionel Messi and Cristiano Ronaldo have played over twice as many games as Van Basten. The great Dutchman's shortened career was at the forefront of FIFA's thinking when they tightened up guidance on tackling from behind and eventually made challenges like Boli's red card offences. That, along with football's best-ever volley, are Marco van Basten's legacy.

35

Paul Gascoigne

ENGLISH PEOPLE love a flawed hero and heroes rarely come more flawed than Paul Gascoigne. Take your pick from what we euphemistically call his 'demons': alcoholism, obsessive compulsive disorder, bulimia and bipolar disorder. He was seven years old when he first became obsessed by dying. He was ten when he was left with a friend's young brother who was knocked over and killed by an ice cream van, leaving Gascoigne with feelings of guilt for years.

He made his debut for Newcastle United aged 17 and became a crowd favourite, usually referred to simply as Gazza. He was a rarity in English football: a skilful, dynamic central midfielder who could dribble past opponents, score and create goals. Fans might love talented midfielders, but the English system could almost have been designed to crush the spirit out of creative players: 'Get it out!' and 'Play the way you're facing!' Rebellious characters were more likely to retain their individuality, and talented English players were often mavericks.

One photograph framed Gascoigne's place in English football: Wimbledon's Vinnie Jones, the epitome of the vulgar midfielders of the era, squeezing the Newcastle youngster's penis mid-match at Plough Lane. Jones is gurning like Mr

Punch while Gascoigne squeals – but he 'took it well' as was expected in a macho world.

England manager Bobby Robson was wary of calling up youngsters, so Gascoigne missed the pitiful Euro 88 campaign in which Bryan Robson, Neil Webb, Glenn Hoddle and Steve McMahon were all used in central midfield.

That summer, Gascoigne broke the British transfer record. His preference was to join Liverpool but they wouldn't match Newcastle's £2m asking price. Manchester United did, and after speaking to Gascoigne Alex Ferguson went on holiday expecting the deal to be sorted. It has been suggested many times that this was Gascoigne's 'sliding doors' moment, that his life might have taken a smoother path had he signed for Ferguson. I'm not sure. United had a core of hard-drinking players and Ferguson didn't magically transform any of them; he managed the situation until he could get rid. Lee Sharpe signed that summer and failed to fulfil his potential, winning only eight England caps. Eric Cantona was a complex character who later thrived at Old Trafford but he was very different from Gascoigne.

Instead Tottenham and Terry Venables got their man after sending Chris Waddle to talk to Gascoigne in a Tyneside pub. An England call-up soon followed, but he hadn't started a competitive international before the 1990 World Cup, despite the media clamour. An excellent performance in a friendly against Czechoslovakia convinced Robson the 23-year-old could be trusted.

England qualified by playing out goalless draws with Sweden and Poland, and the tabloids, in particular, made the manager's life miserable. After a drawn friendly with Saudi Arabia, the *Daily Mirror* headline pleaded: 'IN THE NAME OF ALLAH, GO!' There were stories about Robson's private life on the front pages as well, and there was little surprise or disappointment when he announced he would leave for PSV Eindhoven after the World Cup, come what may.

With England exiled in Sardinia so their fans could be more easily policed, the grim football continued. Their first game was against Jack Charlton's Ireland, and a 1-1 draw prompted *Gazzetta dello Sport*'s headline: 'NO FOOTBALL PLEASE, WE'RE ENGLISH!' Obviously, the Irish objected to being lumped in with England, but seven of their players that day were English-born and they played basic, direct football.

England had the better of another poor game with the Dutch and sneaked past Egypt with a goal by centre-back Mark Wright. The draw fell kindly and Robson's side faced Belgium in the second round in Bologna, another scrappy game that was seconds away from penalties when Gascoigne floated a free kick into the box and David Platt volleyed one of England's best-ever goals.

Had everything gone to form, it would have been Argentina in the quarter-final again, but Cameroon had topped their group and then beaten Colombia, with two goals from the extraordinary Roger Milla. The 38-year-old had been a footballer since 1968, had been named African Player of the Year in 1976 and now played club football on Réunion Island.

The Africans were underrated in England because some brutal tackling against Argentina had masked their ability. Watching the quarter-final again, Cameroon look like the modern team while England kicked lumps out of them – but it was a brilliant match. Platt headed England in front but Milla came off the bench and was clobbered by Gascoigne. Penalty: 1-1. No African side had made it this far before, and after Milla's pass set up Eugène Ekéké Cameroon had one foot in the semis for 18 minutes. Gary Lineker rescued England, winning and converting the penalty to force extra time. Gascoigne's pass released his Spurs club-mate and again Lineker won and scored the penalty to make it 3-2.

The mood change in England was incredible. Robson had listened to his players and abandoned 4-4-2 to use three centre-backs. It was unsophisticated and you would never see

Gascoigne and Platt as a central-midfield pairing now, but one way or another England had reached the final four and then put in their best performance.

The semi-final against West Germany in Turin is Gazza's most famous match. England were the better side, but after an hour Andy Brehme's shot from a free kick deflected off Paul Parker and made Peter Shilton look all of his 40 years, as he backpedalled but failed to stop the ball looping under the crossbar. Lineker equalised with his tenth goal in World Cup tournament football. Gascoigne had been booked against Belgium and just two cautions meant a suspension, even for the final. In extra time he over-ran the ball and clattered into Thomas Berthold. It was a clear yellow-card offence but the German defender's theatrics were undignified. As the tears welled in Gascoigne's eyes, the camera picked up Lineker warning Robson to 'have a word'. Both sides hit the post, and while all the Germans scored their penalties Stuart Pearce struck his straight at Bodo Illgner and Waddle blazed his into the Turin sky.

In football's greatest set-piece anticlimax, Roberto Baggio and Toto Schillaci's goals won the third-place play-off for Italy, but Robson left for Eindhoven revered by the English public and media.

Gascoigne was one of the world's best midfielders. In Spurs' 1990/91 campaign he scored 19 goals, including a stunning long-range free kick past David Seaman, as they beat soon-to-be league champions Arsenal in the FA Cup semi. Lazio offered £8.5m for Gascoigne and debt-ridden Spurs accepted.

Disaster struck in the final against Nottingham Forest. Before the game, Gascoigne had an injection to 'calm him down' – as he put it. Whatever it was didn't work. He studded Garry Parker in the chest and somehow wasn't booked. We will never know whether a yellow card would have calmed him down. He then made a frenzied challenge that looked like he was trying to launch Forest full-back Gary Charles out of Wembley Stadium and ruptured his own cruciate knee ligament. Gascoigne was stretchered off and Forest's Pearce scored from the free kick. Spurs fought back to win the cup with an equaliser from Paul Stewart and a Des Walker own goal. Gascoigne's team-mates visited him in hospital. He cried after they left him and drank champagne the night before his knee operation.

He missed a whole season before eventually joining Lazio. His time in Italy was a failure in football terms, although Gascoigne's charismatic appearances on Channel 4's *Football Italia* augmented his popularity at home. He played only 43 Serie A matches in three seasons. Antics such as wearing comedy breasts and belching into a reporter's microphone amused the English but baffled the Italians. Lazio manager Dino Zoff said Gascoigne 'had ice cream for breakfast and beer for lunch'. Gascoigne later admitted heavy drinking contributed to his persistent injuries. Bad luck played a part too – he suffered a broken leg in a training-ground clash with Alessandro Nesta.

He missed England's awful Euro 92 tournament which finished with new boss Graham Taylor substituting Lineker, who was one short of Bobby Charlton's England scoring record, in the fateful last group game against hosts Sweden. The tabloids revelled in it: 'SWEDES 2 TURNIPS 1' was a funny if harsh headline. The subsequent hounding of Taylor was horrible. He had been successful with Lincoln, Watford and Aston Villa employing direct, high-pressure football but never got to grips with the international game.

The subsequent failed 1994 World Cup qualifying campaign was the subject of the spellbinding documentary *An Impossible Job*. As Taylor dithered, England gave away leads at home to Norway and the Netherlands. I am reluctant to criticise referees but standards were low back then: Jan Wouters broke Gascoigne's cheekbone with a straight-arm smash but somehow the Dutch still had 11 players when they completed their comeback. Taylor's side lost in Oslo to a Norway team inspired by the English long-ball game before his ultimate humiliation in Rotterdam. It could have been so different. Gascoigne was missing but England hit the post twice and Ronald Koeman should have been sent off for fouling Platt, who was through on goal. The cruel irony was that Koeman then scored, exploiting David Seaman's bad positioning. Commentator Brian Moore spotted it: 'He's going to flip one now!' Dennis Bergkamp got a second and Taylor exploded with anger on ITV. He couldn't bring himself to say Koeman's name: 'That blond man shouldn't be on the pitch!' In the interest of balance, Frank Rijkaard had a goal mistakenly ruled offside at 0-0.

In 1995 Gascoigne signed for Rangers for a club-record £4.3m and won two Scottish titles and both domestic cups in three years, although his appearances were limited by injury. Controversy followed him: a sectarian flute-playing gesture he made in an Old Firm derby led to death threats from someone claiming to be the IRA. In typical Gascoigne style, he bought his young team-mate Gennaro Gattuso some tailored suits while pretending the club was paying but he also defecated in the Italian's sock as a prank.

The popular notion that England's relative success at Italia 90 revitalised the game in the country is only partially true. The goodwill towards the national team dissipated under Taylor and the tabloid hostility was feverish in the build-up to Euro 96 to be staged in England. New boss Venables took the squad to play an unofficial friendly in Hong Kong and pictures appeared in the newspapers of players in the so-called 'Dentist's Chair', lying back having booze poured into their mouths. *The Sun* headlined it, 'DISGRACEFOOL. LOOK AT GAZZA ... A DRUNK OAF WITH NO PRIDE'.

Again the public mood followed the results. After a draw with Switzerland, England faced Scotland at Wembley. Alan Shearer headed the opener before Seaman saved Gary McAllister's penalty. Gascoigne wrapped up the victory with his most famous goal, collecting the ball on the run, lifting it over Colin Hendry's head with his left foot before volleying past Andy Goram with his right. He then lay on the ground, mouth open while his team-mates reprised the Dentist's Chair, only this time with Lucozade.

One of England's best-ever performances saw them hammer the Dutch 4-1 with two goals each from Shearer and Teddy Sheringham. In the quarter-final, Spain's Julio Salinas was incorrectly flagged offside before he beat Seaman. It ended 1-1. England took four near-perfect penalties including Pearce's powerful drive that prompted his iconic bawling, fist-pumping celebration. Seaman saved from Miguel Angel Nadal and England faced the now-unified Germans in the semi-final.

Only Gascoigne, Pearce and Platt survived from Turin six years earlier, and though the 1990 side had some talented players I think Venables's team were a stronger unit, chiefly because he was a more accomplished tactician than his predecessors.

Shearer headed an early opener, Stefan Kuntz equalised and an agonising game saw Darren Anderton hit the post and Gascoigne check his stride when a fully committed lunge would have given England the winner. Under Venables, a slower Gascoigne played in a midfield three and in the semi-final his tackling verged on wild.

The first ten penalties were faultless before Andreas Köpke saved the first one within reach, adding Gareth Southgate's name to the list of England penalty villains. Andy Möller smashed in the clincher and the Germans went on to win the final against an excellent Czech Republic side. Former East German international Matthias Sammer was the star of the tournament for the recently unified nation.

It was to be Gascoigne's last tournament. He played six World Cup qualifiers under Glenn Hoddle but was forever in the tabloids. Hoddle took a provisional squad to Morocco and La Manga in Spain, where he broke the bad news to those being dropped in a series of face-to-face meetings. Gascoigne reacted furiously, smashing up the room and punching a glass lamp.

He returned to the English top flight with Middlesbrough in 1998 and Bryan Robson's side finished ninth, but Boro fanzine readers voted Gascoigne the club's most disappointing player. He had two disrupted seasons at Everton before joining First Division Burnley. He played briefly in China with Gansu Tianma and his last league football was for Boston United in League Two in 2004.

His life has remained chaotic. He has made attempts at rehabilitation and been in trouble with the police a number of times. He became a public laughing stock after trying to speak to armed fugitive Raoul Moat in 2010. Literally as I write he is in the tabloids again for another public misdemeanour. As his Rangers team-mate Ally McCoist said, 'Gazza will help anyone but himself.'

I remember yearning for Gazza to fulfil his potential as a footballer. Lots of people did, which was partly why everyone was often so angry with him, but Lineker put it best: 'Part of his genius, part of his magnificence, is that he was so vulnerable. Without that vulnerable side, that carefree side, without all the things that come with Gazza, I don't think Paul Gascoigne would have been the player he was.'

36

Brandi Chastain

THE 1999 FIFA Women's World Cup Final, played at the Pasadena Rose Bowl in California, in front of 90,185 fans, had come down to its tenth penalty. One Chinese player had failed to score, although to be fair to Liu Ying, USA keeper Briana Scurry was so far off her line she all but saved at the midfielder's feet.

Had the USA won a spot-kick in normal play, Brandi Chastain was the nominated taker, even though she hit the bar from the spot in a defeat against China in the recent Algarve Cup. Chastain was surprised the US coaching staff approached her at the end of the goalless two hours and asked if she would take one. She assumed she was first on the list. She was also surprised when coach Tony DiCicco told her to take it left-footed. She played left-back in the game and was comfortable using her left foot but usually took set pieces with her right.

She took his advice and slammed in the winning penalty and immediately whipped off her baggy white jersey, spun around to see her team-mates charging towards her and fell to her knees. The image appeared in newspapers around the world and on the front cover of *Sports Illustrated*, *Time* and *Newsweek* – unprecedented interest in women's football.

THE FIFTY

At the time I missed the significance and took a defensive view: why the fuss? After all, she was wearing a sports bra and male players took their shirts off all the time. I hadn't understood how inspirational the moment could be. *Match of the Day*'s first-ever female commentator Jacqui Oatley explained what it meant to her.

'Brandi whipping off her shirt was a spontaneous act of pure, raw emotion which didn't require translation into a thousand languages to make an impact. It screamed: "We've arrived and women's football is here to stay." It felt like the start of something, genuine recognition that the women's game can be everything we want it to be: quality entertainment which attracts crowds and means just as much as the men's game. It was the start of the recent leg of the slow, painful journey from ridicule to recognition.'

Hostility to women's football was never a peculiarly English thing: UEFA and FIFA only recognised it in the early 1970s. The Germans, future powerhouses of women's football, lifted their ban in 1970. Chastain didn't have a USA women's team to support until 1985, when she was 17.

There had been unofficial international competitions from 1970, including the Italian-organised Mundialito. An invitation to the 1985 tournament was the spark that created the USA women's national team (USWNT). They were the weakest team, although it gave a first taste of international football to future great Michelle Akers. A year later, Norway's Ellen Wille became the first woman to address the FIFA congress and challenged them to stage a World Cup. There was a trial run in 1988 and in 1991 the first women's World Cup was staged, sort of.

Worried that it would be an embarrassment, FIFA kept the tournament at arm's length and saddled it with a ludicrous title: the First World Championship for Women's Football for the M&M's Cup. China hosted and little thought was given to TV rights distribution, although they did get Pelé for the opening ceremony and the hosts mobilised good support in the stadiums.

The USA had come a long way in six years, partly because equal rights legislation forced colleges to offer sports scholarships to women, which helped create a strong base of soccer players despite the game's low status. Chastain came through the college system and was 'Freshman of the Year' in 1986. She then missed two years of football after reconstructive surgery on both anterior cruciate knee ligaments. What would the doctors who supported the FA ban of 1921 have said? But Marco van Basten put his body on the line for football, so why couldn't Chastain? She was named in the squad of 18 that played six 80-minute games in two weeks, although the key roles were taken by Akers, who scored ten goals, and Golden Ball winner Carin Jennings.

The USWNT beat European champions Germany in the semis and Norway in the final. They thought they were on top of the world until they arrived home to be greeted at the airport by a single media outlet. Crucially, FIFA were impressed – the major governing bodies were ahead of the clubs for decades in their support for the women's game.

Chastain struggled to hold down a place as an attacker and missed the 1995 World Cup in Sweden in which the Europeans rallied. Norway beat the Americans in the semis and Germany in the final. Switching to left-back helped Chastain win a place in the squad for the first-ever Olympic women's football competition at the 1996 Atlanta Games. She tore a knee ligament as the US beat World Champions Norway in the semi-final but still lined up for the final against China. Shannon MacMillan scored first, but China's best player Sun Wen beat Chastain's desperate attempt to clear before Tiffeny Milbrett hit the winner. A crowd of 76,489 watched the final in Athens, Georgia, and the potential of the women's game was obvious. There was no professional league but star players such as Mia Hamm signed lucrative sponsorship deals.

THE FIFTY

The US players worked hard on the pitch in a flood of friendly matches and tournaments – and off the pitch in a never-ending promotional push in preparation for the 1999 World Cup in the USA. The original plan had been to use mid-sized stadiums, but the interest in the Olympic victory persuaded organisers to gamble. It paid off spectacularly: 78,972 watched the USWNT beat Denmark in their opener at Giants Stadium, another 65,080 saw them thrash Nigeria in Chicago and 50,484 watched the win over North Korea. No crowd was lower than 14,000, and 78,972 watched Brazil's 7-1 demolition of Mexico.

Chastain's own goal, after a mix-up with Scurry, put Germany in front in the quarter-final, but she later scored at the right end as they came back for a 3-2 win. Another 73,123 were in Stanford for a semi-final victory over Brazil, setting up a showdown with Sun Wen-inspired China who had outclassed Norway 5-0.

The only two goalless draws were the last two games. The TV audience for the final would remain the biggest for any soccer match in the US until 2014, merchandise sales were huge and the tournament made a $4m profit. Ex-USA international Wendy Gebauer was a co-commentator and teed it up: 'This is more than a game. This is a defining moment in sports history.'

Chastain's penalty, and iconic celebration, gave women's football a prominence it had never known. She signed a deal with Nike and appeared in a host of adverts in print and TV and a generation of American girls had soccer-playing female heroes.

The obvious next step was to establish a professional women's league alongside Major League Soccer, which had been played since 1996. The Women's United Soccer Association launched in 2001 and Chastain's Bay Arena CyberRays won the inaugural Founders' Cup against Scurry's Atlanta Beat. Chastain scored the opening goal and after a 3-3 draw it went to penalties. The CyberRays only needed four kicks to win, so the two World Cup heroes didn't face off.

Lots of the world's best players signed for US teams and initially crowds were healthy and sponsorship revenue strong, but it proved to be unsustainable and WUSA only lasted three seasons. It would take another couple of attempts to establish professional women's club soccer in the USA.

Chastain won a silver medal at Sydney in 2000 as the Olympics vied for status with the World Cup. Unlike the men's game, it was an open competition and full international caps were awarded.

The 2003 World Cup was switched from China to the US because of the SARS outbreak. Plans were more modest and attendances were strong, but not as spectacular as four years earlier. Chastain only played in the first game and the US lost 3-0 to Germany, led by Maren Meinert and the magnificent Birgit Prinz.

There was one last hurrah for Chastain and Hamm's generation at the 2004 Olympics when they took the gold medal ahead of Brazil and future six-time World Player of the Year Marta. Average crowds were only around 4,000 and the final, in the original Athens, attracted only 10,416.

Two Olympics gold medals, two World Cup wins and 192 caps is a fantastic haul for a player who had no female soccer role models as a kid and Chastain has no regrets that she is remembered most for a celebration: 'Women's soccer was not anonymous anymore: people were talking about it.'

37

Eric Cantona

NINETY NINETY-TWO changed football for good. Firstly, there was a new back-pass law. Denmark gave the old one a fine send off, frequently passing the ball to keeper Peter Schmeichel to pick up, smothering the life out of opponents and counter-attacking just enough to become 1992 European Champions. Howard Wilkinson, whose Leeds side won the last season of the old Football League in 1991/92, believed the new law would encourage long-ball football. Wimbledon certainly loved it, as defenders and keepers panicked when they got the ball at their feet, but future generations became more technical and the game became faster and more skilful.

Ninety ninety-two also saw the launch of the UEFA Champions League and the FA Premier League, as football belatedly recognised its worth as a TV product. One outspoken socialist condemned the new arrangement in England and the rights deal with satellite channel BSkyB as a 'piece of nonsense' that 'sells supporters down the river and hits hardest at the most vulnerable part of society, the old people'. Still, we all make compromises and Alex Ferguson became the most significant figure in the Premier League's development, getting rich along the way.

ERIC CANTONA

The year 1992 also saw Eric Cantona's debut in English football, although he had already made his mark in France. He had played for six clubs, starting at Auxerre when he and his friends bought old cars and smashed them up, dodgem-style, around a rubbish tip. After his National Service, he was loaned to Ligue 2 side Martigues to stop him from driving the length of the country in pursuit of his future wife Isabelle. His references to poets, painters and philosophers brought him media attention he would later revile. Trouble followed him. He was accused of spitting in the face of an official during a youth tournament in Leningrad. On a pre-season tour in Poland he had to be restrained from going into the crowd to confront an egg-thrower. He punched team-mate Bruno Martini during a dressing-room row and shocked TV viewers with an extraordinary flying kick at Nantes's Michel Der Zakarian in a French Cup match.

In his 2009 biography of Cantona, Philippe Auclair wrote, 'He revelled in thinking of himself as a victim, as if it brought him proof that he too, like the "geniuses" he admired was doomed to be misunderstood and vilified.' Cantona told *France Football* magazine: 'I need to have crazy reactions to be happy – and even to be good on the pitch. You must have strength to be crazy.'

Marseilles's controversial club president Bernard Tapie agreed with Cantona's self-diagnosis after he signed for his home-town club for a French-record fee in 1988. After being substituted in a charity match, Cantona took off his shirt and threw it at coach Gerard Gili. Tapie declared, 'If we need to, we'll put him in a psychiatric hospital.'

Mutual contempt between player and president was undisguised, as Cantona railed against corruption in French football. In his eyes, the club's successes were worthless. Marseilles players were ordered to have injections, which the club insisted were vitamins, but they doubted. Cantona was loaned to Bordeaux where team-mate Clive Allen described him as 'the conductor of our orchestra'. Next stop was Montpellier, where he faced the sack after another fight with a team-mate but was saved by Laurent Blanc and Carlos Valderrama's intervention. Then it was back to Marseilles, where he won the French title for the second time in 1991 before his French league career ended at Nimes. He threw the ball at a referee and when summoned to face the federation's disciplinary panel he walked up to each member one by one and called him an idiot. He was given a two-month ban and in late 1991 he announced his retirement, aged 25.

But Michel Platini and his assistant Gerard Houllier saw Cantona as vital to their Euro 92 plans and helped get him to England, initially to Sheffield Wednesday on trial. His only appearance was in an indoor tournament and, as the South Yorkshire club hesitated, Leeds made a bid. They paid Nimes £100,000 for a loan, with another £900,000 payable if he signed in April.

Wilkinson had got Leeds promoted two years earlier and they were fighting Manchester United for the 1991/92 title. They were physically strong and typically English. Lee Chapman was the target man, backed up by guile and guts in midfield. To the surprise of French observers, Cantona was happy being used largely as a super-sub. Leeds outlasted Ferguson's side and claimed their first championship since Don Revie's days. Cantona had scored only three goals in 15 appearances but became a fans' hero, as the chant 'ooh-aah, Cantona' caught on.

Manchester United's title bid had foundered in a spell of four games in nine days in which they claimed a single point. Ferguson wanted to break the British transfer record for Alan Shearer but lost out to Kenny Dalglish's nouveau riche Blackburn Rovers. He made a series of offers for Wednesday's David Hirst, who was rated as highly as Shearer but soon suffered his first serious injury. Ferguson instead paid £1m to get Dion Dublin from Cambridge United, who had risen from Fourth Division to Second with aggressive long-ball football.

Cantona wasn't happy with a cameo role for long and his relationship with the gruff Yorkshireman Wilkinson deteriorated as the champions struggled. The unfortunate Dublin broke his leg after six games for Manchester United and a chance conversation led to one of the most famous transfers in English football. Leeds chairman Bill Fotherby rang Manchester United's Martin Edwards to ask about Irish full-back Denis Irwin's availability but ended up agreeing to sell the unsettled Cantona for just £1.2m. When Ferguson's assistant Brian Kidd heard the price he asked, 'Has he lost a leg, or something?'

Ferguson got more out of his turbulent star than anyone else had. He gave him a pivotal role and the Frenchman helped transform not only Manchester United but English football. The English were initially more forgiving of Cantona than his countrymen, perhaps because he fitted our view of the stereotypical brooding Frenchman. He was big and strong enough for the English game and was happy to see the ball moved from back to front quickly. In time, though, the value of his intelligent movement, and his ability to drop into midfield, gave United an added dimension. Within a few years the likes of Dennis Bergkamp and Gianfranco Zola were doing similar jobs. His old Leeds colleague Gary Speed told Auclair, 'Maybe we weren't good enough to accommodate him and Manchester United were.' Cantona also positively influenced his new teammates, making it acceptable to work hard. As Gary Neville said, 'There was a vast unspoken respect. We were desperate to impress him.'

There was no collapse this time and Manchester United were champions for the first time in 26 years, since the days of Charlton, Law and Best, and the first Premier League winners. Cantona had won league titles with Marseilles, Leeds and Manchester United in three consecutive seasons – making only 55 appearances.

He revelled in an excellent, aggressive United side that won the double in 1993/94. Cantona was sent off in successive matches against Swindon and Arsenal, and when United lost in the Champions League to Galatasaray he was red-carded and then assaulted by a policeman. Two penalties in the FA Cup Final took him to 25 goals for the season, making him United's top scorer.

Houllier's part in resurrecting Cantona's career didn't bear fruit for France. They needed a single point from two home games against Israel and Bulgaria to qualify for the 1994 World Cup but contrived to fail. They were seconds away from the draw they needed in their final game against Bulgaria when an errant free kick from David Ginola led to a break and goal from Emil Kostadinov. Houllier accused Ginola of 'firing an Exocet missile through French football'. The underrated Bulgarians subsequently reached the World Cup semi-finals, knocking out Germany on the way.

The season 1994/95 was the only one of Cantona's career in England in which he failed to win the league, largely because he missed half of it after an extraordinary incident at Selhurst Park in January. Having been sent off for a retaliatory kick at Crystal Palace's Richard Shaw, Cantona noticed Palace fan Matthew Simmons shouting abuse and launched himself, kung-fu-style, over the advertising hoardings. The shocked expressions of the nearby Palace fans were plastered over the news worldwide. Cantona was quickly banned by United, only for the FA to add to the duration and the fine. He was initially sentenced to prison but a judge over-ruled and gave him community service coaching kids. At a packed press conference Cantona delivered his famous not-so-cryptic analysis of the relationship between celebrities and the media: 'When the seagulls follow the trawler, it's because they think sardines will be thrown into the sea.'

The legacy of the affair is perhaps two-fold: firstly, Manchester United threw a protective ring around Cantona, which became the template for how players are hermetically sealed from the media today. More positive was the reaction to Simmons's apparent use of racist language, which was challenged rather than dismissed as inevitable. Obviously, Cantona was white, a Manchester United player and was contracted to Nike. I cannot recall black players of the day being protected in the same way, but it was progress. Simmons incidentally told *The Sun* he had shouted: 'Off you go, Cantona. It's an early bath for you!' In the 1994/95 title run-in, United drew 0-0 with Leeds, Chelsea and Spurs and finished a point behind Blackburn. The following season's events suggest Cantona would have been the difference.

That summer, Cantona asked United to cancel his contract, prompting Ferguson to fly to Paris for a clandestine meeting at which he persuaded the Frenchman not to quit the game. Cantona eventually returned that October and scored a penalty in a 2-2 draw with Liverpool, but form and fitness took a while to recover. Meanwhile, Kevin Keegan's Newcastle had become the team to beat. They lit up the league with high-tempo, attacking football and became the favourite of many erstwhile neutrals. Ginola, Peter Beardsley, Keith Gillespie and Rob Lee created opportunities for Les Ferdinand, who would be crowned PFA Player of the Year. But the fixture list landed Keegan's side with a run of tough springtime away games. Signing Tino Asprilla upset the balance, although the Colombian did little wrong, and Newcastle began to wilt. Cantona's part was extraordinary. He scored the only goal at St James' Park in March, the first of six consecutive scoring games, five of which United won by a single goal while the other was drawn. The sequence was worth 11 points (and inflicted a defeat on Newcastle).

Keegan's impotent rage boiled over live on Sky Sports. Ferguson had attacked the attitude of Leeds's players who, he claimed, raised their game against his side, effectively 'cheating' their manager. He hinted Leeds would go easy in their next game against Newcastle. After that match, Keegan exploded, jabbing his finger, voice rising and cracking, 'He went down in my estimation when he said that. We've not resorted to that but I'll tell you, you can tell him now if you're watching it, we're still fighting for this title and he's got to go to Middlesbrough and get something and I'll tell you, honestly, I'd love it if we beat them, love it!'

Manchester United went to Middlesbrough and won 3-0. Keegan's 'entertainers' had a final hurrah with a 5-0 thumping of Ferguson's side in October 1996, but Keegan was soon gone, as was Cantona. Manchester United finished seven points clear but defeat in the Champions League against eventual winners Borussia Dortmund prompted him to quit, just short of his 31st birthday. It was a shock to most observers, but this time there was no changing his mind.

His international career remained unfulfilled. Aimé Jacquet didn't have Ferguson's powers of persuasion and failed to talk Cantona into returning for France's Euro 96 campaign and he never won another cap. Auclair suspected he came to regret his decision, which might have hastened his eventual retirement.

Cantona was 32 when France won the World Cup in Paris in 1998. Would they have won it with him? We will never know. He attained legendary status in England but not on the European or international stage. English football was still behind the best of the rest; Cantona's gift to the country was the part he played in bridging that gap.

38

Jean-Marc Bosman

JIMMY HILL lit the fire under footballers' wages, the launch of pay-TV fanned the flames but Jean-Marc Bosman's victory at the European Court of Justice in 1995 poured on the rocket fuel.

Bosman only wanted to earn a decent living playing in the French second division. After two years with RFC Liège in his native Belgium, his contract expired in 1990 and he wanted to leave. No club would pay the fee demanded for an unremarkable midfielder and he negotiated his own move to Dunkerque, only for Liège to insist the whole fee be paid up front. Belgian rules meant the club could keep him and even reduce his wages by 75 per cent, to around £500 a month. Understandably, Bosman took legal action and was advised it could be resolved in weeks. He was granted a free transfer by the Belgian court but struggled to find a club. He believed he was victimised for taking on the football establishment. He played only 14 further competitive matches, despite leaving Liège in his mid-20s.

In December 1995 the ECJ delivered the verdict that shook football. The judges ruled that EU free movement of labour laws meant out-of-contract players should not be subject to a fee. Players would be able to let their contract run down and command huge signing-on fees and wages from other clubs. Money currently set aside for fees could be given straight to players. The implications were obvious: a switch of power from clubs to players and, by extension, agents. As Alex Ferguson put it, 'All hell broke loose.'

In 1994 Chris Sutton had signed for Blackburn on £10,000 a week; seven years later Sol Campbell walked out of Tottenham and joined Arsenal on £100,000 a week. Compared with other sportsmen, footballers had been relatively underpaid: Michael Jordan and Mike Tyson made over $40m in 1995. Okay, those two are all-time greats, but Riddick Bowe, a boxer who didn't like to box, made over $20m that year and stars of American team sports were earning many times more than leading footballers.

As well as freedom of contract, globalisation of the transfer market set the course that eventually saw Messi and Ronaldo become the world's highest-paid athletes. The Bosman Ruling also made the various quotas on foreign player numbers illegal. This was a seismic change and the Premier League, fuelled by Sky TV customers' money, moved farthest and fastest. In the first week of the relaunched league in 1992, only 11 non-British or Irish players started games. By 1999 Chelsea had fielded the first wholly non-British starting line-up. Foreign players routinely outnumber Englishmen (147 to 102 in the latest round of games at the time of writing) and other British and Irish players have also been marginalised (22 last time out). In turn, the global nature of the Premier League contributed to its popularity, helping to sell international TV rights. Wages spiralled upwards: in 1995 clubs spent an average of 43 per cent of their money on wages; that peaked at nearly 70 per cent before UEFA's Financial Fair Play finally put the brakes on.

With touching naivety, Bosman thought he had struck a blow for the little guy, but the richest clubs and leagues were best placed to take advantage of the new freedoms. Ajax won the 1995 Champions League (nine Dutch against Milan's nine Italians) but became the first big losers when Edgar Davids moved to the San Siro for free. On the Ajax bench against Milan was Winston Bogarde, who became the poster boy of idle, rich footballers, spending four years at Chelsea on around £40,000 a week, making just nine league appearances. Bosman himself did receive a settlement, which paid for a Porsche and a house – but they were soon gone and he was left living on benefits.

Agents loved it. Before the ruling they were seen as chancers with big cigars but that generation gave way to slick professional operators and later to global organisations, still led by characters whose chief qualities include ruthlessness. Former DJ Jorge Mendes set up his Gestifute sports agency in 1996 and in 2019 made $118m in commission, with active contracts worth over a billion (according to Forbes.com). The money flows efficiently from fans via TV or turnstiles to clubs, then to agents and players (some of whom give generously to good causes). Owners of big clubs get richer, although sometimes there is a political agenda at play, such as bringing international legitimacy to autocratic states.

The name Bosman soon outgrew the man. Michael Ballack, Robert Lewandowski and Aaron Ramsey have all moved on 'Bosmans', picking up huge wages after letting contracts run down. Agents now typically start renegotiating their clients' contracts in the second year of four, or the third year of five. It is a different story at lower levels where players are often on year-to-year deals, playing for clubs with precarious financial futures. The situation for smaller clubs is set to become more hazardous in the aftermath of the Covid-19 lockdown.

Bosman told *Gazzetta dello Sport*, 'The Bosman Ruling was born to redistribute wealth to everyone, especially the poorest players, but now the gain is in the hands of the few. The decision of the ECJ was right. It is a positive law but now it has been distorted.'

Would this all have happened without Bosman? Probably. The football governing bodies argued that the game was a special case and should be exempt from EU law, but that would surely have been tested at some point, given that the EU demanded markets be as free as possible. The growth of pay-TV was equally as important: without subscribers' money, Messi wouldn't have got a million a week, regardless of his freedom of movement.

Bosman was treated appallingly but his case ran away from him. He believes the distortion of the ruling has made football less healthy. Is he right? The foreign influx certainly changed English football, with obvious benefits when you think of players like Henry, Zola and Cristiano Ronaldo, and managers like Wenger, Guardiola and Klopp. But for every Bergkamp there is a Brolin, for every de Bruyne there's a Djemba-Djemba. The likes of Sergio Agüero, Luis Suárez, Didier Drogba and Mohamed Salah are from outside the EU and had to get work permits anyway. The glut of TV cash, and the ability to spend it anywhere, created a transfer market Wild West with vast sums sprayed carelessly around the world. More common than signing rank-bad players was recruiting good ones who were moved on without being given a proper chance.

Tactics are now more homogenised: games played in England, Spain and Italy don't look radically different, unlike 30 years ago, although TV has influenced that as much as free movement. Big clubs are bigger. In the 25 years since the ruling, the only team from outside the big four leagues to become European champions were Jose Mourinho's Porto in 2004. Last season, former European champions Red Star Belgrade and Celtic entered the Champions League at the first qualifying round, which kicked off on 9 July, two months and eight games earlier than clubs from the bigger leagues joined in, at the lucrative group stage. Too many European leagues are dominated by too few clubs, which soon becomes boring.

JEAN-MARC BOSMAN

None of that was in the Bosman Ruling; it was mainly the result of clubs threatening to form a European Super League. I know of nobody who truly wants that, but UEFA daren't risk it. Jean-Marc Bosman supplied the dynamite for the EU to blow up the transfer system and the big clubs have rebuilt the game to suit themselves. On the upside: the best football ever played is in the Champions League latter stages, by clubs that have gathered together a global elite of players.

39

George Weah

NOBODY ELSE has made George Weah's journey from capital city slums to the Ballon d'Or and on to the presidential palace. Liberia's greatest footballer was born in Monrovia in 1966, one of 13 children. After his parents separated he was brought up by a grandmother and dropped out of school early. He won the Liberian league with two clubs before moving to Cameroon to play for Tonnerre Yaoundé, still as a semi-pro, aged 21. Claude Le Roy's side won the league before the Frenchman recommended Weah to Arsène Wenger, who paid around £50,000 to take him to Monaco in 1988.

Weah held Wenger in such high regard that when he won the Ballon d'Or in 1995 he gave the trophy to his old boss, later saying, 'He was a father figure to me. This was a man who, when racism was at its peak, showed me love.'

Ghana's Abedi Pele, father of André and Jordan Ayew, was another trailblazing African football superstar. His attitude reveals the forbearance expected of African players in France in the 1980s and 90s: 'Sometimes you would train and your own colleagues would tell you "go home to your country" and sometimes they spat on you,' he told the Discovery Channel. 'You go through a lot of hard situations but that makes you stronger, and when you continue making them win you get a place in their hearts and they even think of making you captain, so you can see the tremendous changes.' It was clearly an experience shared by Weah.

Weah's stoicism deserted him before a Champions League game in 1996 when he headbutted Porto's Jorge Costa who, he claimed, was racially abusing him. Costa denied it and nobody backed up Weah's story, so the Liberian got a long ban. He apologised publicly and was awarded that year's FIFA Fair Play award. Weah is often named as the inspiration for the next generation of black African stars, and is the main reason Didier Drogba and Samuel Eto'o are regularly forced to deny any presidential ambitions.

Weah was part of a new breed of all-round strikers capable of tactical flexibility as coaches sought to load their midfields. He scored 66 goals in four seasons with Monaco, who won the French Cup in 1991. Thierry Henry joined Monaco's youth set-up as the Liberian was moving to Paris St Germain. He credits Weah, Romario and Ronaldo with reinventing centre-forward play: 'They were the first to drop from the box to pick up the ball in midfield, switch to the flanks, attract and disorientate the central defenders with their runs, their acceleration and their dribbling.'

Weah's most famous goals involved him running from deep; his best was against Verona in 1996, when he collected the ball in his own box and dribbled the length of the pitch. Almost as spectacular was an effort against Bayern Munich; he finished top scorer in the 1994/95 Champions League, as PSG reached the semis. PSG only formed in 1970 and the 1994 Championship was one of only two in the club's first four decades. PSG's crack at Europe that year was ended by AC Milan, but Fabio Capello saw enough of Weah to want him at the San Siro, along with other recruits Roberto Baggio and Paulo Futre. From finishing 13 points behind Juventus in 1994/95, Milan won the *scudetto* by eight points, with Weah top scorer. That was the last year of Capello's first spell before he was tempted to Real Madrid, where he won La Liga but was seen as too defensive and sent packing. Weah won his second Serie A title in 1999 in Alberto Zaccheroni's attack-minded Milan set-up, before he left to join Chelsea on loan.

Weah wanted to stay in Italy or join Wenger at Arsenal, but Milan loaned him to Chelsea, who were managed by Gianluca Vialli. Weah arrived in England on a January morning in 2000 and that evening came off the bench to head the only goal of a Premiership game against Tottenham. He scored five goals as Chelsea finished fifth and played in the FA Cup Final victory over Aston Villa, missing a great chance early in the game.

That summer he joined Manchester City, who had been promoted in successive seasons under Joe Royle. Having been a great player in France and Italy, Weah unfortunately became an example of post-Bosman English profligacy. He signed a two-year deal on £30,000 a week a couple of months short of his 34th birthday. He and Costa Rica's Paulo Wanchope were added to a squad of hard-working but limited players. A 4-0 opening-day hammering by Charlton set the tone. Weah scored one Premiership goal against Liverpool and three against Gillingham in the League Cup. He was paid off by the end of September, leaving a withering assessment: 'I felt like I was being used for publicity to attract other players. My reasons for leaving were the lack of respect, the lack of communication and the dishonesty shown to me by Joe Royle.'

City were relegated and Royle was replaced by Kevin Keegan, who got them back up at the first attempt, bringing much-needed stability to the club. Weah went to Marseilles and later to Al Jazira in Abu Dhabi, prolonging his club career as Liberia had their best-ever attempt to qualify for the 2002 World Cup. They reached the final stage where they finished a point behind Nigeria. Defeat to Ghana in their last home game proved decisive. Despite going closer than any other Liberian side, fans attacked the team coach and the country's brutal ruler Charles Taylor threatened to disband the team.

Weah was more than just an inspirational player. With Liberian society in chaos, he paid for flights and hotels and organised the national squad. He even funded his team-mates if they got trials with European teams. The Nations' Cups of 1996 and 2002 are the only other ones Liberia have ever qualified for. No player has ever carried a whole country's football like Weah.

The Ballon d'Or had been for Europeans only until 1995 (Eusébio was counted as Portuguese). Weah won it immediately and not through positive discrimination – the next non-European was Gabriel Batistuta in 20th place. No other African has appeared in the top three; Sadio Mane and Mohamed Salah were fourth and fifth in 2019.

It felt like African football was a coming force when Weah was in his pomp. Cameroon had sparkled at the 1990 World Cup and excellent Nigerian sides reached the second round in 1994 and 1998. There were back-to-back African Olympic champions Nigeria in 1996 and Cameroon in 2000. Senegal reached the 2002 World Cup quarter-finals.

Unfortunately the story of African football is one of rise and stall. You can list brilliant individuals and European clubs scour the continent for talent, which is part of the problem as agents, often unscrupulous, move young players to Europe. FIFA has funded football projects with varying success but that failed to turn the tide as European football grew richer, stronger and better organised. At Russia 2018 no African team made it out of the groups. Okay, basing judgments on a short tournament is flawed, but the Africa Cup of Nations has been disappointing in recent years. The 2019 tournament, played in the Egyptian summer, which pleased European clubs, attracted pitiful crowds except for the hosts, and the football reached new lows of negativity with 1.96 goals per game.

When Weah won the Ballon d'Or in 1995, there were 717 million people in Africa; now there are 1.3 billion and projections estimate there will be another billion by 2050, with most of the growth in sprawling cities. It is a huge opportunity for football but it is hard to plot a way through the potential pitfalls.

Solving Liberia's seemingly intractable generational problems is President George Weah's job now. He inherited an economy weakened by years of civil conflict, the Ebola crisis, an over-reliance on selling commodities and a culture of secrecy and corruption. His fame from the football field and his personal generosity towards his country won him votes and will buy him time, but the harsh reality of international politics and global markets will show him no sentiment.

40
Cafu

ON THE day that Gordon Banks made his famous save from Pelé, Marcos Evangelista de Morais was born in Sao Paulo's Jardim Irene favela. Three weeks later, Brazil's captain and right-back Carlos Alberto lashed in the signature goal of the 1970 World Cup. Marcos and his generation grew up hearing all about it, as he set about breaking records and redefining the full-back position.

He adopted his nickname in honour of Botafogo right-winger Cafuringa and, like lots of Brazilian footballers, became a youth futsal player before joining Sao Paulo and breaking into the first team under Telê Santana, coach of Brazil's fantasia sides of the 1982 and 1986 World Cups. Sao Paulo were South American champions in 1992 and 1993 and de facto world club champions after beating Cruyff's Barcelona and Capello's Milan in back-to-back seasons. Between the two Intercontinental Cup victories, Santana converted Cafu from a proficient right-winger into a world-beating right-back.

Despite the success of Santana's expansive Sao Paulo, the Brazil national team went the other way under Carlos Alberto Parreira (not the 1970 skipper) who had led Kuwait and UAE to World Cups. After 24 years of hurt, the pressure to win the 1994 World Cup was ear-splitting and Parreira made his philosophy clear: 'Magic and dreams are finished in football.'

He still picked Romario, the *Pichichi* winner in La Liga and an explosive player – for good and for bad – and the Barcelona striker scored in all three group games. But Parreira came to see playmaker and skipper Rai as a luxury too far and promoted the industrious Dunga for the second-round match with hosts USA. Despite having left-back Leonardo sent off for a bloodcurdling elbow on Tab Ramos, a Bebeto goal sent Brazil through. Cafu was still a bit part, used from the bench, with Bayern Munich's Jorginho first-choice right-back. They beat the Netherlands in the quarter-final, prompting Bebeto's iconic baby-cradling celebration. A Romario goal saw them scrape past Sweden in the semi-final.

The final, against Arrigo Sacchi's Italy, was a disappointment to the neutral. It kicked off at 12.30pm and the temperature in Pasadena, California, was 38°C (100°F). Chances were few and far between and it finished goalless – although it worked out for Cafu who played over 100 minutes after an early injury to Jorginho. Roberto Baggio had been Italy's outstanding player as they stumbled through the tournament but, cruelly, his was the decisive penalty miss, skied high over the bar.

But the 1994 World Cup was an improvement on its predecessor. The Americans turned up to watch despite the *New York Times*' cynical take: 'Our country has been hired as a giant stadium, hotel and TV studio.' FIFA ordered a clampdown on dangerous tackling but inconsistent refereeing was a problem, as was the stifling heat. Brazil scored only 11 goals in seven games.

The tournament's tragic postscript was the murder of Colombia's Andrés Escobar, who had scored an own goal in the game against the USA that saw them eliminated. His killer was the bodyguard of a drug lord who had apparently lost money gambling on the much-hyped national team; 120,000 people attended Escobar's funeral.

CAFU

Cafu had a brief spell with Real Zaragoza where he got a Cup Winners' Cup winner's medal in 1995, despite missing the final against Arsenal through injury. The game was decided by Nayim's 50-yard lob over David Seaman in the 120th minute.

By 1997 Brazil had their famous full-back duo Cafu and Roberto Carlos in tandem. The Real Madrid left-back caught the world's attention with his amazing swerving free kick past Fabien Barthez in Le Tournoi de France, a four-team tournament won by Glenn Hoddle's England. Brazil went from there to the Copa America in Bolivia and won it in style, helping to make them the most hyped football team ever ahead of the 1998 World Cup. Nike produced a memorable TV commercial in a time of less sensitivity about airport security in which, after 90 seconds of tricks, there was a self-effacing denouement with Ronaldo messing up; how prophetic.

Mario Zagallo was back in charge, having won two World Cups as a player, one as coach, and serving as an assistant in 1994. They started by beating Scotland 2-1. Cafu forced the winner when his shot was pushed out by Jim Leighton into the unfortunate Tom Boyd. It would have been impossible to satisfy the astronomic expectations of the side containing Ronaldo, Rivaldo, Bebeto and Denilson (who had just, implausibly, broken the world transfer record joining Real Betis) but Brazil played some attractive football, keeping their worldwide fanbase, FIFA and Nike happy. A 66-year-old Zagallo was accused of indecision by the Brazilian press as he sought ways of protecting his defence while picking his talented stars. Norway beat them in the last group game and coach Egil Olsen damned the reigning champions as being 'as organised as garbage'.

We will return to the final later: Ronaldo's collapse and Zinedine Zidane's goal decided it. We will never know what would have happened had Brazil's best player been fit or replaced. We do know that the final was played between the teams with the best full-backs, although, ironically, the least attacking of the lot, Lilian Thuram, made the biggest mark going forward by scoring the only two goals of his 142-cap France career in a 2-1 semi-final win over Croatia.

Brazilian full-backs had long been ahead of their time. In the 1950s they were early adopters of the backfour but made sure their 'laterals' Nilton Santos and Djalma Santos got forward. In 1982 that came at the expense of the defence, but the 1990s version aimed for more balance with the likes of Dunga and Cesar Sampaio providing midfield cover, while Cafu and Roberto Carlos attacked together. Of the two, I preferred Cafu, who was less prone to ending promising attacks with wild shots.

There had been attacking full-backs before, but Cafu and Roberto Carlos's fitness allowed them to cover the whole flank and that became the benchmark for top clubs. The ultra-cautious, purely defensive full-back still exists but rarely at the top level. See how Liverpool use Trent Alexander-Arnold and Andy Robertson, acting as playmakers, allowing midfielders and attackers to operate inside. Cafu is a particular fan of Alexander-Arnold, insisting the young Englishman is a candidate for the Ballon d'Or: 'I can see a lot of similarities between him and me. I would say he's got a Brazilian instinct in the way he plays. We have to change this paradigm that the Ballon d'Or is only won by attackers.'

Cafu became part of Roma's title-winning side in 2000/01, although Capello couldn't bring himself to employ the Brazilian in a back four. Using him as a wing-back with a back three and holding midfielders was largely designed to get the best out of the brilliant Francesco Totti and Argentina's Gabriel Batistuta, who had cost more than £30m at the age of 31. The resourceful Cafu thrived.

The 2002 World Cup brought redemption for Brazil. Filipe Scolari used Cafu, now the captain, similarly to Capello. This time the formation released the joyous combination of Ronaldinho, Rivaldo and Ronaldo and a tournament of shocks was eventually won by the best team. They won every group game and beat Belgium before Ronaldinho's free kick against England gave Seaman flashbacks to Nayim's lob from seven years earlier. Turkey gave Brazil their biggest scare in the semi-final before Ronaldo slayed some demons and pricked Oliver Kahn's ego against Germany in the final. A beaming Cafu, with '100% Jardim Irene' scrawled on his shirt, tottered precariously on a podium, World Cup aloft.

He was far from done. The man the Italians had dubbed *'Il Pendolino'* (an express train) signed for Milan aged 33 and played five seasons at the San Siro. Carlo Ancelotti's side were arguably the best in Europe but won Serie A only once in Cafu's five seasons, and were on the wrong end of arguably the greatest-ever comeback.

Of the 14 players used by Milan in the 2005 Champions League Final against Liverpool in Istanbul, nine had won it two years earlier against Juventus. The others were Cafu, the World Cup-winning skipper; Jon Dahl Tomasson, who had a winners' medal but didn't play against Juve; Jaap Stam, who had won it with Manchester United; Kaka, whose skilful running from midfield tore Liverpool to shreds in the first half; and Hernan Crespo, who scored the second and third goals before half-time. It seemed utterly unfeasible that a team with 150 trophies between them would buckle, but in an amazing spell between the 54th and 60th minute they did just that.

First Steven Gerrard headed in, then Vladimir Smicer made it 3-2 and, after Gerrard had been fouled, Xabi Alonso scored on the rebound after Dida saved his penalty; 2004 Ballon d'Or winner Andriy Shevchenko had the best chance of extra time for Milan but was denied wonderfully by Jerzy Dudek. Liverpool's Polish keeper was the hero of the eventual shoot-out, dancing on his line as Bruce Grobbelaar had 21 years earlier. Serginho missed, Andrea Pirlo and Shevchenko were denied by Dudek, and Liverpool were European champions, despite having finished fifth in the Premier League, 37 points behind champions Chelsea.

Cafu played his fourth World Cup in 2006, part of a back four again and still sprinting up and down the right flank, until France again knocked out Brazil – this time in the quarters.

The 2007 Champions League Final was a repeat of two years previously: two clubs expert in Europe but miles off winning their domestic leagues. Liverpool had finished 21 points behind Manchester United. Milan were 36 points behind Inter and positively ancient. Pippo Inzaghi, who missed the Istanbul final through injury, scored twice and Dirk Kuyt's header didn't spark anything dramatic. Paolo Maldini lifted the trophy a month short of his 39th birthday.

The Cafu express finally ran out of steam in 2008, a month before his 38th birthday. He is the only player to have appeared in three consecutive World Cup finals, winning two and setting the standards for future generations of full-backs.

41
Zinedine Zidane

THERE WAS a time when it was hoped Zinedine Zidane's legacy might be heralding an era of racial harmony in French football and society, but he didn't want to be that sort of hero. Instead he will be remembered for his football. He dominated two World Cup finals, for better or for worse. He scored the most famous goal in any Champions League Final and was the player of the tournament when France became European Champions.

Marcello Lippi, who coached him to two Serie A titles and benefitted from his extraordinary dismissal in the 2006 World Cup Final, believed Zidane was peerless in his generation. 'He's the greatest player of the next 20 years. The previous 20 was Maradona and the next 20 is Zidane. I'm convinced of that.'

Lippi hadn't foreseen the emergence of Lionel Messi and Cristiano Ronaldo with their superhuman consistency. Zidane won everything – but not repeatedly. He was a football genius but needed clever management to draw out his best form. He was hailed as a shining example of racial and religious harmony, but he left that to others. In common with many geniuses, he had a self-destructive trait – in his case a temper that would flare from seemingly nowhere and threaten everything.

Zidane was 13 years old and still known to friends and family as Yazid when he first headbutted an opponent. There were similar incidents before he made his First Division debut for Cannes in 1989, aged 16. He was the son of Algerian immigrants and grew up in the run-down La Castellane district of Marseilles. One Cannes director objected to 'putting an Arab in the team'.

When Cannes wanted to cash in on their French youth international, Newcastle, Blackburn and Monaco were asked to bid but instead allowed Bordeaux to snap up a bargain. He was sent off for the first time as a professional for punching Marseilles's Marcel Desailly, and was later suspended for the first leg of Bordeaux's UEFA Cup Final against Franz Beckenbauer's Bayern Munich – which should have been the pinnacle of his club career in France.

Zidane was red-carded 13 times but was generally regarded as diligent and respectful, if shy and wary of the media. A coach's main challenge was whether to build a side around him. Aimé Jacquet tried at Euro 96 but that might have felt like a mistake when he was far from outstanding, although he was still recovering from the effects of a car crash. They drew their quarter and semi-finals 0-0, going out on penalties to a Czech Republic side, inspired by Pavel Nedvěd.

Zidane joined Juventus that summer and his first challenge was matching the physical standard of Marcello Lippi's European Champions. Zidane had thalassemia – a mild blood disorder – while Juve were subject to a whirl of allegations from opponents. Zdenek Zeman, who coached both Lazio and Roma, said Italian football 'had to come out of the pharmacy'. More than one of the Ajax team, losing finalists in the 1996 Champions League Final, said the Juve players' ability to run for 120 minutes was unnatural. A police raid found 281 different substances at Juve's training ground that resembled 'a small hospital'. Proving illegality was difficult and the only person sentenced to prison, club doctor Riccardo Agricola, was cleared on appeal. Zidane admitted taking supplements as recommended by Juve's medical staff in what he described as a 'relationship built on trust'.

Juve won the Italian title in Zidane's first season but the Champions League Final was lost to Borussia Dortmund, who used Paul Lambert to man-mark the Frenchman. The 1997/98 season brought the same half-wanted double: Serie A won amid corruption allegations and defeat in the Champions League Final, this time to Real Madrid, who reclaimed their European crown after a 32-year gap. This was pre-Galacticos, but Madrid had Raúl, Redondo, Seedorf and goalscorer Predrag Mijatović.

Going into the 1998 World Cup, Zidane's status was high but French morale was low, with Jacquet's negativity the butt of criticism. A 3-0 victory over South Africa lifted spirits and they were coasting 2-0 up against ten-man Saudi Arabia when Zidane was sent off for what looked like an utterly pointless stamp on Saudi skipper Fuad Anwar.

Without their best player, France beat Denmark to top the group and then Paraguay, thanks to a 'golden goal' from centre-back Laurent Blanc in the 114th minute. Zidane was back for the quarter-final against Italy, which was settled by Luigi Di Biagio's shot against the bar in the shoot-out. Jacquet persisted with Stephane Guivarc'h – who was soon to become a Newcastle flop – as his first-choice striker, reluctant to trust youngsters Thierry Henry and David Trezeguet. He was grateful that Lilian Thuram became an unlikely goalscoring hero in the semi-final against Croatia.

The final was France's most comprehensive performance, helped by Brazil's implosion after Ronaldo played, despite suffering a fit in the afternoon. Zidane delivered on the biggest stage, although not as expected. He was 185cm (6ft 1in) but not regarded as an obvious aerial threat. He out-jumped Leonardo to head the first and just before half-time he benefitted from Dunga's slip to head a second. Emmanuel Petit, who had scored just twice for Arsenal in their double-winning season, got the third. France were World Champions for the first time. Zidane won the Ballon d'Or and the FIFA World Player of the Year, which, irritatingly, had been launched as a rival award.

He was also hailed as a model of French integration when he was spotted with tears in his eyes singing 'La Marseillaise' and 'Merci Zizou', which was projected onto the Arc de Triomphe. The squad had players born outside of the country such as Patrick Vieira (Senegal) and Desailly (Ghana), the sons of immigrant families (such as Henry, Djorkaeff and Trezeguet) and others from French overseas territories (Thuram, Karembeu). Fans singing of 'Black, Blanc, Beur' (black, white, Arab) was taken as evidence of harmony but not everyone celebrated the diverse nature of the squad: far-right political leader Jean Marie Le Pen said it made France's victory 'artificial'.

Zidane, who has described himself as a non-practising Muslim, has never had much to say on anything perceived as political. Thuram was more forthcoming, arguing that a country is hypocritical if it celebrates people from diverse backgrounds only if they are famous footballers: 'The French team was composed of players of different colours and different religions; can we also accept this is our society outside of sports?'

In rich countries, football – the ultimate meritocracy – has integrated people from immigrant communities better than almost any other walk of life, although it is not a magic wand for creating multi-racial harmony, as Le Pen's subsequent rise in polling numbers showed.

The next two seasons were far from magical for Zidane. Juventus finished seventh in 1998/99 and the following season, under Carlo Ancelotti, collapsed in the title race. They were nine points clear in March, and five clear with three games to play, only to be overhauled by Sven-Göran Eriksson's Lazio.

Zidane's redemption came in style as he played the starring role as France became European champions in 2000. New boss Roger Lemerre trusted Henry, Trezeguet and Nicolas

Anelka, while the likes of Vieira, Petit and Didier Deschamps still offered a solid base for Zidane to operate as a number ten or drift to the left. France were more entertaining, although they didn't blow opponents away: a penalty miss by Raúl killed Spain in the quarter-final before a closely fought semi-final against Portugal ended in chaos. Abel Xavier's attempt to con the officials out of giving a penalty for handball sparked a furious reaction from his team-mates, who had fallen for his play-acting: Xavier, Nuno Gomes and Paulo Bento all received massive suspensions. Zidane kept his nerve to hammer in the golden-goal penalty.

All the goals in the final were scored by substitutes: Marco Delvecchio for Italy, after two bad misses by Alessandro Del Piero, Sylvain Wiltord equalised in the 93rd minute and Trezeguet smashed in the golden goal. Silvio Berlusconi – who was in between his first two terms as prime minister – blamed coach Dino Zoff for not having the 'intelligence' to have Zidane man-marked, which shows his influence on France's win.

Juventus finished behind Roma in 2001 and Zidane set his heart on a move to Real Madrid. *Los Blancos* had won the Champions League Final in 2000 and President Lorenzo Sanz called an election, hoping to ride the wave of success. However, building magnate Florentino Pérez beat him with the twin promises of sorting out the club's debts of around €278m and bringing the world's greatest stars to the Bernebéu. He delivered. Madrid City Council would pay €447m for the club's training ground and Pérez exploited the club's popularity to increase revenue. He broke the world record to pay Luis Figo's €62m buy-out clause, symbolically snatching him from Barcelona. They won La Liga, and Figo was awarded the Ballon d'Or in 2000 and FIFA World Player of the year in 2001.

Pérez spent the best part of a year pursuing Zidane before a bid of €77m again broke the world transfer record. Pérez tried to dub his project '*Zidanes y Pavones*' – a melding of expensive superstars and home-grown talent, characterised by Paco

Pavon, a Madrid-born centre-back who made 167 appearances for the club. Everyone else preferred 'Galaticos'.

In La Liga, they finished behind Valencia and Deportivo but stormed through the Champions League, finishing top of both group phases and beating Barça in the semi-final after chipped goals from Zidane and Steve McManaman in the first leg at the Camp Nou.

The final was in Glasgow against Bayer Leverkusen, doomed to be remembered as 'Neverkusen' after surrendering a five-point advantage in the Bundesliga and losing the finals of both the German Cup and Champions League. Zidane's goal was Real's 35th in the competition and one of the greatest-ever volleys. Roberto Carlos hooked the ball towards the edge of the box, where Zidane watched it down onto his left boot, sending it searing into the top corner – a rival to Van Basten's 1988 effort for technique and timing.

That was the peak for the Galaticos. Pérez bought Ronaldo the following year and they won La Liga in 2003 but lost in the Champions League semi-final to Juve, who had reinvested Zidane's transfer fee on Nedvěd, Thuram and Gianluigi Buffon.

As Pérez added Galaticos, the balance of the team was lost, especially after defensive midfielder Claude Makélélé was sold to Chelsea, where he later became the lynchpin of their expensively assembled title-winning squads of 2005/06 and 2006/07. Pérez sacked Vicente Del Bosque and inexplicably replaced him with Manchester United assistant manager Carlos Queiroz, the first of five coaches in Zidane's last three seasons. His last club medal was the Spanish Super Cup of 2003.

The 2002 World Cup was miserable for France. A fatigued Zidane was injured in a warm-up match with co-hosts South Korea and missed the champions' humiliating defeat to Senegal in the opening match – the first and most eye-catching shock in a tournament defined by them. Henry was sent off early in a 0-0 draw with Uruguay and a half-fit Zidane made little difference as the misery was compounded by Denmark.

At Euro 2004 France topped their group after two Zidane goals in added time, a brilliant free kick and a penalty, helped them beat England. But like every other team who faced Greece in the knockout phase they lost, as Otto Rehhagel masterminded one of football's greatest shocks. The Greeks had been 150-1 to win the tournament.

Zidane initially quit international football but changed his mind to join France's faltering qualification campaign for the 2006 Germany World Cup. Before the tournament he announced his retirement from football. Diego Maradona pleaded for him to change his mind: 'We don't love him for the cups he's won but because of how he's played and how he makes us feel,' he said. 'Watching him control the ball with his long body is the most amazing thing.'

Bookings in the first two games meant Zidane needed a 34th birthday present from his team-mates as he watched them play Togo. In the knockout stages he laid low some of his old Galatico mates: Spain's Raúl and Iker Casillas, Brazil's Ronaldo and Roberto Carlos and, in the semi-final, Figo's Portugal. His farewell would be the World Cup Final in Berlin against Italy.

The *Azzurri* played the tournament in the shadow of *calciopoli*, the revelation of deep-rooted, widespread cheating in Italian football, with Juventus's general manager Luciano Moggi, the Moriarty at the centre of a complex conspiracy. A different criminal investigation had led a judge to order Moggi's six mobile phones to be tapped. The cheating unearthed ranged from club officials at Milan, Fiorentina, Lazio and Reggina to referees and their administrators and even TV producers, who made decisions about which replays should be shown. As John Foot wrote in *Calcio*, 'Most Italians were not shocked. The affair simply confirmed their suspicions.'

Italy's Juve players went to the World Cup not knowing what punishment the club would face. The draw was kind and with Lippi in charge Italy were difficult to beat. They defeated Ghana and the Czechs and drew with the USA in the group before beating Australia, with a 95th-minute penalty, and Ukraine. Two goals at the end of extra time beat hosts Germany, who had won lots of admirers under Jurgen Klinsmann.

In the final, Argentine referee Horacio Elizondo did Italy no favours by awarding France a soft penalty after Florent Malouda's tumble in the box. Zidane went for the Panenka but over-hit it and was grateful the assistant referee saw it bounce down off the bar and just over the line.

I have just watched the game again and, in truth, Zidane was unimposing: credit to Lippi and to Gennaro Gattuso, who marked him. France struggled against Andrea Pirlo's set pieces and Italy equalised inside 20 minutes with a powerful header from Marco Materazzi, Zidane's co-star.

Fast forward to the second period of extra time when a France attack came to an end and Materazzi took a very light hold of Zidane. The Frenchman made a comment along the lines of waiting until after the game to swap shirts; Materazzi suggested it was said with arrogance and aggression. TV viewers didn't see the flashpoint live because the ball was cleared – the match officials also clearly followed the action. Only when a free kick was given at the other end was the referee's attention drawn to Materazzi on the ground. Quick work from replay operators revealed that Zidane had stepped towards the Italian and headbutted him in the chest, knocking him off his feet. We then witnessed the first – unofficial – use of video refereeing. The minute-and-a-half delay between the incident and the red card is clear-enough evidence for me that officials at pitch-side must have watched a replay or been advised by someone who had. It was, of course, the right decision, but FIFA denied it had been made using TV evidence.

Why did Zidane do it? Materazzi insulted his family, definitely his sister and perhaps his mother, depending on whose account you believe. He said it happened three times and he had to react; Materazzi insists it was a commonplace exchange in football. Zidane seemed strangely calm for a man who had lost his temper. You can see on the replay the players arguing but there was no sign that Zidane was about to do what he did.

The game went to penalties. Trezeguet's shot hit the bar and bounced in front of the line. Fabio Grosso smashed in the decisive spot-kick and Fabio Cannavaro lifted the World Cup for Italy, a day before his club Juventus were demoted. Lippi resigned a few days later. Zidane didn't play again.

He was never comfortable in the spotlight and, by his own admission, wasn't a natural leader, but he became a hugely successful coach, winning the Champions League at the first three attempts with Real Madrid. He left after the 2018 final against Liverpool but was back the following March, and won La Liga in 2020. He is a pragmatic coach who likes to emphasise the need to 'suffer' – such a contrast to Zidane, the beautifully enigmatic footballer. He was more admired as a player but, in terms of winning trophies, he has been more successful as a coach, which probably tells us a lot about how to win at football.

42

Ronaldo

I SHOULDN'T have to write this but I do: Ronaldo was a great player.

If you only remember him post-injury, overweight, with an underactive thyroid, and cruelly dubbed 'Fat Ronaldo' then take a minute to watch some videos of the extraordinary kid at Cruzeiro, PSV Eindhoven and Barcelona.

He could run 100 metres in 10.3 seconds and wasn't much slower with the ball. At 17 he was a non-playing member of Brazil's 1994 World Cup-winning squad and soon, on Romario's advice, he went to PSV Eindhoven and scored 54 goals in 57 games.

Ronaldo's single season at Barcelona coincided with Bobby Robson's year in charge of the team. Despite winning the Cup Winners' Cup and Copa del Rey, the Englishman never won over the Catalan press. He wasn't helped by not learning the language, instead relying on his assistant Jose Mourinho to translate. In England, managers were directly involved in transfers, but at Barcelona Robson could only make requests to the club hierarchy. He persuaded them to break the world record and pay PSV around £13.2m for Ronaldo and was rewarded with a sensational campaign from the Brazilian, who turned 20 en route to 47 goals in 49 games, time and again breaking through the defensive lines and either dribbling or shooting past the keeper. Team-mate Luis Enrique described him as 'the most spectacular player I have ever seen'.

The local press took against his lifestyle and when Inter offered roughly £19.5m he was happy to leave and reclaim the world transfer record from Newcastle's Alan Shearer. After Robson had been 'moved upstairs' for Louis van Gaal's arrival, he spoke to Jimmy Burns about Ronaldo: 'I have nothing but admiration for that player, the fastest thing I've ever seen running with the ball. But how is it possible that having bought the finest, best goalscorer in the world at a cost of $20m we let him go one year later? No one here has the courtesy to sit down and explain it to me.'

Italian defences curbed Ronaldo to the extent that he scored 34 in 47 games in his first season, but were darker forces responsible for Inter's failure to win Serie A in 1997/98? The *calciopoli* evidence related only to the two years when Luciano Moggi's phones were tapped, but rumours had long circulated that Juventus benefitted from more than big-club bias – after all, he had been in post since 1994.

In April 1998 Inter went to Juve a point behind the leaders and were a goal down when Ronaldo was body-checked by Mark Iuliano in the penalty area. Referee Piero Ceccarini waved away the appeals and the home side broke forward. Zidane found Alessandro Del Piero in the other box and when he was knocked over by Taribo West, the referee gave the penalty. All hell broke loose. To be fair to Ceccarini, West's challenge was a foul, and he could have sent off a number of Inter players for their reactions. Del Piero missed the penalty and the rebound was cleared by an Inter player who had been yards inside the box when it was taken. However, the original decision not to award the penalty to Ronaldo still rankles with Inter. Juventus won seven *scudetti* while Moggi was employed and were only stripped of the last two. Ceccarini continues to deny wrongdoing. Ronaldo still maintains he 'suffered a conspiracy' while he was in Italy.

Ronaldo was mesmerising as Inter hammered Lazio in the UEFA Cup Final. He got the third goal after two other fine South Americans Ivan Zamorano and Javier Zanetti had scored. By the time of the 1998 World Cup, Ronaldo had 179 goals in 200 club games across four leagues and another 25 for his country, including five as Brazil won the 1997 Copa America. He was the reigning Ballon d'Or winner and expectation was extraordinary.

His part in the tournament is usually remembered as a personal disaster, but he scored four goals and converted Brazil's first penalty in the semi-final shoot-out with the Netherlands – in a side poorly marshalled by the veteran Mario Zagallo. Johan Cruyff argued it would be bad for football if such a badly organised team became world champions.

The arrival of the team sheets, minus Ronaldo's name, was the first the outside world knew of the drama in the Brazilian camp on the day of the final. We now know that while he was having a post-lunch sleep he started convulsing. His roommate Roberto Carlos called for help and Edmundo and Junior Baiano were the first to arrive and attempted first aid. Ronaldo came round and initially didn't know what had happened. He was taken to hospital for tests and the team management assumed their star striker would miss the game and named Edmundo instead. Zagallo outlined a new game plan. Then after tests on Ronaldo revealed nothing untoward, he went to the stadium and told Zagallo he was available. The players clashed over whether he should play.

Nike were forced to deny rumours that they had pressurised Brazil into picking Ronaldo, and Zagallo insisted the decision was his. The team sheet was amended and Ronaldo took the field to play the worst game of his career. No reason for his fit was ever established. He had been given painkillers but that wasn't unusual for a footballer. Ronaldo needed rest and it is tempting to blame Zagallo, and conclude that he should have been stronger and left his young striker on the bench – but, as Luiz Felipe Scolari found four years later, Ronaldo was usually worth the gamble. But not in 1998 when Brazil lost to France in that final.

Inter's next season was a shambles as they used four coaches and finished eighth with an injury-hit Ronaldo figuring in only 19 league games (still scoring 14). Brazil bounced back to retain the Copa America in 1999, with five goals from Ronaldo, but his fatal flaw was that his desperation to play outweighed his wisdom.

He ignored persistent knee pain and that November suffered his first serious injury, rupturing a patella tendon in a game against Lecce. He attempted a comeback in the 2000 Coppa Italia Final, but after just six minutes as a substitute he collapsed, this time with a completely ruptured knee tendon. His personal physiotherapist, Nilton Petrone, told *FourFourTwo* that Ronaldo's kneecap had moved to the middle of his thigh. He argues that Ronaldo's long and painful recovery advanced medical science because such injuries are no longer necessarily career-ending.

He missed the entire 2000/01 season and played only three full matches for Inter in the following campaign. He only played consistently from April, before Brazil went to the 2002 World Cup. Scolari turned a deaf ear to demands to turn elsewhere for a striker, and how his faith was rewarded!

Ronaldo scored in every game except against England, when Rivaldo and Ronaldinho delivered. I think that Brazil team is underrated. They scored wonderful goals and had enough steel to go all the way. Ronaldo was decisive. He turned up for the semi-final against Turkey with a weird monk's haircut, designed, he said, to take the media's focus off his injuries. Okay, whatever it takes. He scored the only goal, taking Brazil to the final.

In Yokohama, when his team-mates went for an afternoon nap, he persuaded substitute keeper Dida to sit up with him, fearing a repeat of the drama of Paris. The final brought redemption: he scored both goals and, as he put it, 'I could bury all the traumas.'

Real Madrid paid €46m to make him a Galatico and he scored a minute after coming on as a substitute on his debut against Alaves that October. He was applauded by both sets of fans at Old Trafford after scoring a stunning hat-trick to eliminate Manchester United from the Champions League, but he was missing from Real's elimination against Juventus. The 2003 La Liga victory finally gave him a national title but his four and a half seasons at the Bernebéu were light on trophies, despite him scoring over 100 goals.

He was forced out after Fabio Capello was recruited from Juventus post-*calciopoli*. The Italian challenged Ronaldo about his increasing weight – 96kg or 15 stone – and sold him to Milan in January 2007. He got a second La Liga winner's medal after he had gone, when Madrid dramatically beat Barcelona on head-to-head, but he was cup-tied and unavailable for Milan's Champions League revenge against Liverpool.

He supplanted Gerd Müller as the top scorer in World Cup tournament football as he got three goals at Germany 2006, producing a brilliant long-range effort against Japan and enough step-overs to bamboozle the Ghanaian keeper and claim his 15th goal at the finals, out of 62 in 98 appearances for Brazil.

At Milan he discovered he had an underactive thyroid, which slowed his metabolism, and the discipline he had shown when recovering from his knee injury at Inter was also a thing of the past. Another serious knee injury ended his unhappy stay.

He moved back to Brazil, upsetting Flamengo fans by rejecting the club he supported as a kid for Corinthians. He got heavier, partly because he feared the drugs normally used to treat hypothyroidism would fall foul of testing. He still produced flashes of brilliance and scored 35 goals in 69 games, winning the Brazilian Cup and the Paulista state championship.

RONALDO

He was given the rare honour of an international farewell game, playing 15 minutes of a friendly against Romania. He now owns La Liga club Real Valladolid.

Ronaldo was a better player than George Weah or Marco van Basten. He fought excruciating pain, illness and hurtful ridicule to become a record-breaking, world-beating striker, arguably the best number nine of all time. Ronaldo was one of the greats.

43

David Beckham

THE MANCHESTER United sides from the FA Youth Cup finals of 1992 and 1993 contained, between them, ten players who went on to win 588 international caps and 51 Premier League winners' medals. Ryan Giggs, Paul Scholes, Gary and Phil Neville, Nicky Butt and David Beckham allowed Alex Ferguson to create the second wave of United's domination of the early years of the Premier League. Giggs won 13 championship medals and Scholes 11; but neither is nearly as famous as Beckham, the doyenne of modern superstar footballers.

On his third birthday, Beckham was given a Manchester United kit. His family were part of the club's huge nationwide fanbase and his dad, Ted, was a local league footballer who later coached David's youth team. Beckham was a United mascot and gave Gordon Strachan a tub of hair gel and Alex Ferguson a pen. He was good young: on a Bobby Charlton Soccer School he won a trip to stay and play at Barcelona's La Masia academy, and rejected Spurs to sign for United on his 13th birthday.

The six most prominent of United's kids all played over 30 games in the double-winning season of 1995/96. When they had lost to Aston Villa on the opening day, BBC pundit Alan

Hansen infamously pontificated, 'You can't win anything with kids.' To be fair to the ex-Liverpool skipper, United's output of youth players reverted to normal and that group remained outliers.

Beckham scored eight times that season and took the corner from which Eric Cantona scored the only goal of the 1996 FA Cup Final. On the opening day of the following season, he scored from halfway in a 3-0 win over Wimbledon. He made his England debut under new manager Glenn Hoddle that September. He was well known as a promising young footballer but his fame was about to be amplified.

The Spice Girls were extraordinarily successful in 1996 and 1997: 'Wannabe' was number one around the world and their first six singles were all top of the UK charts. Beckham was introduced to Victoria Adams, aka Posh Spice, by the band's manager Simon Fuller and, after keeping their relationship secret for a while, they were soon in every newspaper and glossy magazine. The media were obsessed by the fusion of football and pop embodied by two beautiful young people.

The 1997/98 season wasn't good for United. Arsenal won the double in Arsène Wenger's first full season with a rock-solid English defence, a French centre-midfield of Vieira and Petit and Dutchmen Dennis Bergkamp and Marc Overmars as top scorers. United missed Roy Keane who injured a cruciate knee ligament in a clash with Leeds's Alfie Haaland. He played on at first – but he was hurt and exacted grim revenge four years later, inflicting a career-threatening injury on the Norwegian.

Beckham played in all of England's 1998 World Cup qualifiers but Hoddle left him out of the first two games in France, accusing him of not being focussed, which the player took as a reference to his relationship with Victoria. After badly mishandling Paul Gascoigne's omission from the squad, Hoddle made Beckham attend the pre-match media conference, despite knowing he was being dropped. He got back in by replacing the injured Paul Ince in a defeat against Romania and kept his place for the decisive group game against Colombia, in which he scored his first international goal, swinging in a sensational 30-yard free kick. Four days later he was public enemy number one.

Michael Owen's wonder goal was one of four in a brilliant first half against Argentina in the second round. Two minutes after the restart, Beckham was fouled by Diego Simeone. He said Simeone pulled his hair while pretending to apologise. Beckham's flick of the leg, while prone, was petulant rather than violent: ITV commentator Brian Moore expected a yellow card but co-commentator Kevin Keegan correctly predicted red. The ten men held out for a 2-2 draw but Ince and David Batty had penalties saved in the shoot-out and England were out.

Beckham discovered fame is a double-edged sword. The anger directed his way was wildly disproportionate to his actions. A media pack formed outside his parents' house, their phones were bugged and Piers Morgan's *Daily Mirror* produced David Beckham dartboards.

Much of the bile directed at Beckham the following season was pantomime stuff, but some of it was genuinely threatening. He responded impressively as United, rejuvenated by the big-money signings of Jaap Stam, Dwight Yorke and Jesper Blomqvist, launched a dramatic bid for the treble.

They went unbeaten in the league after December and knocked Arsenal out of the FA Cup after a classic semi-final replay. Peter Schmeichel saved a Bergkamp penalty before Giggs scored a sensational winning goal for ten-man United, running from his own half, weaving through the Gunners' defence.

In the Champions League that season Beckham got a measure of revenge when United beat Inter in the quarter-final and he swapped shirts with Simeone. Keane's inspirational performance in the semi-final saw off Juve, and United would be able to complete all three legs of the treble inside 11 days. They beat Tottenham to finish a point above Arsenal and brushed aside Newcastle in the FA Cup Final.

Bayern Munich led for 85 minutes of the Champions League Final at the Camp Nou after Mario Basler's free kick beat Peter Schmeichel in his last game for United. The Germans hit the woodwork twice, but United's substitutions were decisive. Teddy Sheringham turned in a mis-hit Giggs shot following Beckham's corner in the first minute of injury time. Two minutes later, Sheringham flicked on another Beckham corner and Ole Gunnar Solskjaer stabbed in the winner. As Ferguson said on TV, 'Football: Bloody Hell!'

United won the next Premiership at a canter after refusing to defend the FA Cup because the FA asked them to play in the first FIFA World Club Championship, which was won by the Brazilians Vasco de Gama.

Hoddle was sacked in 1999 after sharing his outrageous thoughts about reincarnation, karma and people with disabilities with a newspaper. He was replaced by Keegan and England qualified for Euro 2000, courtesy of a play-off against Scotland.

It was a poor tournament for England. Their only victory, against Germany, was marred by hooligans fighting in Charleroi. Keegan's side led against Portugal and Romania but lost both 3-2. Phil Neville was the new fall guy after his clumsy challenge gave away a decisive late penalty against Romania, but the deeper concern was that English players lacked the technical ability to succeed in major competitions. Keegan left after 18 months in charge, quitting immediately after a defeat to Germany in a World Cup qualifier that autumn, the last game at the old Wembley.

After the Portugal defeat, a photo appeared of Beckham giving some England fans the middle finger. Instead of being hammered by the media, this time there was sympathy after Keegan revealed Beckham had reacted to vile abuse about Victoria and their son Brooklyn. Beckham felt that was a turning point in his relationship with England fans and the media. Another soon followed when caretaker-manager Peter

Taylor made him captain, and he kept the job after Sven-Göran Eriksson's appointment.

Manchester United won the league in 2001 but were beaten by Arsenal the following season, in what was originally meant to be Ferguson's final campaign. The Gunners completed another double, no longer such a rare achievement as power concentrated with a couple of clubs in the Premier League era. We will never know how United would have fared had Ferguson left then rather than 11 years later. Journalist and United fan Michael Crick claims Eriksson was lined up for the job; leaving England in such circumstances sounds like a recipe for chaos and recrimination.

In September 2001 Beckham played in one of England's best-ever games, a 5-1 victory over Germany in Munich as Eriksson reinvigorated the side, despite his low-key personality and relatively simplistic tactics. English football was facing up to its technical and tactical shortcomings but a Swede, who had won the Portuguese and Italian leagues, decided the smartest solution was to pick the best XI and squeeze them into a 4-4-2.

One of the restrictions was getting Beckham into the team. He wasn't quick enough to play as a winger and, although he was happy to play centrally, England's other top midfielders were Scholes, Steven Gerrard, Frank Lampard and later Joe Cole.

Beckham abandoned his right-midfield role in his most feted England performance, against Greece at Old Trafford. Needing to equal Germany's result against Finland to qualify for the World Cup, Eriksson's side were trailing, despite Beckham's feverish running. Then deep in added time he fired a brilliant free kick to equalise. He celebrated wildly, although he didn't know at the time that Germany had indeed drawn against Finland. I was in the media seats after the game when Beckham walked by and was given an unprecedented standing ovation from the hard-bitten hacks, a reflection of the great affection for a modest, hard-working man.

He then educated a nation on the physiology of the human foot when he suffered a broken metatarsal in a Champions League game with Deportivo La Coruña. The will-he-won't-he saga continued until he took to the pitch in England's opener in Japan in the 2002 World Cup, against Sweden, which finished 1-1. The group of death next served up Argentina and Owen stumbled over Mauricio Pochettino's outstretched leg, giving Beckham the chance to exorcise some four-year-old ghosts. It wasn't a good penalty but the relief was palpable as the ball hit the net. A sweltering draw with Nigeria was followed by a rain-sodden win over Denmark, but it all came to a Ronaldinho-inspired end in the quarter-finals.

Beckham's relationship with the club he supported as a boy and the coach he had revered came to a bitter conclusion in 2003. Ferguson became increasingly frustrated with what he saw as Beckham's showbiz lifestyle, while the player felt unfairly treated, given that he was hard-working and clean living. It came to a head after an FA Cup defeat against Arsenal in which Ferguson harshly blamed Beckham for a conceded goal. When the player argued, Ferguson kicked a boot that somehow hit Beckham just above the eye and drew blood. He was photographed driving with his hair scraped up so the injury was plain to see. Europe's big clubs were put on alert: Joan Laporta promised to land Beckham if he was elected as Barcelona president and the player was furious that Manchester United were prepared to negotiate. He chose instead to become Florentino Pérez's next star.

The Englishman was probably a Galatico too far, although that depends how you measure the project's success. He sold shirts and added English-speaking stardust, and it wasn't his fault Pérez made a series of bad managerial appointments. He certainly fared better than fellow Englishmen Owen and Jonathan Woodgate.

Beckham's determination saw him finally win a major Spanish trophy in his last season. A new regime replaced

Pérez, and after Beckham agreed to sign for LA Galaxy Fabio Capello announced he wouldn't play again. But the Italian was impressed by Beckham's professionalism and recalled him for the run-in. In the 2006/07 season finale against Mallorca, the Englishman limped off and his replacement José Antonio Reyes scored twice to clinch La Liga.

Major League Soccer changed its salary cap rules to get Beckham to America, and when LA Galaxy sold a quarter of a million shirts it looked like good business. He signed with Fuller's management company and his commercial interests became increasingly interlinked with Victoria's post-pop career, as they rubbed shoulders with Hollywood's A-listers.

But Tom Cruise couldn't help LA Galaxy win football matches and nor could Beckham when he was sidelined with ankle and knee injuries. His first couple of seasons were frustrating and he grabbed the chance to join AC Milan on loan in 2009, alienating Galaxy fans by staying longer than initially advertised and admitting he would join permanently if the Italians paid the asking price. They didn't but he was back in Milan in 2010 before a torn Achilles tendon ended his season.

Beckham's last two seasons in MLS were his best. Galaxy improved under former USA national team coach Bruce Arena and Beckham formed an impressive partnership with America's best player Landon Donovan, who had previously been an outspoken critic. Galaxy lifted the MLS Cup in 2011 and 2012.

Beckham won 115 caps, skippered his country, had moments of inspiration and scored some fine goals. But since 1966 England's tournaments have always ended badly. The so-called 'Golden Generation' lost to Portugal in successive quarter-finals. At Euro 2004, where 18-year-old Wayne Rooney was a revelation, England beat Switzerland and Croatia. But in the last-eight shoot-out Beckham's slip on a loose patch of turf sent his penalty skywards before Portuguese keeper Ricardo ripped off his gloves, saved from Darius Vassell and scored the winner himself.

Beckham became the first Englishman to score at three World Cups when he got the winner against Ecuador in the second round in 2006. Rooney again didn't get to the end of the quarter-final, this time sent off for stamping on Ricardo Carvalho. Beckham was off injured before the penalties this time and Ricardo was again England's nemesis as he saved from Lampard, Gerrard and Jamie Carragher.

Eriksson's replacement, Steve McClaren, originally dropped Beckham but relented and the former captain played twice in the doomed Euro 2008 qualifying campaign. England were 2-0 down against Croatia at the new Wembley when 32-year-old Beckham came off the bench in the pouring rain and set up Peter Crouch's equaliser, only to see Mladen Petric beat Scott Carson and deny England a place at the finals. The England job had transformed McClaren from highly rated coach to 'the wally with the brolly' in less than 18 months.

Beckham played for England under Capello until an injury ended any chance of him making the 2010 World Cup, except as an overqualified cheerleader. Even the Italian serial winner couldn't lighten the load of the England shirt. They had bad luck against Germany when Lampard was denied a good goal, hastening the introduction of goal-line technology, but England had come up short again, the players desperate to succeed but paralysed by the burden of representing their country.

Beckham signed off with a brief spell at Paris St Germain, who spent their Qatari oil and gas money on the likes of Zlatan Ibrahimovic and strolled to the French title. Beckham donated his wages to a children's charity and collected a champion's medal in his fourth country, a unique achievement for an Englishman. As I write, he is a football entrepreneur getting his club Inter Miami off the ground in MLS.

Beckham is here because his successful career lets me tell some stories. He wasn't nearly as good as most of the others in this book, but it is a relief to tell a happy story of a working-class lad who had success – it is not easy. He made the most of his talent as a footballer and is enduringly popular because, even though he had everything, he didn't become a prima donna ... a nice guy who won.

44

Cristiano Ronaldo

I'M GOING to take a leap at arguing that Cristiano Ronaldo is the modern-day Stanley Matthews – in terms of their shared obsession with improvement. Matthews set the template for future footballers' technical and physical training; Ronaldo is doing the same. Matthews's hours of practice and lifestyle sacrifices were abnormal; Ronaldo is an outlier now but I suspect the future footballer will look something like him.

Obviously, football has changed: Matthews wasn't paid £26m a year and he stayed at Stoke until he was 32 years old. Ronaldo is incredibly rich but his journey has been tough. He left his home island of Madeira to move 600 miles across the Atlantic Ocean, without his family, aged just 12. At Sporting Lisbon's academy he lived in dorms with older boys and made his own way to school, where he struggled and was teased about his accent, prompting frequent tearful calls to his mother.

He played only 25 league games in Portugal. Arsenal tracked him but refused to meet Sporting's price, one of many false economies they made around then. So Manchester United swooped. They originally intended to loan him back but Alex Ferguson changed his mind after the 18-year-old tortured John O'Shea in a curtain-raising friendly at Sporting's new stadium in

August 2003. The most expensive teenager in English football was given the number-seven shirt vacated by David Beckham.

Young Ronaldo was eye-catching but maddening. He overused tricks and took the occasional dive. In training sessions, United's players literally tried to kick him into line. In his first season they finished third, behind Arsenal's Invincibles, for whom the magnificent Thierry Henry scored 30 in the league.

Portugal hosted Euro 2004 when Ronaldo was 19. Against Greece in the opener and Holland in the semi-final he scored near identical headers from Luis Figo and Deco corners. Luiz Felipe Scolari blended Portugal's so-called 'Golden Generation' with younger players, many of whom had just won the Champions League under Jose Mourinho at Porto. They lost the final to Angelos Charisteas's header. Some major tournaments are won by great teams; in others we are reminded that it is a few games at the end of a long season. Greece kept it tight and nicked goals, mainly from crosses: analysis over – but it is important for football that we believe underdogs can succeed. We need hope.

Mourinho's arrival in England that summer, bankrolled by Roman Abramovich, threatened to strip everyone else of their dreams for years to come. The core of the Porto team arrived, as did Didier Drogba and Arjen Robben, while Frank Lampard scored freely from midfield. I remember a caller to a radio station arguing the rules should be changed or Chelsea would never be caught again.

In Ronaldo's first three seasons, United finished 15, 18 and 8 points behind Arsenal and then Chelsea twice. Their only silverware was the 2004 FA Cup, in which they hammered Millwall in the final, and the 2006 League Cup when they beat Wigan. Ronaldo scored in both finals but frustrated his teammates, especially Ruud van Nistelrooy, who complained that it was impossible to make the right runs when the Portuguese winger was in possession. Van Nistelrooy had scored 110 goals in his first three seasons in England, including 44 in total as United won the title in 2002/03. He scored 40 in his last two seasons before Ferguson was forced to choose between the two.

The 2006 World Cup was a watershed for Ronaldo. Portugal lost the semi-final to France but it was his part in his club-mate Wayne Rooney's dismissal in the quarter-final that would dominate the agenda in England. It was Rooney's fault – no one made him stamp on Ricardo Carvalho's nether regions – and his red card was inevitable. Ronaldo led the Portuguese protests and was caught on camera winking to someone on the bench, which was taken as evidence of subterfuge. National characteristics were questioned. Ex-England striker Alan Shearer, by then a BBC pundit, asked, 'Are we too honest?'

On his return to England, Ronaldo walked into a storm but Ferguson had been there before and, as with Cantona and Beckham, drew on the external hysteria to build internal unity and the phlegmatic Rooney didn't make a fuss. Ronaldo worked obsessively and became bigger, stronger and better. Van Nistelrooy was sold to Real Madrid after relations between the two players hit rock bottom when the Dutchman made an insensitive remark in a training ground row after Ronaldo's father had died. United thrived and regained the title, playing fluid, attacking football.

The 2007/08 season was Ronaldo's pinnacle in England. He scored 42 goals as United retained the title and won the Champions League. According to Gary Neville, 'That season all the negative aspects of his game disappeared. He was breathtaking. He won us match after match. I'd never seen anything like it on the pitch at Old Trafford. We had the best player in the world that season.' The Ballon d'Or judges agreed.

In the Champions League Final United faced Chelsea, somehow managed by Avram Grant. Ronaldo headed the opener and Lampard equalised. In the shoot-out, Ronaldo took a terrible penalty, easily saved by Petr Cech. It would have been decisive but for John Terry's slip in the Moscow rain as he took

Chelsea's fifth kick. Edwin van der Sar saved from Nicolas Anelka and United were European champions again.

It seemed that English club football was back on top, but Ronaldo wanted out. Real Madrid made an offer but Ferguson persuaded him to stay another season, partly so he and United could save face in the light of the Spanish club's discourteous public pursuit.

United won the league again in Ronaldo's final season but failed to retain the Champions League. They faced Barcelona and Lionel Messi in the final, as the two men who would bestride the era met for the second time. United started well but the under-appreciated Samuel Eto'o nicked a goal and Barça were then the better side, clinching victory with, of all things, a towering header from Messi – his first goal of many against English clubs.

Neville argued that Messi emerged at the perfect time for Ronaldo, who was beginning to lose focus on important aspects of the game such as running off the ball and positioning. The two outstanding footballers of the age, playing for great clubs and bitter rivals, drove everyone around them to new heights. Barcelona's brilliance under Pep Guardiola prompted the returning Real Madrid president Florentino Pérez to kickstart a second Galatico era, although Ronaldo's transfer had been agreed while he was out of office.

Ronaldo had some tense times at the Bernebéu, clashing with team-mates and being booed by the home crowd. At £80m, he may have been the world's most expensive player but he was joining the world's most successful club and lining up with great players, who weren't ready for subservient roles.

No player had been as single-minded about his own wellbeing within a team environment as Ronaldo. He openly admitted he wanted to be the best player in the world and was irked that Messi won the Ballon d'Or for four straight seasons. Ronaldo wanted teams built around him, so that the collective pathway to success matched his. Despite an injury-hit first season, he scored 33 goals and Madrid amassed 96 points, but that wasn't enough to win La Liga or save Manuel Pellegrini's job.

Mourinho, who had been snubbed by Barça before Guardiola's appointment, ushered in a period of great football and great conflict, characterised by a run of bad-tempered *Clásicos*. Ronaldo also sought control in the politicised atmosphere at Real Madrid. He spoke of his 'sadness' (which was soothed by more money), demanded a role that would facilitate his goalscoring and wanted the club to actively campaign for him to win the Ballon d'Or. As a Real Madrid player, he won the personal award four times but La Liga only twice in nine seasons.

He and Messi traded records like no two footballers have ever done. Ronaldo scored 450 goals in 438 games for Real Madrid, including 105 in 101 Champions League games. For a player of such ability, the striking thing about Ronaldo's finishing is its simplicity; his goal attempts are usually uncomplicated, first-time shots taken early, hard and low. And if the only way to score is a volleyed back-heel (against Valencia) or a perfectly executed overhead kick (against Juventus) he can do that too.

By 2014 Real Madrid had waited 12 years for *La Decima*, their tenth European title. Their opponents in the final were Diego Simeone's Atlético Madrid, fresh (or not) from breaking the Barça-Real La Liga duopoly. Diego Godín, who had clinched the title the previous weekend, headed Atleti in front. They led until the 93rd minute when Sergio Ramos equalised. Real scored three more in extra time: Gareth Bale, Marcelo and then Ronaldo from the spot.

Ronaldo didn't join the wild celebrations that followed the first two – crucial – goals but when he added the gloss he whipped off his shirt and demanded centre-stage. The irony is that his obvious yearning for adulation is precisely why lots of people withhold it: the boy who left home just after he stopped believing in Father Christmas and lost his alcoholic father aged 20 is seen as a strutting peacock, too arrogant to be loved. He has millions of fans (237 million on Instagram) but his public perception is complicated: his generous philanthropy is weighed against unproven allegations of sexual misconduct and an admission of tax avoidance (he is definitely not alone in that last regard).

The 2016 Champions League Final was another Madrid derby in a period of Spanish domination of Europe's big prizes. This time Ronaldo's penalty in the shoot-out was decisive. The following season they beat Atleti in the semi-final before overrunning Juventus, with Ronaldo scoring two of their four goals.

Zinedine Zidane's first three seasons as Real's coach brought three Champions League wins, but regular viewers of La Liga will appreciate that only in the middle of those three seasons were they consistently good. They were, however, a great cup team, capable of finding a way to win on big European nights. In 2018 they also benefitted from some calamitous goalkeeping: Sven Ulreich's awful misjudgement in the semi-final helped defeat Bayern. In the final, Liverpool's Loris Karius, suffering from concussion but still on the pitch, under-armed the ball to Benzema, who had an open goal. Karius then lost track of a long-range Bale shot. In between, the Welshman scored a magnificent overhead.

Winning ugly is still winning, and Ronaldo's international career peaked long after Portugal's 'Golden Generation' faded. The 2014 World Cup was an injury-hit misery, but glory, of a sort, followed. The expanded Euro 2016 was a poor tournament. Portugal failed to beat Iceland, Austria or Hungary in their group but knocked out Croatia with a 117th-minute Ricardo Quaresma goal and won a penalty shoot-out against Poland. Meanwhile, Bale had inspired Wales to an unprecedented semi-final and the Real Madrid duo squared up in Lyon, where a prodigious Ronaldo leap saw him head the first in a 2-0 victory.

His perfect script would have seen him score the winner in the final against France in Paris but there was a twist in the tale, and in his knee. He went off in tears, recovering sufficiently to act as a surrogate coach, bellowing instructions and encouragement to his team-mates. The unlikely hero was Eder, a goal-shy striker who had previously failed to score in 15 games for Swansea. His first-ever competitive international goal was a brilliant long-range shot that won Portugal their first trophy.

Ronaldo's chief contribution to the 2018 World Cup was a hat-trick in a thrilling draw with Spain, capped off with a superb free kick (his conversion rate from set pieces is poor for a player of his calibre). His relentlessness, incredible physique and willingness to play through pain have allowed him to show more commitment to international football than many lesser players. A hat-trick against the Faroe Islands can be seen as easy pickings – or reward for unprecedented determination. His 99th international goal came against Luxembourg.

There was another trophy in 2019. Ronaldo had missed Portugal's Nations League group phase but returned as they hosted the inaugural finals tournament, in which he scored a hat-trick against Switzerland in the semi-final. It was another 1-0 in the final against the Netherlands, but this time Gonçalo Guedes stole the limelight.

It transpired the €94m Real Madrid paid was a bargain because nine years, 450 goals and four Champions League wins later, they turned a profit. After winning seven consecutive Serie A titles, Juventus paid €100m for the 33-year-old. They obviously saw no sign of Ronaldo fading. He won Serie A in each of his first two seasons as Juventus continued their domination of Italy, smashing 31 league goals in 2019/20 as he turned 35. A man who gets back from a Champions League away tie in the early hours of the morning and goes straight for an ice bath clearly still has mountains to climb and future generations to inspire.

45

Xavi Hernández

THIS WAS the hardest call: who should tell the story of Spain's rise to global football dominance, Xavi or Iniesta? The elegant Andrés Iniesta produced the ultimate moment, the winning goal in a World Cup Final, and his dribbling skills were crucial for Spain and Barcelona to break disciplined opposition lines. I did a Twitter poll, thousands voted and it came out 50/50, so I asked Graham Hunter, who chronicled the rise of Spain and Barça in book and film. He agonised, then chose Xavi: 'His play and mentality marked the philosophy/style: the possession school. If I'm honest, I think he had the slightly bigger football brain and his character was what was needed.'

Xavi wasn't as extravagantly talented as Iniesta and was a long way short of Messi and Cristiano Ronaldo, but his influence changed how football is played. He was the epitome of intelligent football. I see it watching youth football in England; kids are encouraged to get on the ball, pass and move, even on pitches that would make Xavi weep – he wasn't averse to measuring the length of the grass when he turned up at a stadium.

It took him a long time to become a sensation. When he broke into Barcelona's team in 1998 he won La Liga but didn't win over the club's supporters. He was billed as Pep Guardiola's replacement, which he hated because, as a Barça fan, he had great reverence for the stylish deep-lying midfielder. The club was in chaos but Xavi had success with Spain's youth teams, winning trophies and forming a friendship with Iker Casillas, which would later be critical for national team unity when the *Clásico* wars hit their peak.

In his first World Cup in 2002, he scored in the penalty shoot-out defeat against co-hosts South Korea, who had benefitted from some highly dubious decisions. In 2006 he was subbed in the second-round game against France at 1-1, and watched a Zidane-inspired defeat from the bench. Spain were like England: periods of dominance at club level, a taste of glory on home turf in the mid-1960s but lots of tales of misfortune, underpinned by the nagging doubt that the country's players simply weren't good enough.

It changed for Spain in Euro 2008 qualifying, although the roots of success ran deeper. An emphasis on coach education and the high status of the national age-group teams had produced a generation of superbly technical, intelligent players with experience of winning tournaments. Veteran coach Luis Aragonés had a long record of highs and lows and his last gamble was to trust in the diminutive Xavi, Iniesta, David Silva and Cesc Fabregas when Europe's top midfielders were powerhouses like Patrick Vieira, Michael Ballack and Steven Gerrard. Qualifying defeats against Northern Ireland and Sweden left Aragonés hanging by a thread, and reviled for jettisoning Real Madrid legend Raúl. *El Pais* newspaper called him 'a clueless coach with a bunch of characterless players'.

They rode their luck in the tournament, as most winners do. Casillas saved them in the penalty shoot-out against Italy, but by the time Xavi set up Fernando Torres to score the only goal of the final against Germany in Vienna, it was clear that this time the European champions were Europe's best team. Xavi still had detractors, such as the *Daily Mail*, who captioned a picture of that year's Ballon d'Or top five as 'The Best Players in the World (and Xavi)'.

Xavi's future at Barcelona was uncertain. Frank Rijkaard had brought success to the Camp Nou, winning La Liga twice and beating Arsenal in the 2006 Champions League Final. Gunners' keeper Jens Lehmann was sent off but they took the lead through Sol Campbell. Substitutes Iniesta and Henrik Larsson changed the game and Samuel Eto'o and Juliano Belletti goals secured Barça's second European title. Xavi stayed on the bench, having only recently returned from a thigh injury.

The laidback Rijkaard couldn't maintain the discipline from there and Barça's high-profile stars were soon having a better time off the pitch than on it. The Dutchman went and Guardiola was promoted from the B team. Xavi asked his old team-mate if he was needed or whether he should accept an offer from Bayern Munich. Guardiola saw Xavi as central to his plans, and in 2008/09 Barça produced some of the best football ever: high-tempo passing, purposeful possession, controlling and dominating opponents with the cutting edge from the sensational Messi. They put six past Atlético Madrid, Sporting Gijón, Valladolid, Malaga and, most satisfyingly, Real Madrid. They won the domestic double and faced down the muscular forces of England's Premier League – with a little help from Tom Henning Øvrebø. The Norwegian refereed the second leg of the Champions League semi-final at Stamford Bridge and turned down three clear and two debatable Chelsea penalty appeals, prompting an apoplectic Didier Drogba to yell into the live TV cameras, 'It's a fucking disgrace!' They were bad decisions but the subsequent personal abuse suffered by Øvrebø was unacceptable. Football ended up with VAR because we couldn't accept mistakes.

Such moments do matter in the course of history, but Guardiola's team was the best in the world for three years. They beat Manchester United in the Champions League finals of 2009 and 2011 and a defeat against Jose Mourinho's Inter in the 2010 semi-final doesn't change that perspective.

Mourinho brought down Guardiola in the end after pursuing him to Spain. Xavi was inspirational as Barça thumped Real Madrid 5-0 in Mourinho's first *Clásico* and the Portuguese decided to play nasty. His antics helped to drain the joy out of Guardiola, who quit in 2012. Barça only hit those heights again in the second half of 2014/15, Xavi's last season, when Luis Enrique's team, with Messi, Luis Suárez and Neymar up front, won the Treble.

Spain went into the 2010 World Cup as favourites. Vicente del Bosque had replaced Aragonés but stuck with the principle of picking intelligent players, whatever their height. Possession football is not necessarily attacking football and, in truth, Del Bosque used his side's technical ability and positional sense to strangle the life out of opponents, winning all of their knockout games 1-0. David Villa's goals got them past Portugal and Paraguay before Carles Puyol's meaty header beat Germany, the second-best team around.

Before the final, Johan Cruyff, now a revered observer, said he couldn't lose: the two nations whose football culture he helped shape were on top of the world. Afterwards he described the Netherlands' performance as 'ugly, tough, vulgar and barely watchable'. England's Howard Webb was an excellent referee who earned his place in the final, but he seemed too intent on keeping 22 players on the pitch. Nigel de Jong should have been sent off in the 28th minute for studding Xabi Alonso in the chest. He was one of eight Dutchmen booked along with five Spaniards. Webb showed the red card eventually, in the 109th minute for Johnny Heitinga's second obviously bookable offence. Justice was done when Iniesta scored in the 116th minute. He took off his shirt to show his tribute to his friend Dani Jarque, the former Espanyol captain, who had died of a heart attack a year earlier. Iniesta's yellow card for that was the same punishment as de Jong's for his assault on Alonso.

Spain were the best team in the world. Foreign clubs were desperate for Spanish players and football associations wanted the secrets of youth development. Michel Platini asked for Xavi's number-eight shirt and the *Daily Mail* published an apology to the midfield mastermind. Xavi and co had changed the game.

In the 1970s, West Germany had fallen short of a tournament treble, so Spain broke new ground by retaining the European title in 2012. Villa was out with a broken leg; Torres was there but a knee injury had robbed him of his lightning pace. Del Bosque did away with strikers altogether in key games, using Fabregas as a false nine. They needed penalties to beat Portugal but were magnificent when Italy went toe-to-toe with them in the final. It was already 2-0 when the Italians went down to ten men because of injury and 4-0 was the biggest margin of victory in a final, capping a wonderful era in which Spain had proved technical football could be winning football.

It unravelled at Brazil 2014, a tournament too far for 34-year-old Xavi. Spain led in their first game until Robin van Persie equalised for the Netherlands with a fabulous diving header in the 44th minute. The Dutch went on to score five. By the 43rd minute of their second match against Chile, Spain were 2-0 down and heading out. They had conceded seven goals inside 90 minutes of action – more than in all 19 games they had played during their hat-trick of tournament wins.

Xavi quit international football with 133 caps and Del Bosque graciously conceded the Catalan midfielder had been more important than him. Xavi's next stop was Qatar, where he played for Al-Sadd and won his ninth league title before taking over as manager. He upset people in Spain when he favourably compared Qatar's autocratic regime to his home country's democracy.

He turned down an offer to manage Barcelona in 2019 but remains a likely candidate for the job in the near future when the club's toxic political situation better suits his arrival. He would have the backing of Messi, who said, 'As a player he saw the whole picture from the pitch. As a coach watching from the sidelines he would see more clearly.' And when a coach has the backing of Lionel Messi anything is possible.

46

Lionel Messi

LIONEL MESSI has spent his career winning trophies, scoring goals, dominating matches and being compared to two other footballers.

He and Cristiano Ronaldo have dominated world football for over a decade, prompting an obsessive debate: choose your champion and define your philosophy. So who is your man: Ronaldo, with his manufactured, muscular efficiency, or Messi, with his carefree creativity? It is a false choice. There are more similarities than differences. Both left their mothers and flew across the Atlantic Ocean at a heartbreakingly young age. Acceptance in their new world came from their genius for football but there were still tearful phone calls to mum. Both had early medical interventions without which they might never have become footballers at all. Ronaldo had laser surgery to correct a racing heart when he was 15. Messi had a hormone deficiency that stunted his growth. His family knew it would be tough to move to Spain aged just 13 but couldn't pay for the treatment or find an Argentine club to do so. Messi and his dad relocated, leaving the rest of the family behind. By the way, both interventions were correcting defects: we're not yet in the era of the bionic footballer.

It is also nonsense to suggest Ronaldo is all about grafting in the gym while Messi was born nutmegging defenders. In common with most of the greats, Messi had an early obsession with football and a remarkable work ethic. He hasn't played 900 games without being extremely fit. In fact, Barcelona's hierarchy got rid of Ronaldinho and Deco partly because they were fearful young Messi might get a taste for the hedonistic lifestyle enjoyed by two men he had huge respect for and had welcomed him into the first team.

Messi was the main difference between the hugely effective but occasionally dull Spain teams and the thrilling Barcelona of the Guardiola years. Xavi, Iniesta, Busquets controlled; Messi slayed. A measure of his genius is that as well as being a record-breaking goalscorer he also orchestrates games. He starts moves, he finishes moves. Guardiola is a system addict but he moulded his team around Messi. Years later, a pithy answer in a Champions League media conference summed up his regard for the Argentine: 'Which team is favourite? Who does Messi play for? There's your answer.'

Guardiola wants that team to be remembered for its emotional impact on fans, but Messi's stats are worth a quick look. In those four seasons ending in 2012, he scored 38, 47, 53 and 73 goals. The 2011/12 season was a personal best, even though Barça finished second in La Liga and were dramatically knocked out of the Champions League by Chelsea, who went on to win the competition, despite having declined as a team. Messi scored a remarkable 91 goals for club and country that calendar year. The two seasons immediately after Guardiola left were chaotic and traumatic: former assistant Tito Vilanova took over and the early form set Barça on the path to 100 points and the Spanish title. But Vilanova was diagnosed with parotid gland cancer and took breaks for radiotherapy and chemotherapy. He stood down that summer and died in April 2014.

Messi scored 60 in Vilanova's season and despite niggling muscular injuries he hit 41 in Tata Martino's only campaign when Atlético Madrid won La Liga. The MSN: Messi, Suárez and Neymar put Barça back on top of European football under Luis Enrique.

Suárez cost £65m from Liverpool even though he was suspended from all football for biting Giorgio Chiellini at the 2014 World Cup, the third such incident in his career. He didn't play until October and by January Enrique was close to the sack. He survived, and soon his side was playing thrilling, beautiful football, completing the treble and interrupting Real Madrid's run of four Champions League wins in five years. It was hard for the Premier League to maintain its claim to be the best in the world as Sevilla and Atlético also won the Europa League in six out of nine seasons between 2010 and 2018.

In Enrique's three years, he won the Champions League, Club World Cup, La Liga twice and the Spanish Cup three times, but, such are the demands on a coach at a modern SuperClub, he was gone after winning only one trophy in 2016/17. Ernesto Valverde won La Liga in both of his full seasons but strangely similar second-leg collapses in the Champions League against Roma and Liverpool made his job untenable. It got worse after he was replaced by Quique Setien and Barça were humiliated 8-2 by Bayern Munich in the 2020 Champions League quarter-final played in neutral Lisbon, during the Covid-19 pandemic.

Many Barça fans would tell you four Champions League winner's medals are not enough for Messi (he missed the 2006 final because Rijkaard didn't trust he was fully fit). Barcelona hasn't been a well-run club in recent years: the record-breaking €222m received for Neymar's move to Paris St Germain was squandered; the supply of La Masia graduates dried up; and there was a feeling that Messi was carrying the club. Under Valverde the plan sometimes looked suspiciously like keep it tight, get the ball to Leo.

And that brings us to Messi's frustrating international career. It started well with victory at the 2005 under-20 World

Cup in which he was top scorer, best player and got both Argentina goals (from the spot) in the final against Nigeria. Argentina won the Olympic Gold in 2008 after Guardiola made one of his first big decisions to over-rule his bosses and allow Messi to go to China.

But what really matters is the World Cup, and Messi's lack of impact meansthat in the eyes of many Argentina fans he remains second best to Diego Maradona. Messi's stats, the goals, assists and trophies won dwarf Maradona's but Diego had timing. He played his best when it mattered most and he played his best for Argentina.

Messi has never done that. The best Argentina team of his era was in 2006 and 2007. He made his World Cup debut in a fabulous victory over Serbia & Montenegro, coming off the bench to set up the fourth and score the sixth. They looked like potential champions but lost to the hosts, largely thanks to coach Jose Pékerman's poor substitutions, as he took off the influential Juan Roman Riquelme and didn't use Messi. Germany equalised and won the shoot-out. It was largely the same Argentina team that swept all before them in the 2007 Copa America, only to collapse in the final against Brazil. That is one of four major finals Messi has lost with Argentina, including in two Copa America penalty shoot-outs against Chile.

One thing Messi had to contend with in his international career that Maradona didn't was having Maradona as his coach. Diego was every bit as bad in the dug-out as he was brilliant on the pitch. He took over during the 2010 qualifiers and used 55 players in 13 games. When Argentina sneaked through, Maradona told the press to 'Suck on it and keep sucking!' Argentina fell at the same stage to the same opponents as four years earlier: Germany in the quarters – but this time it was 4-0 and well deserved.

Maradona's failure as a coach did little to harm his reputation and his chaotic charisma was juxtaposed with Messi's measured, almost dispassionate persona. Argentina longed for Messi to win a World Cup single-handed, but he couldn't. I have never seen a less enthusiastic recipient of an award than when he trudged up to receive his Golden Ball as the best player of the 2014 World Cup. He had been decisive in all three group games and scored four goals but his contribution in later games was to be the focus of the opposition's tactical plans. Germany were Argentina's nemesis again. Higuain missed a great chance and Mario Götze volleyed in an extra-time winner. It is hard to argue the Germans didn't deserve it.

Messi was back in 2018, where he scored an excellent goal against Nigeria but was on the losing side against the eventual champions again: 4-3 against France. Messi has had no luck in tournaments but that is not the whole story. We know so much more about his game than we did about Pelé's or Kempes's. Every coach has a plan for him and Argentina haven't been well led for years. Their production of players has been comically top-heavy; Messi has played internationals with Agüero, Tevez, Lavezzi, Dybala, Di Maria, Crespo, Aimar, Riquelme, Pastore, Veron and Saviola but precious few top defenders.

His relative failure with Argentina makes Messi human; it is almost reassuring that we haven't yet seen the perfect footballer. Diehard Maradona fans will never accept it but if you were a club's director of football you would surely sign the guy who follows a vegan diet to stay lean in the football season, in preference to the one who snorted cocaine with mobsters; at least I would. Maybe Maradona has more stardust, maybe Cristiano Ronaldo is the more relentlessly impressive physical specimen; maybe if you combine those two, you get Lionel Messi. Cristiano seems to have come to terms with his rival's brilliance: 'We've had this battle for 15 years. He pushed me and I pushed him as well, so it's good to be part of the history of football.' I hope they become friends when they retire.

47

Mesut Özil

MESUT ÖZIL won the World Cup and La Liga. He finished top of the assist chart in England and Spain, and joint top at successive major international tournaments. He is also here because he has spent the second half of his career at a club that doesn't know how to use his mercurial talent but threw money at him in a blind panic. In many ways, Özil is the archetypal post-Bosman footballer.

He learned to speak Turkish before he could speak German. His grandfather moved to Gelsenkirchen in the 1960s as a migrant worker and when Mesut was called up to Germany's under-17s he had to go to the Turkish consulate and renounce his citizenship. An official told him only traitors do that. It was the beginning of a relationship with the German national team that would hit the top and end bitterly.

He moved acrimoniously from Schalke to Werder Bremen before he came to England's attention at the 2010 World Cup. Fabio Capello's team qualified impressively but were awful in South Africa, drawing with the USA, Algeria (in one of football's all-time stinkers) and sneaking past Slovenia. Capello's disciplinarian stance didn't work; England's players wanted takeaway food and shark-spotting jaunts. They played

Joachim Löw's Germany in the second round and there was little sign of Italian-inspired defensive discipline as Miroslav Klose made it 1-0 to Germany. The Polish-born striker was a steady goalscorer in club football but hit a record 16 goals in World Cups, claiming the Silver Boot in 2002 and upgrading to gold in 2006.

Germany scored a superb second before Matthew Upson made it 2-1. Moments later, Frank Lampard's shot hit the underside of the bar and bounced well over the goal line, but somehow the assistant referee failed to see what happened. Who knows how the game would have panned out but England's defending was hapless and Thomas Müller scored twice. Germany's fourth was made by Özil who made Gareth Barry look like he was running the wrong way up an escalator. It was a shame Germany's match with Spain wasn't the final.

Özil promptly joined Real Madrid who had just hired Jose Mourinho. The €15m fee was a bargain compared to the €65m they paid for an injury-prone Kaka a year earlier. Cristiano Ronaldo was among Özil's admirers as he topped La Liga's assist chart in each of his three full seasons. He played more than 50 games a season and won his only league title to date in 2012. In Mourinho's third and final season the Portuguese fell out with Ronaldo, Sergio Ramos, Iker Casillas, referees, UEFA, the Spanish media, club officials and half of the fans. In one changing-room confrontation he called Özil a coward. That perceived lack of guts, fire or *cojones* has stuck and despite the change of management, Real Madrid were prepared to listen to offers.

Arsenal had, by then, developed a miserly reputation, by the breathtaking standards of the Premier League. Building the Emirates Stadium was cited as the main reason but the club's owners, and manager Arsène Wenger, were wary of an inflationary transfer market, stoked by rich foreign owners at the likes of Chelsea and Manchester City. Arsenal also had rich owners but they seemed content with regular Champions

League qualification. Remarkably, from 2005/06 to 2014/15 the Gunners finished either third or fourth, hardly ever threatening to win the league. From 2010/11 they were knocked out of the Champions League round of 16 for seven straight seasons. Disengagement from the Premier League's transfer madness might sound sensible but it wasn't replaced by smart scouting, great youth development or inspired coaching and Arsenal slipped out of the elite.

By the summer of 2013, they hadn't won a trophy since the FA Cup eight years earlier and their fans were desperate. They offered £40m plus one pound to trigger Luis Suárez's release clause at Liverpool but the Uruguayan was persuaded, partly by Steven Gerrard, that it would be a sideways move.

Deadline day was now a media circus in England, and Arsenal had only two free transfers to show for that summer's efforts until they paid £42.5m for Özil, a record for a German. He won six and drew one of his first seven Premier League games, and Arsenal were unbeaten and top of the Premier League when they visited Old Trafford in November. The only scorer that day was Robin van Persie, a walking symbol of Arsenal's decline. The Dutchman had scored 37 goals for them in 2011/12 but refused a new contract and was sold to Manchester United for just £24m. He then hit another 30 goals, dragging a relatively poor United team to Sir Alex Ferguson's 13th Premier League title in his final campaign.

After losing in Manchester, Arsenal fell away in the league in a manner that became depressingly familiar to their supporters, but Özil's first season ended well. The Gunners came from two goals down to beat Hull City in the FA Cup Final. I wondered at the time whether Wenger might leave on that high, but far from it, he stayed for four more seasons as Arsenal became FA Cup specialists, winning it again in 2015 and 2017.

Too much of the business of football is based on fear and short-termism. Özil was a classic example. The loss of Van

Persie haunted Arsenal and both Özil and Alexis Sánchez were set to be out of contract in the summer of 2018. The club panicked and in January 2018 offered to double the German's wages in a deal that lasted until 2021. Sánchez was swapped with Manchester United's Henrikh Mkhitaryan, a good player but nowhere near the level at which the Chilean had been operating.

Wenger left a few months later and neither of Arsenal's subsequent coaches, Unai Emery or Mikel Arteta, appeared to want Özil, a player on £350,000 a week. Sympathy for struggling footballers is in short supply but Özil has become a well-paid shadow of his former self. Mkhitaryan and Sánchez both spent last season on loan in Italy, wages subsidised by their English clubs. Arsenal lost Aaron Ramsey to Juventus on a Bosman free in 2019. If you are looking for winners, then the foreign clubs being subsidised by the Premier League probably see it as reasonable wealth redistribution. The richer European clubs are not immune to making reckless decisions about finances: Gareth Bale at Real Madrid and Philippe Coutinho at Barcelona have been cast into similar wage traps. The real champions of the post-Bosman Wild West, of course, are the agents.

Özil's international career went to even greater extremes. He was Germany's top scorer in qualification for the 2014 World Cup and had been named the national team's best player for three straight seasons. But their success in Brazil was a genuine team effort: Mario Götze volleyed the winner in the final; Müller, Phillip Lahm, Mats Hummels and Toni Kroos were nominated for the Golden Ball; and Manuel Neuer, who rescued them in the second round against Algeria, was named as the best keeper.

The semi-final with Brazil was one of the World Cup's most extraordinary matches. Host-nation hype almost hit 1950 levels ahead of the game in Belo Horizonte. Brazil were without suspended captain Thiago Silva and star player

Neymar, who had fractured a vertebra in the quarter-final, but hadn't lost a competitive home match in 62 games, since 1975. Müller scored early and the period between the 23rd and 29th minutes defied everything we know about modern international football: for a team of Brazil's calibre to capitulate on that stage was shocking. With half an hour gone, it was 5-0. Germany eased off until Andre Schürrle came on and scored twice. Özil should have made it 8-0 but his late miss allowed Oscar to salvage the tiniest shard of pride. Brazil's fans wept and David Luiz joined them, openly sobbing throughout his post-match interview.

Few people begrudged Germany's World Cup win, which was built on strong youth development, coach education, fan-friendly Bundesliga clubs – and an unapologetically academic level of interest in tactics, still scoffed at in England. Of course, none of that guarantees victories in major tournaments.

In the quarter-finals of Euro 2016 Özil scored in a 1-1 draw with Italy but was one of the seven players who failed from the spot. His was one of the more normal misses in a bizarre series, headlined by Simone Zaza's dressage-style approach and blast over. Germany won but it was all for nothing as Antoine Griezmann's double won the semi-final for France.

Löw's side were terrible at Russia 2018, and became the fourth of the last five World Cup winners to go out at the group stage of the following tournament. They lost both games in which Özil played, against Mexico and South Korea. They were one of the early victims of VAR (Video Assistant Referee) when Kim Young-gwon's 93rd-minute goal was given after a review of the original offside decision. South Korea got a second when Son Heung-min benefitted from Neuer's hubris, when the keeper was caught in possession on the German left wing.

Özil's 92nd cap was his last. He quit the national team citing racism: 'I am German when we win, but I am an immigrant when we lose.' The German FA had joined the tide of criticism after he took part in a photo opportunity with

Turkey's controversial president Recep Tayyip Erdoğan, who had also been at his wedding.

Özil walked into more controversy when he tweeted in support of the Uyghurs, against China's treatment of the largely Muslim minority group. Amnesty International said the footballer had taken an 'important stand' but it was one that terrified the English game's powerbrokers. Chinese TV cancelled plans to show Arsenal's match with Manchester City and his club quickly distanced itself from Özil's stance.

The position of Muslims in English football is intriguing but hopeful. In 1992 Tottenham's Nayim was the only Muslim in the Premier League; now you could pick an excellent side including Özil, Mohamed Salah, Sadio Mane, Paul Pogba and N'Golo Kanté. English Muslim footballers such as Hamza Choudhury are few and far between, largely because the game has failed to tap the British South Asian community for players.

Football has the same contradictory currents as wider society where greater tolerance is opposed by a vocal minority. The football media has no equivalent of the click-baiting bigots who make a living in the political forum, although some racist groups use the cloak of football supporters. A Stanford University study found evidence of a decline in Islamophobic incidents on Merseyside correlated with Salah's arrival at Liverpool FC. The influence of Muslim footballers like Salah and Özil juts up against politicians who use Islamophobia as an easy way to mobilise voters. Football clubs like non-drinking, clean-living players but are less keen when someone like Freddi Kanouté objects to gambling adverts, the drug football cannot wean itself off.

There is an obvious pitfall in the charting of the history of current players. Maybe Özil might revive his Arsenal career or find a new challenge. It would be a shame if he is remembered for his money-sodden latter years rather than as the inventive assist specialist and World Cup winner.

48

N'Golo Kanté

ONE NIGHT after playing for Chelsea in Cardiff, N'Golo Kanté tried to get to Paris by train but missed the last Eurostar. Instead of booking into a hotel, he found the nearest mosque and ended up staying with a local football fan, eating chicken curry and playing the FIFA video game.

A humble hero, rejected by the big clubs, Kanté became a World Cup winner. He is so small he was literally mistaken for a child when he first came to England but went on to play a pivotal role in the most stunning of all Premier League campaigns. He is a vital figure for modern football: a sign of hope for the little guy, a beacon that it is not all about the money.

The Premier League has been a roaring success when it comes to generating revenue. Overseas TV rights and commercial partnerships help but it has been underpinned by the willingness of English fans to pay handsomely to watch football, either in the stadium or via subscription TV. In turn, some of the world's wealthiest people have got involved for complex reasons including, but not limited to, generating an international profile, making money and creating legitimacy for questionable autocratic regimes. Since the old toffs of

Highbury's oak-panelled boardroom celebrated Arsenal's 'Invincibles' season, no English-owned club has won the English league.

Chelsea won 16 major trophies from Roman Abramovich's arrival in 2003 to the 2019 Europa League. After the Glazer family bought Manchester United in 2005 and loaded it with debt, there were five more Premier League titles – but none since Sir Alex Ferguson's retirement. Manchester City should have capitalised but despite the financial muscle of Abu Dhabi's royal family, progress was haphazard until Pep Guardiola's arrival. City did win the Premier League under both Roberto Mancini and Manuel Pellegrini, giving the competition its most exciting finishes.

When the full-time whistle went in Manchester United's final game of the 2011/12 season, they had beaten Sunderland and were sitting top of the league, only for City to snatch the title. Edin Dzeko and Sergio Agüero both scored in added time to beat QPR and claim the three points they needed. It was amazing, matching Michael Thomas's goal for Arsenal at Anfield in 1989 for drama. Two years later, City benefitted from Liverpool's agonising late slip.

For all the inconsistency of the top clubs, evidence suggested only the richest could feasibly win the modern Premier League. The champions always came from the top five clubs in terms of budget. That was why Leicester's remarkable triumph in 2015/16 transcended the normal rules of football rivalry.

When Agüerooooooo scored his goal in 2012, Jamie Vardy was at Conference club Fleetwood Town and both Riyad Mahrez and N'Golo Kanté were trying to force their way into the first teams at French second division clubs Le Havre and Boulogne respectively. That summer, Leicester made Vardy the first million-pound non-league player. Mahrez joined a year later for just £400,000 and helped win promotion under manager Nigel Pearson. By March 2014 it looked like rapid relegation was inevitable, but a stunning sequence of seven wins from nine games saved them; the only defeat was against Jose Mourinho's title-winners Chelsea.

Leicester's owner was Vichai Srivaddhanaprabha, owner of the King Power duty-free chain. He was from Thailand, which was the location of the squad's fateful end-of-season tour. Three players, including the manager's son James Pearson, were sacked after the *Daily Mirror* revealed a 'racist sex tape' recorded on the trip. That, added to the manager's erratic behaviour, which included a bizarre press conference in which he asked a journalist if he was an ostrich, meant it was no great surprise when Pearson was sacked. His replacement was met with a collective shrug.

In a 27-year career, Claudio Ranieri had managed Juventus, Inter, Roma, Atlético, Valencia, Chelsea and Monaco but never won a league title. Most recently he had been sacked by Greece after losing to the Faroe Islands. In England he was regarded, unfairly, as something of a clown because of his amusing press conferences conducted in broken English.

One of his first decisions was to pay Caen £5.6m for Kanté. The 5ft 6in (168cm) midfielder had been repeatedly disregarded by big French clubs because he was too small, even in the age of Xavi and Iniesta. He played one full season for Boulogne in the third division, while studying to be an accountant, then moved to second division Caen, who were promoted in his first campaign. Leicester's head of recruitment Steve Walsh had been impressed by Kanté's running and ball recovery statistics and travelled to watch him in his only season in the French top flight. Walsh successfully convinced his new boss to prioritise the little-known Frenchman over a list of available international midfielders.

After his second training session at Leicester, Kanté was hanging around looking lost when he was approached by the training-ground manager who asked if he needed help. When Kanté said he needed a taxi to the Hilton Hotel, the club official asked, 'Are your parents not coming to pick you up?'

He admitted mistaking the club's new midfielder for a 12 or 13-year-old academy kid.

Kanté didn't go straight into the starting line-up as Leicester, 5,000 to 1 outsiders for the title, made a positive and entertaining start. The theme of those early weeks was their inability to keep a clean sheet. The Italian manager promised his players pizza when they managed their first shut-out, which happened in their tenth match, by which time Kanté's midfield presence was obvious. The pizza-making trip to a local restaurant, Ranieri's jocular press conferences and Leicester's underdog status helped create a hugely positive vibe. They were top at Christmas but publicly, almost comically, he refused to budge his target from the 40 points needed for survival.

Vardy had managed only five goals in his first top-flight season but went on a record-breaking run, scoring in 11 straight Premier League games. Leicester defended deep and used their centre-forward's devastating pace and aggression. Mahrez was fabulous. The Algerian mainly played from the right, cutting inside to use his left foot; defenders knew what was coming but couldn't stop him. Kanté was the other star: his positioning was exquisite, his running and ball recovery were breathtaking. The joke was that Leicester played with three midfielders: Danny Drinkwater in the centre with Kanté either side of him. Without him they wouldn't have won the league.

The script for Leicester's end-of-season video suggests their title victory changed the sport – but really it was a marvellous outlier, the exception that proves the rule. Everything fell right. After a close defeat against Arsenal, Ranieri gave his players time off and they came back refreshed and kept a series of clean sheets. Their enduring underdog status allowed for counter-attacking football, which was unusual for title contenders. Not playing European games gave them time for rest and preparation.

The usual contenders were all in transition: Pellegrini was a lame duck at City who lined up Guardiola to replace him. Mourinho signed a new contract at Chelsea ahead of his third season but was gone by Christmas. Manchester United finished eighth, won the FA Cup but sacked Louis van Gaal. Liverpool fired Brendan Rodgers and replaced him with Jurgen Klopp, who ran the players ragged. Tottenham emerged as Leicester's main contenders. Mauricio Pochettino's side played stylish football and Spurs hadn't won the league since 1961 but Leicester were the neutrals' favourites: even rival players and managers openly wished for them to become champions. Spurs faded (finishing behind Arsenal), and Leicester had pulled off their barely believable title heist. It was brilliant for the Premier League, giving credence to the notion that titles can be won with bargain signings, sound tactics, hard work and good luck – rather than always bought by billionaires. Was it English football's greatest shock? Yes, given the new financial realities – but Brian Clough's Nottingham Forest went on to win two European Cups, which is now unimaginable.

Ranieri was sacked the following February as Leicester suffered a hangover and there was a tragic postscript. Vichai Srivaddhanaprabha and four other people were killed when his helicopter crashed following a match at the King Power stadium in 2018.

By then Kanté was long gone. Chelsea paid £30m for the engine of Leicester's title triumph – less than they spent on Michy Batshuayi. It was Antonio Conte's first season in English football and he made easy work of it. A switch to a back three during a defeat at Arsenal in September sparked a run of 13 straight wins and they never looked back. Kanté had seamlessly carried his energy and know-how from one title-winning team to another.

Conte's second season was wasted amid Mourinhoesque turmoil. Another Italian, Maurizio Sarri, followed, and, typical of Chelsea, won a major competition despite a season of angst. Sarri was pilloried for using Kanté further forward to allow Brazilian-born Italy international Jorginho to act as a deep playmaker. They won the Europa League and Sarri left for Juventus.

And from a trainee accountant too small to play professional football, Kanté became a world champion. First there was disappointment: he started for France at Euro 2016 but lost his place, partly through suspension, and was on the sidelines as the hosts lost the final to Portugal.

The FIFA corruption years reached a peak (or trough) with the awarding of the 2018 World Cup to Russia (and the simultaneous decision to take the 2022 competition to Qatar). Didier Deschamps joined Mario Zagallo and Franz Beckenbauer by winning the World Cup as a player and coach. France had pace throughout their team and Kanté covered his usual midfield miles. Right-back Benjamin Pavard lashed in the goal of the tournament in a 4-3 win over Argentina but Kylian Mbappé was the star: the teenager's performances drew justifiable comparisons with Pelé and Ronaldo.

France's victory in the final was controversial. Croatia's Mario Mandžukić headed an own goal before Ivan Perišić equalised. VAR had been generally well used until Blaise Matuidi failed to connect with a corner and the ball struck Perišić's arm. The French appealed and Argentine referee Néstor Pitana checked on the pitch-side monitor. The process took two minutes to complete; it hadn't looked like a deliberate handball in real time but 'rock-and-rolling' the replay changed the perspective. VAR is here to stay and hopefully its use will improve. Antoine Griezmann converted the penalty and, thankfully, Paul Pogba and Mbappé scored good goals so it didn't feel like the outcome was solely down to VAR.

The influence of players from immigrant communities on the France squad was stronger in 2018 than it had been 20 years earlier; a majority were black and Kanté was one of seven Muslims. The political pushback to the changing world was also stronger: Marine Le Pen, leader of right-wing National

Rally and daughter of Jean-Marie, got 34 per cent of the vote in France's presidential election.

Kanté had his worst game of the tournament in the final and was subbed ten minutes into the second half. Outsiders didn't know but he had a stomach bug. In the celebrations the French players took turns to be photographed with the trophy but Kanté almost missed out; apparently he was too shy and didn't want to push himself forward. It took Steven N'Zonzi to grab the trophy and pass it to Kanté so he got his moment in front of the flashlights.

49

Megan Rapinoe

I SUSPECT that of the 50 influential footballers in this book Megan Rapinoe will be the most contentious. Search her name on YouTube, Twitter, whatever, and you will see the hate that America's 2019 World Cup-winning captain inspires.

These two examples took almost no time to find:

Alexander: 'I wish that gross thing would climb back up the ugly tree she fell out of.'

Larry: 'She is not a person, not a woman, she is not relevant to anything that matters to human existence, just more trash to carry to the curb.'

Rapinoe's lack of relevance didn't stop Larry from taking the time to comment on a YouTube video in which a man insulted the footballer/activist for views and likes. Rapinoe doesn't seem to mind. She knew what she was getting into when, for example, she joined American footballer Colin Kaepernick's kneeling protest against racism and the American police. She chose to take on the US President: her casual dismissal of a question about a potential invitation from Donald Trump to a victory party flashed around the world: 'I'm not going to the fucking White House.' She apologised, but only to her mother and only for the language.

MEGAN RAPINOE

If you don't like Megan Rapinoe appearing in the history of football ask yourself these questions: Is women's football on the rise? Is Rapinoe its most high-profile and articulate advocate?

The first answer is a clear 'yes'. Viewers per match at the 2019 World Cup were more than double the previous edition, and the increase was most marked for group games, suggesting deeper engagement. The commitment of TV companies and corporate sponsors to the women's game is stronger than ever. Attendances for the tournament in France were down to an average of 21,756 (from 26,029 in Canada 2015, and 37,218 at China 2007) but league games are more indicative of the deeper state of health. Attendances rose after the World Cup: at Rapinoe's club OL Reign the average jumped from 3,824 to 5,213, having fallen slightly for the previous two years. In England's WSL, average crowds rose from 1,010 to 3,401 after the tournament. The challenge for women's football is to maintain that World Cup momentum.

But how important is the paying spectator to modern football? Rapinoe plays league games in front of 5,000 people but has millions of social media followers and commercial deals with Nike, Samsung, Bodyarmor and Procter & Gamble, among others: the corporate world doesn't seem too freaked out by an outspoken, left-wing, liberal, gay, women's rights activist. It helps that she is currently the best female footballer in the world, although it took her a long time to get there.

Rapinoe started playing soccer because of her elder brother Brian. She idolised him and was devastated when he began a descent into drug dependency that would see him spend years in prison for a series of crimes. She won a scholarship to Portland University and made her international debut aged 20. Two anterior cruciate ligament injuries forced her to miss almost two years of football, including both the 2007 World Cup and the 2008 Olympics. After university, she joined the WPS, an ill-fated first attempt at professional women's football in the US. She also played for Sydney and in France for Lyon, where she was on the losing side in the Champions League Final. Since 2013 she has played for Seattle Reign, which later became a partner of Lyon.

Her big breakthrough came at the 2011 World Cup. She came on as a substitute in the second game and thumped in a goal before picking up a pitch-side sound-effects microphone and singing 'Born in the USA'. In the quarter-final the USWNT were 2-1 down to Marta's Brazil when, in the 122nd minute, Rapinoe set up Abby Wambach's equaliser, and then converted her penalty in the shoot-out. She started in the final against outsiders Japan, who played excellent, controlled, attractive football. Rapinoe was substituted and had to watch her team-mates lose on penalties.

They bounced back at the London 2012 Olympics where Rapinoe scored twice in a 4-3 semi-final win over Canada. The final was played at Wembley in front of 80,203 and the USWNT took revenge on Japan with two goals from Carli Lloyd.

Lloyd also scored a hat-trick in the 2015 World Cup Final against the Japanese in Vancouver. This became the most watched soccer match in US history and the successful team were given a ticker-tape victory parade in New York, a far cry from the semi-anonymous return for the first world champions in 1991.

But were they paid fairly compared to their male counterparts, who reached the second round in 2014 and failed to qualify for Russia 2018? Lines were drawn for the bitter battle that currently rages far from the soccer field. At the time of writing, the women have lost but plan to appeal against the court ruling that they voluntarily entered into contracts that were different from the men's, but not fundamentally discriminatory. 'In the beginning it was for the team,' said Rapinoe, 'but then I realised we're the lightning rod for this whole movement. You can lose but you have to keep fighting.'

Two arguments commonly raised against equal pay are: *1.* Women don't bring in as much revenue, and *2.* They're not as good.

The first is true as far as FIFA is concerned, but no longer in American soccer. Also, as not-for-profit organisations charged with promoting the game, there is no requirement for sports governing bodies to match income with specific expenditure.

As for the second point: it depends how you measure it. Feel free to say this out loud if it makes you feel better: Megan Rapinoe is not as good at football as Lionel Messi. It's not the point. It doesn't even matter that the USWNT had a kickabout with a Dallas Boys under-15 team in 2017 and lost. It was played for fun – but no matter what age of men would beat them, the US are unquestionably the best in the world at women's football, and they believe that entitles them to earn as much as the nation's men, who didn't even make the last World Cup.

There was an air of defiance about the Americans at the 2019 World Cup. They had lost to Sweden in the 2016 Olympic quarter-finals but were still the smart bet to retain their crown in France. They won their opener 13-0 against Thailand and were criticised for their raucous celebrations. They were in no mood to apologise. Rapinoe scored decisive doubles in the knockout games against Spain and France. Her celebration against the hosts, arms stretched in balletic pose, demanded adulation. It was confident, defiant and arrogant, telling the world she knew she was good.

Rapinoe missed the semi-final against England but her replacement Christen Press scored before Ellen White equalised and USWNT's Alex Morgan got the goal that proved to be the winner. Morgan celebrated by sipping imaginary tea, allowing the team's critics to take offence. White had an equaliser disallowed because she was an inch offside, not spotted by the assistant referee but by the VAR, technically correct but not the original intention of the offside law. England almost benefitted from the VAR but Steph Houghton's penalty was saved by Alyssa Naeher.

Rapinoe was fit for the final against the Netherlands and scored the opener from the spot, her sixth goal of the finals, enough to win her the Golden Boot, to go with the Golden Ball. In her post-match interviews she sent a message to her brother who was watching her win the World Cup from a rehabilitation centre, rather than prison, for the first time.

Images of the victory celebrations in Manhattan beamed around the world. A bleary-eyed Rapinoe entranced the crowds with a message ostensibly of hope but also taking the fight to President Trump – and his supporters and her critics, who were very much the same: 'This is my charge to everyone: we have to do better. We have to love more, hate less. We have got to listen more and talk less … it's our responsibility to make this world a better place.'

Her lack of humility fuelled her critics but their hate fuels Rapinoe and her team-mates, giving them a sense of mission stretching beyond winning matches. 'It's so much bigger than soccer,' she said of their World Cup victory. 'It was just so inspiring to people. We have an incredible opportunity here to shift a national narrative on who we want to be.'

50

Raheem Sterling

RAHEEM STERLING lived almost in the shadow of the old Wembley Stadium, until they started demolishing it when he was seven years old. At 12 years old he was a youth player at Queen's Park Rangers and his sister took him to training, three bus rides away. Bigger London clubs wanted him but his mum thought he would be better able to shine at QPR. When he was 15, Liverpool bought him for £600,000 up front, with an appearance clause and a 20 per cent sell-on – QPR eventually got around £10m.

He was attacked and racially abused for the first time on Merseyside but he still thought it was a good idea to have left West London because of the power of gangs in his neighbourhood. He told the *Players' Tribune*, 'I thought I needed to get away. At that time there were a lot of stabbings, a lot of silly crime going on.'

The fear of violence was understandable: Sterling's father Phillip had been shot dead in Jamaica when Raheem was two years old. His mother, Nadine, moved to England to study, leaving him and his sister Kima-lee with their grandma until she was settled. He made his Liverpool debut aged 17 and became a regular as they finished seventh under Brendan

Rodgers in 2012/13. The following season was dramatic. Liverpool hadn't been champions of England since 1990 but the brilliance of Luis Suárez, backed up by Daniel Sturridge and Sterling (the S.A.S.A.S), saw them surge to the top, with 11 straight wins in the spring. Sterling got the opener as they beat rivals Manchester City to gain a potentially decisive advantage. They went into their third-to-last game knowing a draw at home to Chelsea would leave them two wins from the title. But football is often cruel and it was Liverpool-born-and-bred skipper Steven Gerrard, in his 16th season at the club, who slipped, allowing Demba Ba to score for Chelsea, who later added a second. Rodgers's side could still pressurise City by winning at Crystal Palace on the Monday of the final week. All seemed fine when they led 3-0 in the second half, only to collapse and ship three goals in eight minutes. They finished two points behind City.

Suárez left for Barcelona after the 2014 World Cup, at which he battered England and bit Giorgio Chiellini. Without him, Liverpool lost six of their first 12 Premier League games and Sterling's relationship with Rodgers fractured. He rejected a contract worth £100,000 a week and a public spat between player and club made the situation irretrievable. City offered £30m, then £40m and, after Sterling asked not to join Liverpool's summer tour, a deal was done: £44m up front (with £5m in extras) made him the most expensive Englishman until Harry Maguire moved to Manchester United for £80m in 2019.

City finished fourth in 2015/16 and Sterling struggled with a groin injury before Euro 2016. By the end of that tournament he was English football's public enemy number one. Pep Guardiola's arrival was timely. The new boss observed, 'He obviously had a problem with the £49m in the eyes of the people.'

Guardiola and his assistant Mikel Arteta found a willing student who worked hard on his technical flaws. City won their first ten games but later faded, finishing third and losing to an exciting Monaco team in the Champions League. The French club were plundered that summer; City took Bernardo Silva for £43m and solved their defensive problems by spending £120m on three full-backs, Kyle Walker, Benjamin Mendy and Danilo, and, crucially, Brazilian keeper Ederson for another £35m. Centre-back Aymeric Laporte arrived in January for £57m. Unpicking a manager's influence from his financial backing is tough and Mourinho led the sceptics questioning how Guardiola would fare without Abu Dhabi's money. Sterling certainly flourished: he used his pace to devastating effect and became a 20-goal-a-season winger. A record-breaking City side scored over 100 goals and claimed 100 points.

Liverpool finished fourth, 25 points back, but Jurgen Klopp was given time to lead the club back to the very top and create what we might look back on as a great rivalry. Mohamed Salah was devastating, attacking from the right, and centre-back Virgil van Dijk proved to be a £75m bargain. After Loris Karius's nightmarish Champions League Final against Real Madrid in 2018, Klopp also decided his missing jigsaw piece was a Brazilian goalkeeper. With Alisson behind Van Dijk, two superb energetic full-backs, a hard-working midfield and Salah, the equally speedy Sadio Mane and the selfless Roberto Firmino up front, Liverpool were set for an epic battle with City.

In 2013/14, City got 86 points to Liverpool's 84; five years later it was 98 to 97. Liverpool's draw at Everton on 3 March was the last time they dropped points. After an early FA Cup exit they lost only once – 3-0 at Barcelona, a setback spectacularly overturned at Anfield. They beat Tottenham in the Champions League Final with goals from Salah and Divock Origi, and English club football could claim to be on top; long overdue given their financial clout.

Klopp's side dominated the 2019/20 Premier League from the off, only kept waiting for the yearned-for title by the Covid-19 lockdown. Their tactics were not especially sophisticated, essentially a German-style pressing game adapted for English football, with wise recruitment and a tremendously charismatic leader. They also sold brilliantly, most notably getting £142m from Barcelona for Philippe Coutinho. Sterling is a rare recent example of a player who thrived after leaving Liverpool.

His England career has summed up recent generations: enough ability to foster hope but not enough to deliver success, yet. It began in November 2012, when he was 17. Before Euro 2012, Roy Hodgson had taken over from Fabio Capello, who had resigned in protest at the FA stripping John Terry of the captaincy after he was charged with racially abusing Anton Ferdinand. Terry was later cleared in court but suspended by the FA. Hodgson's England lost to Italy on penalties in the second round – it was his high point.

Sterling started in defeats against Italy and Uruguay and came on in a draw with Costa Rica, as England finished bottom of their group at the 2014 World Cup. They won all ten qualifiers for Euro 2016, raising expectations of fans and media. It was a familiar pattern: giddy excitement followed by bitter recrimination.

Hodgson's side were hard on the eye. Sterling struggled: he was subbed before England conceded an unnecessary late equaliser against a dreadful Russia side in Marseilles. Tooled-up Russian thugs attacked England fans at the end of the game. Against Wales, Sterling was taken off at half-time with his side trailing; Jamie Vardy and Sturridge gave England their only victory.

Sterling was dropped for a goalless draw with Slovakia but returned for England's elimination against Iceland, who had brilliant fans and enthusiastic players. Sterling won an early penalty which was converted by Wayne Rooney. The rest was truly awful. Iceland scored from a long throw and again from an 18th-minute Kolbeinn Sigþórsson shot that Joe Hart should have saved. There was plenty of time left but the subsequent

72 minutes summed up everything wrong with England. The public reaction afterwards suggested the players hadn't tried, were overpaid and somehow 'didn't want it'.

I saw a team of young men, desperate to succeed but overwhelmed by pressure. Hodgson's gloomy outlook didn't help; it is hard to be creative in a cycle of negativity. Fans and media act like wounded partners in a dysfunctional relationship with England teams – over-eager then quick to lose faith. Supporters in the stadium chanted, 'You're not fit to wear the shirt!' The BBC website described England's performance as 'shameful'. All big football countries put pressure on their players but the British tabloid press adds a moral dilemma to sporting failure. The *Daily Mail* splashed a story condemning Sterling for 'showing off' about having bought his mother a house: '£180,000-a-week England flop Raheem Sterling shows off a blinging house he bought for his mum complete with jewel-encrusted bathroom hours after flying home in disgrace from Euro 2016.'

Here 'in disgrace' means 'having lost a football match'.

We will never know how Sam Allardyce would have fared. Hodgson's replacement was caught in a *Daily Telegraph* sting, in which he appeared willing to offer advice on how to get around a ban on third-party ownership of players. No charges ever followed and much of the media focus was on whether or not Allardyce was drinking wine by the pint during the faked meeting. He was sacked after one game and replaced by Gareth Southgate, the under-21 manager whose previous experience was getting Middlesbrough relegated. While Allardyce was an ultra-pragmatist, Southgate espoused possession football, which was more in line with the FA's 'DNA for English Football' project.

He understood the media better than his predecessors. Bad performances bring inevitable criticism but positive relationships can mitigate the reaction. Lower expectations at the 2018 World Cup helped, as did the luck of the draw: had

England gone out at the group stage, the cheerful chat about Gareth's waistcoats would have disappeared.

Harry Kane got an injury-time winner against Tunisia, and by the time Panama had been dispatched the Tottenham striker was on his way to winning the Golden Boot. England lost to Belgium before finally winning a World Cup penalty shoot-out, against Colombia.

The drama-free quarter-final victory over Sweden was England's best at a major tournament in years but Croatia ended the ride in the semi-final. Kieran Trippier scored an early free kick but England didn't have midfielders to match Barça's Ivan Rakitić, Inter's Marcelo Brozović or Golden Ball winner Luka Modrić of Real Madrid. Ivan Perišić of Inter equalised and Juventus's Mario Mandžukić got an extra-time winner. The praise for Croatia was justified but they needed penalty shoot-outs to beat both Denmark and Russia. World Cup legends are made by fine margins.

The two teams met again in the inaugural Nations League and England's victory at Wembley, thanks to Kane's late goal, relegated the World Cup finalists. Southgate's side finished third after losing their semi-final against the Netherlands and winning (another) penalty shoot-out against Switzerland.

There are promising signs for England fans that talented players are at last coming through the academy system in good numbers, although playing time for home-grown kids remains a sticking point. Can England win the World Cup or Euros sometime soon? Yes, of course, if Denmark (1992), Greece (2004) and Portugal (2016) can, but in my lifetime England have never been consistently excellent – like Spain (2010), and maybe Brazil (2002), Germany (2014) and France (2018) – or even like Italy, a perennial candidate if no likelier force steps up.

Sterling has played his best international football as he has matured, although it is hard to evaluate the criticism he gets because of the inevitable issue of race. Before the Russia World Cup, he was all over the media because of a tattoo of a rifle on his right leg. He explained it was an anti-gun message, inspired by the death of his father. Overt racism is now rare in the mainstream media but Sterling is certain he and other black players are treated differently from white contemporaries. He has been a constant source of front-page headlines: contracts, relationships, where he shops and what he buys. When he was pictured smiling at a gaggle of Chelsea fans, whose contorted faces told of deep hatred, the media took his side. Sterling then used the power given to famous people by social media to confront the tabloids, posting on Instagram juxtaposed images of headlines about Tosin Adarabioyo and Phil Foden. Both City youngsters had bought their mum a house but the headline for Adarabioyo's story had a negative barb: 'Despite never having started a Premier League match' while Foden's didn't. Adarabioyo is black and Foden is white. Sterling's post was impactful; it challenged the media to give more thought to its biases. He was voted the 2019 Football Writers' Player of the Year.

He has also spoken out about the lack of black or mixed ethnicity managers in the English league. Again he compared treatment of whites such as Gerrard and Frank Lampard, who were appointed by top clubs, with black contemporaries Sol Campbell and Ashley Cole. When Sterling took on abusive, racist Montenegro fans, England supporters sang in support of their black players: we've come a long way from Viv Anderson being told to suck it up. The road isn't straight but with players like Sterling speaking out, we are travelling in the right direction.

Bibliography

Is videography a word? It should be. Thanks to YouTube and Sky Sports for many hours of football content.

- The Greatest Team and Football's Greatest series by Pitch International (no relation, like the Baggios)
- Premier League Years, Sky Sports
- Premier League Icons, Sky Sports
- FIFA TV for interviews, history documentaries and match action
- YouTube's anarchic football content
- BBC Sport
- Al Jazeera TV
- The Discovery Channel
- The Olympic Channel
- STV (Kenny Dalglish)
- UEFA.com
- When English Football Ruled Europe (ITV Sport)
- Diego Maradona (Asif Kapadia)
- Take the Ball, Pass the Ball (Duncan MacMath/Graham Hunter)
- George Best: All by Himself (Daniel Gordon, BBC)
- Graham Taylor: An Impossible Job (Ken McGill, Patrick Collins, Chrysalis, Cutting Edge 1994)

BIBLIOGRAPHY

- Pele, Argentina and the Dictators (Goalhanger Films)
- Kenny (Stuart Sugg)
- Ronaldo's Redemption: 2002 World Cup documentary (FourFourTwo)
- History of African Football (EnVagency)
- Hillsborough Remembered (Discovery)
- Hillsborough: Anatomy of a Disaster (The Guardian)
- When Lineker Met Maradona (BBC)
- Fearless Foxes: Our Story | Leicester City's 2015/16 Premier League Title (LCFC)
- Soccer Star Rapinoe Is Completely Obnoxious (Daily Wire)
- USA Champions: The Story of the 2019 Women's World Cup (Yohn Voker)
- Raheem Sterling ft Megan Rapinoe (Raheem Sterling)

Agnew, P., *Football Legend: the Authorised Biography of Tom Finney* (Milo, 2002).
Anderson V., Guest, L., *First Among Unequals* (Fullback Media, 2010).
Andrews, G.R., *Blackness in the White Nation, a History of Afro-Uruguay* (University of North Carolina Press, 2010).
Auclair, P., *Cantona: The Rebel Who Would be King* (MacMillan, 2009).
Balague, G., *Cristiano Ronaldo: The Biography* (Orion, 2015).
Balague, G., *Messi* (Orion, 2013).
Ball, P., *Morbo: The Story of Spanish Football* (WSC Books, 2011).
Beckham, D., Watt, T., *My Side* (Collins Willow, 2003).
Best, G., *Blessed – The Autobiography* (Ebury, 2001)
Bolsmann, C., Mason, T., Porter D., *English Gentlemen and World Soccer: Corinthians, Amateurism and the Global Game* (Routledge, 2018).
Booth, K., *The Father of Modern Sport, The Life and Times of Charles W. Alcock* (Chequered Flag, 2015).
Brown, P., *Victorian Football Miscellany* (Goal-Post, 2013).
Burns, J., *Barça* (Bloomsbury, 2016).

Burns, J., *La Roja* (Simon & Schuster, 2012).

Burns, J., *The Hand of God: The Life of Diego Maradona* (Bloomsbury, 2002).

Castro, R., *Garrincha: The Triumph and Tragedy of Brazil's Forgotten Football Hero* (Yellow Jersey, 2013).

Charlton, Sir Bobby, *My Life in Football* (Headline, 2009).

Clarke, G., *Soccer Women* (Bold Type Books, 2019).

Clough, B., *Clough, the Autobiography* (Corgi, 1995).

Conn, D., *The Fall of the House of FIFA* (Yellow Jersey, 2017).

Cox, M., *The Mixer: The Story of Premier League Tactics from Route One to False 9s* (Harper Collins, 2017).

Cox, M., *Zonal Marking: The Making of Modern European Football* (Harper Collins, 2019).

Crick, M., *The Boss: The Many Faces of Alex Ferguson* (Pocket Books, 2002).

Cruyff, J., *My Turn: The Autobiography* (MacMillan, 2017).

Dalglish, K., Winter, H., *Dalglish: My Autobiography* (Hodder & Stoughton, 1996).

Edwards, L., *The History of the Southern League* (Paper Plane, 1993).

Foot, J., *Calcio: The History of Italian Football* (Fourth Estate, 2010).

Fort, P., Philippe, J., *Zidane: the Biography* (Ebury, 2018).

Freddi, C., *The Complete Book of the World Cup* (Harper Collins, 2006).

Goldblatt, D., *The Ball is Round*: A Global History of Football (Penguin, 2007).

Gullit, R., *How to Watch Football* (Penguin, 2017).

Harding, J., *Football Wizard: the Story of Billy Meredith* (Breedon Books, 1985).

Henderson, J., *When Footballers Were Skint* (Biteback, 2018).

Hewson, A.K., *Megan Rapinoe: Soccer Star* (Press Box, 2020).

Hunter, G., Spain: *The Inside Story of La Roja's Historic Treble* (Backpage Press, 2013).

Hunter, G., Barça: *The Making of the Greatest Team in the World* (Backpage Press, 2012).

BIBLIOGRAPHY

Jones, R., *The Essential History of Middlesbrough* (Headline, 2002).

Lowe, S., *Fear and Loathing in La Liga, Barcelona vs Real Madrid* (Yellow Jersey, 2014).

MacGregor, N., *A History of the World in 100 Objects* (Allen Lane, 2010).

McCarra, K., *Celtic, a Biography in Nine Lives* (Faber & Faber, 2012).

McNeill, B., *Hail Cesar, the Autobiography* (Headline, 2005).

Matthews, S., Millar, D., *Life of Stanley Matthews* (Pavilion, 1990).

Matthews, S., *The Way it Was, my Autobiography* (Headline, 2001).

Millar, C., *The Frying Pan of Spain* (Pitch Publishing, 2019).

Murray, S., *The Title: the Story of the First Division* (Bloomsbury, 2017).

O'Mahony, M., *The Art of Goalkeeping: Memorializing Lev Yashin* (University of Bristol, 2017).

Parkinson, M., *George Best: A Memoir: A unique biography of a football icon* (Hodder, 2019).

Pelé, *Pelé: The Autobiography* (Pocket Books, 2007).

Powell, H., *Hope: My Life in Football* (Bloomsbury, 2016).

Riddoch, A., Kemp, J., *When the Whistle Blows: the Story of the Footballers' Battalion in the Great War* (Haynes, 2011).

Roodt, G., *The DNA of Rugby Football: A Short History of the Origin of Rugby* (Partridge Africa, 2015).

Sanders, R., *Beastly Fury, The Strange Birth of English Football* (Bantam, 2010).

Shackleton, L., *Clown Prince of Soccer* (Nicholas Kaye, 1956).

Smith, J., *The Deal: Inside the World of a Super Agent* (Constable, 2017).

Steen, R., *Floodlights and Touchlines: A History of Spectator Sport* (Bloomsbury, 2015).

Wagnerin, D., *Soccer in a Football World* (Temple University Press, 2008).

Wallechinsky D., Loucky, J., *The Complete Book of the Olympics* (Aurum Press, 2012).

Williams, J., *A Contemporary History of Women's Sport* (Routledge, 2014).

Wilson, J., *Angels with Dirty Faces. How Argentinian Soccer Defined a Nation and Changed the Game Forever* (Bold Type Books, 2016).
Wilson, J., *Inverting the Pyramid: The History of Football Tactics* (Orion, 2010).
Wilson, J., *The Outsider: A History of the Goalkeeper* (Orion, 2013).
Wisden Cricketers' Almanack 1980 (John Wisden, 1980).
Yallop, D., *How They Stole the Game* (Constable, 2011).

Websites:
Wikipedia – which should get a Nobel Prize. (And yes, I've paid.)
Athletic News
Daily Chronicle
Daily Express
Daily Mail
Daily Mirror
Daily Telegraph
El Pais
Football Star
France Football
Glasgow Herald
Lancashire Daily Post
Lancashire Evening Post
L'Equipe
Miroir des Sports
O Mundo
Newsweek
New York Times
Sports Illustrated
Sunday People
Sunday Times
The Blizzard
The Guardian
The Independent
The Observer (article about José Andrade)
The Scotsman
The Sun

BIBLIOGRAPHY

The Sporting Chronicle
The Times
Time

Albiceleste Stories (Eduardo Cantaro)
Beyondthelastman.com
British Newspaper Archive
Britishpathe.com
Decelesteyblanco.blogspot.com
European-football-statistics.co.uk
ESPN.co.uk
Footballandthefirstworldwar.org
Forbes.comTheHardTackle.com
IFFHS.de
Infobae.com
Islamique Magazine
Joe.Com
GQ Magazine
La Gazzetta dello Sport
Mancityfan.tv
Medium.com
Nutmeg Magazine
Liverpoolfc.fandom
Leicester City FC
The Players' Tribune
PlayupLiverpool.com
Puskas.com
RealMadrid.com
Rsssf.com
Staff.city.ac.uk
Taleoftwohalves.co.uk
The42.ie
Thehardtackle.com
Thefootballhistoryboys.com
Thetemporalwisdom.wordpress.com
Theversed.com

THE FIFTY

Toffeeweb.com
Tottenhamhotspur.com
Worldfootball.net
Worldometers.info